A Treasury of Virtues

and

One Hundred Proverbs

Letter from the General Editor

The Library of Arabic Literature is a new series offering Arabic editions and English translations of key works of classical and pre-modern Arabic literature, as well as anthologies and thematic readers. Our books are edited and translated by distinguished scholars of Arabic and Islamic studies, and are published in parallel-text format with Arabic and English on facing pages. The Library of Arabic Literature will include texts from the pre-Islamic era to the cusp of the modern period, and will encompass a wide range of genres, including poetry, poetics, fiction, religion, philosophy, law, science, history, and historiography.

Supported by a grant from the New York University Abu Dhabi Institute, and established in partnership with NYU Press, the Library of Arabic Literature will produce authoritative Arabic editions and modern, lucid English translations, with the goal of introducing the Arabic literary heritage to scholars and students, as well as to a general audience of readers.

Philip F. Kennedy
General Editor, Library of Arabic Literature

دستور معالم الحِكَم ومأثور مكارم الشِّيَم

من كلام أمير المؤمنين عليّ بن أبي طالب

صلّى الله تعالى عليه وآله وسلّم

من تأليف

القاضي محمّد بن سلامة القُضاعي

ويليه

مائة كلمة

من كلام أمير المؤمنين عليّ بن أبي طالب عليه السلام

المنسوب إلى

الجاحظ

LIBRARY OF
المكتبة
ARABIC
العربية
LITERATURE

A Treasury of Virtues

Sayings, Sermons and Teachings of ʿAlī

AL-QĀḌĪ AL-QUḌĀʿĪ

with the

One Hundred Proverbs

attributed to

AL-JĀḤIẒ

Edited and translated by
TAHERA QUTBUDDIN

NEW YORK UNIVERSITY PRESS
New York and London

NEW YORK UNIVERSITY PRESS
New York and London

Library of Congress Cataloging-in-Publication Data

'Ali ibn Abi Talib, Caliph, ca. 600-661
[Selections. English. 2013]
A treasury of virtues : sayings, sermons and teachings of 'Ali
al-Qadi al-Quda'i : with the one hundred proverbs attributed to
al-Jahiz / edited and translated by Tahera Qutbuddin.
p. cm.
Includes bibliographical references and index.
ISBN 978-0-8147-7185-3 (e-book) -- ISBN 978-0-8147-2925-0 (e-book)
-- ISBN 978-0-8147-2914-4 (cl : alk. paper)
I. Qutbuddin, Tahera. II. Jahiz, d. 868 or 9. III. Quda'i, Muhammad
ibn Salamah, d. 1062. IV. Title.
PJ7698.A5A2 2013
892.7'8209--dc23
2012030286
CIP

New York University Press books are printed on acid-free paper,
and their binding materials are chosen for strength and durability.

Series design by Titus Nemeth.

Typeset in Tasmeem, using DecoType Naskh and Emiri.

Typesetting and digitization by Stuart Brown.

Manufactured in the United States of America
c10 9 8 7 6 5 4 3 2 1

dedicated to
Syedna Mohammad Burhanuddin (T.U.S.)
with deepest gratitude

Table of Contents

Acknowledgements

Many people helped bring this project to fruition, and I take this opportunity to gratefully acknowledge their kindness:

My father Syedi Khuzaima Qutbuddin, a venerable scholar, has tutored me on ʿAlī's sermons on a regular basis since childhood, and throughout my work on this book, he and my mother Sakina Qutbuddin have been a rock of support. My husband, Abduz-Zahir Mohyuddin, was a constant sounding board for precision of ideas and clarity of writing. My project editor at LAL, Professor Shawkat Toorawa, spent innumerable hours reviewing each line of the text in great detail, offering excellent advice and expert critique; my fellow LAL editors—Professors Philip Kennedy, James Montgomery, Joseph Lowry, Julia Bray, Michael Cooperson, and Devin Stewart—lent a willing hand in solving some of the text's cryptic utterances; LAL managing editor, Chip Rossetti, efficiently kept me on track through the process; Stuart Brown, LAL digital production manager, Mariam Bazeed, copy editor, and Wiam El-Tamami, proofreader, helped bring the project to its final form. My brothers and sisters—Dr. Bazat-Saifiyah, Bazat-Tyebah, Taher, Dr. Abde-Ali, Fatema, Arwa Qurratulain, Dr. Husain, and Dr. Aziz Qutbuddin—scholars of Arabic in their own right, gave valuable feedback on various parts of the translation. Professor Beatrice Gruendler offered insightful suggestions in the early stages of the project. My colleagues at the University of Chicago—Professors Franklin Lewis, Ahmed El-Shamsy, Dennis Pardee, Noha Aboulmagd Forster, and Muhammad Eissa—answered questions on assorted aspects of the text. Dr. Marlis Saleh, Middle East Librarian at the University of Chicago, aided in procuring manuscripts. Dr. Farhad Daftary and Mr. Alnoor Merchant facilitated access to a manuscript in the library of the Institute of Ismaili Studies in London. Scholars from different parts of the world answered queries: adabiyat listserv members from the US and Europe on transcriptions of Arabic and Persian names; Professor Ramzi Baalbaki of the American University of Beirut on fine points of Arabic grammar and orthography; and Mr. Mahdi Alizadeh, Director of the Center for Research in Ethics and Moral Education in Qom, on the source of the epigraph to the Introduction. My graduate students assisted in different ways: Ayshe Polat located a Turkish translation of the *One Hundred Proverbs* in Istanbul; Lyall Armstrong answered Bible-related questions; and Jeremy Vecchi lent a hand with technical aspects of microforms. My son Hyder helped too, he brightens each and every day for me with his sweet smile.

I thank you all sincerely. جزاكم الله خيرا

Abbreviations

For Arabic abbreviations of manuscripts used in the edition, see A Note on the Text.

AD	*anno Domini* = Gregorian (Christian) year
AH	*anno Hegirai* = Hijrah (Muslim) year
Ar.	Arabic
BC	before Christ
c.	century
ca.	*circa* = about, approximately
cf.	*confer* = compare
ch.	chapter
d.	died
ed.	editor, edition, edited by
fl.	flourished
ibid.	*ibidem* = in the same place
lit.	literally
n.d.	no date
no.	number
n.p.	no place
p., pp.	page(s)
Q	Qur'an
r.	ruled
s.v.	*sub verbo* = under the word
viz.	*videlicet* = namely
vol., vols.	volume(s)

Introduction

تنطق الحكمة على لسانه

"Wisdom speaks upon his tongue"

Ḍirār ibn Ḍamrah, a companion of ʿAlī, describing him[1]

ʿAlī ibn Abī Ṭālib (d. 40/661) was an acknowledged master of Arabic eloquence and a renowned sage of Islamic wisdom. When ʿAbd al-Ḥamīd al-Kātib (d. 132/750)—who has been called the "father of Arabic prose," and who was a chancery official for the intensely anti-ʿAlid Umayyads—was asked, "What enabled you to master the science of eloquence; what formed your training in it?", he replied, "Memorizing the words of ʿAlī."[2] Over the centuries, ʿAlī's sermons, sayings, and teachings were avidly and assiduously collected, quoted, and studied, and extensively anthologized, excerpted, and interpreted. There are in fact tens of collections, in thousands of pages, of ʿAlī's compiled words. Among the earliest and best known extant compilations are *A Treasury of Virtues* (*Dustūr maʿālim al-ḥikam wa-maʾthūr makārim al-shiyam*) collected by the Fatimid Shafiʿī judge, al-Quḍāʿī (d. 454/1062), and the *One Hundred Proverbs* (*Miʾat kalimah*), attributed to the eminent Abbasid litterateur, al-Jāḥiẓ (d. 255/869). They include some of ʿAlī's most moving sermons and a number of his pithiest maxims. In this volume, I present both these important compilations in new critical editions of the Arabic text using several original manuscripts, and in the first English translation.

ʿAlī ibn Abī Ṭālib (d. 40/661): Life and Personality

ʿAlī is a well-known figure in Islamic history. Cousin, son-in-law, and ward of the prophet Muḥammad, he was the first male to accept Islam. The Shia believe him to be the Prophet's legitimate successor in both his spiritual and temporal roles, and thus the first "Imām." Sunnis regard him as the last of the four "Rightly

Guided Caliphs." Both Shia and Sunni Muslims laud him for his deep personal loyalty to Muḥammad, his valorous role in the early battles of Badr, Uḥud, Khandaq, Khaybar, and Ḥunayn, and his profound piety, learning, and justice. They recount numerous hadiths from the Prophet praising him, among the most famous of which are: "I am the city of knowledge and ʿAlī is its gateway"; "ʿAlī is to me as Aaron was to Moses, except that there is no prophet after me"; "You, ʿAlī, are my brother in this world and the next."

To better understand ʿAlī's words, it is important to examine the historical, religious, and political context from which his teachings arise. Most, perhaps all, of ʿAlī's recorded sermons are said to be from the four turbulent years of his caliphate (36–40/656–61). His harsh censure of this world, his many death-themed sermons, and his urgent exhortations to prepare for the hereafter, clearly resonate the difficult reality of those years.

Born in Mecca around AD 600, ʿAlī was raised by his older cousin Muḥammad. He was about ten years old when Muḥammad began the call to Islam, twenty-three at the time of the Muslims' migration to Medina, and thirty-three when Muḥammad died. He participated actively in the setting up of the Medinan polity, playing a key role in establishing Islam in its nascent stage. Early in his time in Medina, he married the Prophet's youngest daughter Fāṭimah, and had four children with her: al-Ḥasan, al-Ḥusayn, Zaynab, and Umm Kulthūm. Muḥammad's line continued solely through ʿAlī's two sons, a line which would become an important locus for the Shia doctrine of the imamate.

After Muḥammad's death in 10/632, ʿAlī took a back seat in government during the reigns of the caliphs Abū Bakr, ʿUmar, and ʿUthmān. The Shia say he spent those twenty-five years collecting the Qur'an and imparting wisdom to al-Ḥasan and al-Ḥusayn. After ʿUthmān's assassination in 36/656, however, he was thrust into the limelight when the community pledged allegiance to him as the new caliph. During the four short years of his reign, he fought three major battles against groups of Muslims who had revolted against him: (1) The Battle of the Camel against the people of Basra, led by the Prophet's widow ʿĀ'ishah and the companions Ṭalḥah and Zubayr (the battle is named after the camel ʿĀ'ishah rode onto the battlefield); (2) the Battle of Ṣiffīn against the people of Syria, led by the governor of Damascus, the Umayyad Muʿāwiyah ibn Abī Sufyān; and (3) the Battle of Nahrawān against a group of renegades from ʿAlī's own army who came to be known as the Khārijites. In these battles, ʿAlī was supported by many of the Prophet's companions from Medina, as well as the people of

Kufa and Basra. Many of his close associates played key roles in his administration,[3] and some are named as interlocutors in the *Treasury of Virtues*. ʿAlī had moved to Kufa from Medina immediately after assuming the caliphate in order to intercept the first group of rebels, and thereafter remained in Iraq, occupied with the Syrian conflict. He spent his last few months unsuccessfully urging the Kufans to regroup and fight Muʿāwiyah. In 40/661, ʿAlī was killed by a Khārijite assassin while he was praying in the mosque in Kufa. His shrine in present-day Najaf, near Kufa, has become an important site of Shia pilgrimage, scholarship, and activism.

An account of ʿAlī by his close companion Ḍirār ibn Ḍamrah al-Ṣudāʾī al-Nahshalī nicely sums up his personality and image. Not only does it encapsulate his companions' affectionate yet reverent regard, it also highlights the austere lifestyle and the concern with the hereafter that underpin ʿAlī's pietistic teachings. Moreover, it comments appositely for our purposes on ʿAlī's wisdom and exposition. The report is as follows:[4]

> Ḍirār came to Damascus to pay a visit to Muʿāwiyah (now caliph after ʿAlī's death).[5] Muʿāwiyah said: Ḍirār, describe ʿAlī to me. Ḍirār replied: Let it go, please. Muʿāwiyah insisted and Ḍirār complied, saying:
>
> ʿAlī was farsighted and strong. When pronouncing judgment, he was discerning. When commanding, he was just. Knowledge gushed from his person. Wisdom spoke upon his tongue.[6] He shied away from the ornaments of this world, taking solace in the lonely night. He wept copiously in prayer, thought deeply, and turned his hands one over the other, admonishing himself before admonishing others. He favored simple food and plain clothes. He lived amongst us as one of us, responding when asked, and answering when questioned. But despite our intimacy, we would approach him with reverent awe, hesitating to call him out for a casual conversation.[7] He respected the pious and was kind to the poor. The powerful did not dare presume upon a favorable ruling and the weak never despaired of his justice.
>
> I saw him once when the night had let down its curtain and the stars had set. He stood in his place of prayer with a hand on his beard, writhing as one who had been stung by a snake. Weeping grievously, he exclaimed: "O world! Tempt someone other than me! Is it me you have come to seduce? Is it me you long for? Far be it! Far be it! I have divorced you thrice, a divorce that does not permit reconciliation. Your life is short, your value little. Alas! My provisions are scarce, the distance long, and the journey must be made alone!"

> Moved to tears, Muʿāwiyah responded: May God have mercy on ʿAlī, truly he was as you describe! How do you grieve for his loss, Ḍirār? Ḍirār replied: My sorrow is akin to the anguish of a mother whose only child has been butchered in her lap.

Orality, Authenticity, and Collection of ʿAlī's Words: Layered Sources

While writing was known in ʿAlī's time—in fact, he is reported to have been one of the Prophet's scribes who wrote down Qur'anic passages as they were revealed—his society was primarily oral. Accordingly, the principal mode of verbal production, transmission, and collection was oral, and ʿAlī's words were initially related for a century or more chiefly by word of mouth. This long period of oral transmission left room for errors in communication and even outright fabrication.[8] Nevertheless, the existence of a genuine core of materials from the period is far from inconceivable. The robustness of the indigenous oral tradition gives us good reason to believe in the validity of the oeuvre. Mary Carruthers has shown that members of oral societies had prodigious memories on which they relied to transmit lengthy pieces of their artistic verbal production.[9] Moreover, Gregor Schoeler has demonstrated that oral transmission in this society was increasingly supplemented by scholarly note-taking.[10] Because ʿAlī was an important figure in early Islamic history who preached often and in many different contexts to large public audiences, the early Muslims had good reason and ample opportunity to remember and pass on his teachings. So it is quite feasible that a portion of the words in our two texts were spoken—with some variation or even verbatim—by ʿAlī himself.[11]

ʿAlī's words were collected and passed down through the centuries by many individuals. We are told of a written collection by a man named Zayd ibn Wahb al-Juhanī (d. 96/715) who fought in his army at Ṣiffīn,[12] but this is perhaps an anomaly. Writing became widespread in the Islamic world after the introduction of paper-making techniques to it from China in the mid eighth century AD, and it was only then that ʿAlī's words—along with prophetic traditions, historical reports, and poetry—were systematically transcribed.

In the eighth and ninth centuries AD, historian-compilers such as Abū Mikhnaf (d. 157/774), Abū Naṣr al-Minqarī (d. 202/818), Ibn al-Kalbī (d. 205/820), al-Wāqidī (d. 207/822), al-Madā'inī (d. 225/840), and al-Thaqafī (d. 283/896) are reported to have collected ʿAlī's sermons, speeches, and epistles in independent works. In the tenth century, the Fatimid jurist and historian al-Qāḍī al-Nuʿmān (d. 363/974) is reported to have collected ʿAlī's sermons and written a commentary on them.[13] None of these early compilations survive. But ʿAlī's words were also transcribed into synthetic historical works by the same historians mentioned above, as well as by several others, and many of these are extant.[14]

ʿAlī's words were culled from these historical works (and perhaps also copied from the earlier independent works) by literary anthologists such as al-Jāḥiẓ (d. 255/869), Ibn ʿAbd Rabbih (d. 328/940), and many other scholars. In the tenth, eleventh, and twelfth centuries AD, major independent compilations of ʿAlī's words were put together from the earlier written sources, still extant today: The celebrated compilation by al-Sharīf al-Raḍī (d. 406/1014), *The Path of Eloquence* (*Nahj al-balāghah*) has attracted over four hundred commentaries. Al-Quḍāʿī (d. 454/1062), the compiler of *A Treasury of Virtues*, was of the generation after al-Raḍī, and the contents of his collection overlap to a certain extent with *The Path of Eloquence*. Other extant compilations of ʿAlī's words include *Scattered Pearls* (*Nathr al-laʾālī*) by al-Ṭabarsī (d. 548/1153), and *Radiant Maxims and Pearly Sayings* (*Ghurar al-ḥikam wa-durar al-kalim*) by al-Āmidī (d. 550/1155).[15]

As a result of the early oral transmission of these materials, assorted renderings of the same piece appear in different works. There are even multiple renderings of the same piece within one collection, including a number of near-identical passages and maxims in the *Treasury of Virtues*. This phenomenon derives from the nature of compiling similar materials from disparate sources, as al-Quḍāʿī has done. Moreover, some proverbs (and also some sermons), are attributed to more than one person.[16]

The Literary Style of ʿAlī's Words: Oral Patterns, Islamic Ethos, and Arabian Context

Eloquence is a crucial component of preaching, and as Richard Lanham has argued, it "tacitly persuades."[17] A brilliant exposition is more effective than a clumsy harangue, beautiful language more likely to evoke a positive response than a plodding lecture. In combination with Qurʾanic validation and rational argumentation, ʿAlī attempted to stir the hearts and minds of his audience with his verbal artistry, rhythmically expounding his lessons in cadenced parallelisms and vivid metaphors.

Understanding the orality of ʿAlī's milieu is also crucial to parsing his literary style. In a study that addresses issues of both authenticity and technique, Walter Ong has shown that verbal expression in an oral culture is mnemonic.[18] He argues that to retain carefully articulated thought, rhythmic patterns must be used. By and large, the materials in the present volume display such oral patterns (as do sermons and sayings attributed to the prophet Muḥammad and other prominent early Islamic orators). Parallelism, which is the hallmark of ʿAlī's verbal creations, produces a strong acoustic rhythm, and pithy sentences, repetition, assonance, and prose-rhyme augment this rhythm. Several other features of oral-based verbal production are also discernible, including vivid imagery, testimonial citation, additive rather than subordinative phrases, aggregative rather than analytic expositions, an agonistic tone, and closeness to the human lifeworld, shown through the use of mundane objects and daily activities as metaphors physically showcasing abstract ideas.[19] (Arabic prose produced after writing became widespread, such as the sermons of the tenth-century Syrian preacher Ibn Nubātah, would have a very different feel, including longer sentences, consistent rhyming, and much less parallelism.) To Ong's list of features of orality, we can add an abundance of audience engagement features: direct address, emphatic structures, rhetorical questions, and prescriptive phrases. Together, these elements create a dense web pulling in the audience toward participation in the speech act—and thus the persuasive goal—of the orator. Moreover, the elegance of Ali's words is apparent in their dignified yet simple language and their apposite positioning.

Growing up under Muḥammad's care, ʿAlī was continually exposed to the Qur'anic revelation; consequently, his words are permeated by its vocabulary and themes. From time to time, he also cites Qur'anic verses verbatim, endorsing the gravity of his teachings with divine authority. There is a religious flavor, a focus on piety, in all modes of ʿAlī's speech, undergirding even the material produced in a political or military context. At the same time, his words also have a distinctly local flavor, a cultural texture grounded in the desert topography, tribal society, nomadic lifestyle, and rich poetic tradition of the Arabian Peninsula. In his verbal production, Qur'anic themes merge with nature imagery to produce a distinctive template of Islamic preaching. Directives to contemplate the purpose of life and the majesty of the creator combine with the vocabulary and images of camel caravans, racing horses, and watering holes. Cultural, geographical, and religious strata converge, coming together in a single, seamless, whole.[20]

Al-Qāḍī al-Quda'ī (d. 454/1062): Career and Books

The compiler of *A Treasury of Virtues*, al-Qāḍī al-Quḍā'ī, was a Sunni-Shāfi'ī jurist, and a scholar of hadith and history who lived and died in Fatimid Cairo. His full name was Abū 'Abdallāh Muḥammad ibn Salāmah ibn Ja'far ibn 'Alī ibn Ḥakmūn al-Quḍā'ī, an affiliate of the Quḍā'ah, a tribe of Ḥimyar.

A senior government official, al-Quḍā'ī performed several singular functions for the Fatimids: He was judge over their Sunni subjects;[21] he traveled in 447/1055 to Constantinople as Fatimid emissary to the Byzantine court; and he served in their chancery, being scribe for a time for the vizier 'Alī ibn Aḥmad al-Jarjarā'ī (d. 436/1045). Al-Quḍā'ī would presumably also have had close contact with the eminent Fatimid scholar al-Mu'ayyad al-Shīrāzī (d. 470/1078), who was head of the chancery from 443/1051 to 448/1056; although the sources do not mention specific interactions, al-Mu'ayyad's dates at the chancery overlap with al-Quḍā'ī's time there.

Al-Quḍā'ī's scholarship was highly respected, especially in the collection and transmission of hadith. His student Ibn Mākūlā (d. 475/1082) praised his teacher saying: "He was a master of many different sciences . . . I don't know anyone in Egypt who approaches his stature."[22] Writing a century later, the jurist al-Silafī (d. 576/1180) said of him: "His fame absolves me from lengthy expositions . . . he is counted among the trustworthy and reliable transmitters."[23] Following Ibn Mākūlā and al-Silafī, several medieval biographers chronicled al-Quḍā'ī's career and writings, and recorded the names of his teachers and students. Numerous hadith works cite him in their chains of transmission.[24] We are told that al-Quḍā'ī heard and transmitted hadith in his homeland, Egypt, as well as during his travels to Constantinople, in Syria en route to Constantinople, and in Mecca and Medina, when he performed the Hajj in 445/1053.[25]

A prolific author, al-Quḍā'ī produced at least seven major books on a range of subjects, namely:

1. *The Blazing Star* (*Kitāb al-Shihāb fī l-ḥikam wa-l-ādāb*, also called *Musnad al-Shihāb*, *Shihāb al-akhbār*, or *al-Shihāb al-nabawī*), a book of "testaments, maxims, counsels, and directions for refined behavior" ascribed to the prophet Muḥammad. This is al-Quḍā'ī's most famous work, and is published in several editions and commentaries.

2. *A Treasury of Virtues* (*Dustūr maʿālim al-ḥikam wa-maʾthūr makārim al-shiyam min kalām amīr al-muʾminīn ʿAlī ibn Abī Ṭālib*), published in several editions, and newly edited and translated in the present volume.
3. *Al-Quḍāʿī's History* (*Kitāb al-Inbāʾ ʿan al-anbiyāʾ wa-tawārīkh al-khulafāʾ wa-wilāyat al-umarāʾ*, also called *Tārīkh al-Quḍāʿī: min khalq Ādam ḥattā sanat 427 AH*, and *ʿUyūn al-maʿārif wa-funūn akhbār al-khalāʾif*), a book on the history of the prophets and the caliphs up to the reign of the Fatimid caliph al-Ẓāhir. It has been published in several editions.
4. *The Merits of al-Shāfiʿī* (*Kitāb Manāqib al-Imām al-Shāfiʿī* or *Kitāb Akhbār al-Shāfiʿī*), a lost hagiographical work on the merits of the founder of al-Quḍāʿī's legal school.
5. *Compendium of Teachers* (*Muʿjam al-shuyūkh*), a lost biographical listing of the scholars from whom al-Quḍāʿi transmitted hadith.

The above five books are listed in Ibn ʿAsākir's *Tārīkh Madīnat Dimashq*, the earliest listing I have found of al-Quḍāʿī's books.[26]

6. *Institutions of Egypt* (*Kitāb Khiṭaṭ Miṣr*, also known as *al-Mukhtār fī dhikr al-khiṭaṭ wa-l-āthār*), a lost book on the history of Egypt ascribed to al-Quḍāʿī by Ibn Khallikān and al-Maqrīzī, both of whom cite numerous reports from it.[27]
7. *Qurʾan Commentary* (*Tafsīr*), now lost, first mentioned by al-Silafī then by al-Maqrīzī;[28] this is possibly the same work as the *Book of Numbers* (*Kitāb al-ʿAdad*) ascribed to him by Ibn ʿAṭiyyah.[29]

Two other works are ascribed to al-Quḍāʿī in rather late sources, perhaps erroneously: A work on preaching, *The Preacher's Pearl and the Worshiper's Treasure* (*Durrat al-wāʿiẓīn wa-dhukhr al-ʿābidīn*),[30] and a work on wisdom sayings, *Details of Reports and Gardens of Lessons* (*Daqāʾiq al-akhbār wa-ḥadāʾiq al-iʿtibār*), the latter now published.[31] Al-Silafī also reports that Ibn Mākūlā preserved his notes from al-Quḍāʿī's lectures, a "work" which does not appear to have survived.[32] Yet other titles which editors of al-Quḍāʿī's various works have ascribed to him are variant titles of al-Quḍāʿī's *History* or *The Blazing Star*, which they list incorrectly as independent works.[33]

A Treasury of Virtues: Form and Content

A Treasury of Virtues is lengthily titled in rhyming Arabic, *Dustūr maʿālim al-ḥikam wa-maʾthūr makārim al-shiyam min kalām amīr al-muʾminīn ʿAlī ibn Abī*

Ṭālib (ṣalla Allāhu taʿālā ʿalayhi wa-ālihī wa-sallam], literally "A Compendium of Signposts of Wisdom and a Documentation of Qualities of Virtue from the Words of the Commander of the Faithful ʿAlī ibn Abī Ṭālib." The Indian manuscript used for this edition also titles it *al-Shihāb al-ʿalawī* (*The Blazing Star of ʿAlī*), to mirror *al-Shihāb al-nabawī* (*The Blazing Star of the Prophet*). It is listed among al-Quḍāʿī's works by Ibn ʿAsākir, al-Silafī, al-Dhahabī, and al-Maqrīzī.[34] In the introduction, al-Quḍāʿī tells us about the impetus for compiling the work. He explains that the success of his collection of the Prophet Muḥammad's sayings prompted a friend to solicit a similar work featuring ʿAlī's wise words. Al-Quḍāʿī himself describes the compilation as a collection of "ʿAlī's words and eloquent sayings, his wise maxims and counsels, his directions for refined behavior, his answers to questions, his prayers and communions with God, and his preserved verse and allegories, nine chapters in varying genres."

The contents of the *Treasury of Virtues* are ethical and humanitarian, encouraging their audience to such virtues as honesty, sincerity, and moderation, and warning against such vices as greed, oppression, and stinginess. But they also contain supplications to God, directives to worship him, censures of this world, warnings of the transitory nature of human life, and exhortations to prepare for the hereafter by performing good deeds. A few pieces support a predestinarian position,[35] and a few other sections profess eschatological beliefs in the appearance of Dajjāl, the antichrist, at the end of time.

Al-Quḍāʿī's love for the family of the Prophet is evident not only in his collection of ʿAlī's words, but also in his selection of materials. Some of the pieces in the *Treasury of Virtues* laud them, mention ʿAlī's special status as Muḥammad's legatee, and confirm the special knowledge conferred on him by the Prophet. Al-Quḍāʿī's reverence for the Prophet's family may have its origin in the fact that the founder of al-Quḍāʿī's school, al-Shāfiʿī, composed numerous poems in praise of them.[36]

The wide-ranging themes of the *Treasury of Virtues* are presented in several distinct genres and forms, including sermons, testimonials, and homilies focused on the hereafter, prayers for forgiveness and salvation, theological discourses on the oneness of God, dialogues about a variety of ethical and religious topics, epistles with pietistic counsel, and ad hoc teachings in the form of legal dicta, prescriptions, proscriptions, and nutritional advice. The work includes a chapter comprising verses composed as a spontaneous response to the battles fought by the early Muslims, as well as gnomic verses, and verses proclaiming

ʿAlī's closeness to the Prophet. There is also a chapter on sayings that use rare words or phrases. Proverbs are the single most prominent genre in the book, presented in three separate chapters, occurring in distinct grammatical and rhetorical patterns, and containing mostly moral advice.

Al-Jāḥiẓ (d. 255/869) and the *One Hundred Proverbs*

Abū ʿUthmān ʿAmr ibn Baḥr al-Jāḥiẓ ("Pop-eyed") is one of the best known figures of Arabic literary history. Born and raised in Basra in a humble family of possibly African origin, he was a self-educated litterateur who wrote some 240 books and essays on diverse topics, of which 75 survive in whole or in part. His writings include: (1) books of literary criticism which also anthologize much prose and poetry such as the 4-volume *Book of Eloquence and Exposition* (*Kitāb al-Bayān wa-l-tabyīn*), and the 7-volume *Book of Living Beings* (*Kitāb al-Ḥayawān*); (2) vivid portrayals and incisive critiques of society in shorter books and essays such as *The Book of Misers* (*Kitāb al-Bukhalāʾ*), *The Virtues of the Turks* (*Manāqib al-Turk*), and *The Epistle on Singing Girls* (*Risālah fī l-Qiyān*); (3) rationalist theological and sectarian Sunni treatises, such as the *Epistle on the Createdness of the Qurʾan* (*Risālah fī Khalq al-Qurʾān*), and *The Epistle on the Position of the Supporters of ʿUthmān* (*Risālah fī Maqālat al-ʿUthmāniyyah*); and (4) expositions legitimizing the ruling Abbasids, such as the *Epistle on the Abbasids* (*Risālah fī l-ʿAbbāsiyyah*).

Several manuscripts of the *One Hundred Proverbs* (*Miʾat kalimah*)—sometimes called *One Hundred Select Proverbs* (*Miʾat kalimah mukhtārah*) or *Maxims of ʿAlī* (*Amthāl ʿAlī*)—credit al-Jāḥiẓ with their compilation. These manuscripts cite the Abbasid scholar Ibn Durayd (d. 312/933), who says he obtained it from Ibn Abī Ṭāhir Ṭayfūr (d. 280/893), a friend of al-Jāḥiẓ according to the report, who had himself solicited it from al-Jāḥiẓ. In this report, Ibn Abī Ṭāhir tells Ibn Durayd the following:

> For years al-Jāḥiẓ had been saying to us that the commander of the faithful ʿAlī ibn Abī Ṭālib had produced a hundred proverbs, each one worth a thousand of the best proverbs produced by the Arabs. I asked him many times to collect and dictate them to me. He would promise to do so, but deliberately, stingily, forget. One day toward the end of his life, he brought out several earlier drafts of his own works, culled from them ʿAlī's proverbs, wrote them down with his own hand, and gave them to me.

The *One Hundred Proverbs* is also transcribed in full and attributed to al-Jāḥiẓ by three medieval scholars: al-Thaʿālibī (d. 429/1038) in *Inimitability and Pithiness* (*al-Iʿjāz wa-l-ījāz*),[37] Abū l-Muʾayyad al-Muwaffaq al-Khwārizmī (d. 568/1172) in *The Book of Virtues* (*Kitāb al-Manāqib*),[38] and Ibn al-Ṣabbāgh (d. 855/1451) in *Important Chapters on Recognizing the Imams* (*al-Fuṣūl al-muhimmah fī maʿrifat al-aʾimmah*).[39] The compilation and its ascription to al-Jāḥiẓ are also mentioned by al-Āmidī in his introduction to the *Radiant Maxims* (*Ghurar al-ḥikam*).[40]

And yet, the attribution of the collection to al-Jāḥiẓ is uncertain, perhaps even unlikely. Charles Pellat, who compiled a critical listing of al-Jāḥiẓ's works, expresses skepticism at the ascription (although he does not explain why),[41] and when I looked through the indices of al-Jāḥiẓ's published works, I found just five maxims of the *One Hundred Proverbs* cited in them.[42] If al-Jāḥiẓ culled the proverbs from his own works, this low number appears to belie the attribution. One possibility might be that al-Jāḥiẓ culled the hundred proverbs from earlier drafts of his own works (*musawwadāt taṣānīfihī*, according to al-Khwārizmī), and perhaps these drafts had materials not included in the final versions. Another important consideration is that only a fraction of al-Jāḥiẓ's works has survived, and the missing maxims might be from his lost books.

Whatever the authorship, the *One Hundred Proverbs* is a text that has attracted much attention. There are numerous commentaries in Arabic, as well as Persian and Ottoman Turkish translations, supercommentaries, and verse renditions, typically one or two couplets per saying, with handsome calligraphy and beautiful illumination.[43] The work continues to be studied assiduously by Muslims across the globe. Two well-known commentaries are: (1) al-Rashīd al-Waṭwāṭ (d. 578/1182), *What Every Student Needs, to Understand the Words of ʿAlī ibn Abī Ṭālib* (*Maṭlūb kull ṭālib min kalām ʿAlī ibn Abī Ṭālib*); and (2) Maytham al-Baḥrānī (d. 679/1280), *Commentary on the One Hundred Proverbs* (*Sharḥ Miʾat kalimah*).[44] The *One Hundred Proverbs* has also been translated into modern Turkish as *Hazrat-i Ali'nin Yüz Sözü*.

ʿAlī's Wisdom in the West

ʿAlī's words, particularly his proverbial sayings, were among the earliest pieces of Arabic literature with which the Western world engaged, presumably because of their universal ethical appeal. Following the first edition in the seventeenth century, there are at least two translations and four editions with translations from the eighteenth and nineteenth centuries, of ʿAlī's gnomic maxims and verse into Western languages, including Old English, Latin, and German (these are listed in the Bibliography). Al-Ṭabarsī's *Scattered Pearls* seems to have been a particular favorite. In the twentieth century, no further translations of those specific compilations appeared. Al-Raḍī's *Path of Eloquence*, however, was translated several times in Iran and India, unfortunately in rather lackluster translations; the one accurate and idiomatic partial rendition is Thomas Cleary's English translation of its wisdom section.

The first Western translator of ʿAlī's words was Simon Ockley, Professor of Arabic at the University of Cambridge in the early eighteenth century. He extolled the humanitarian grounding of ʿAlī's sayings, adducing them as proof against accusations of "gross ignorance" leveled at the Arabians by eighteenth century Englishmen. His words are an appropriate characterization with which to conclude:

> The Sentences are full, and to the Purpose: They breathe a Spirit of pure Devotion, Strictness of Life, and express the greatest Gravity, and a most profound Experience in all the Affairs of Human Life . . . All that I say, is, That there is enough, even in this little Handful, to vindicate, in the Judgment of any Man of Sense, the poor injured Arabians, from the Imputation of that gross Ignorance fastned upon them by Modern Novices.[45]

A Note on the Text

I. Al-Quḍāʿī, *Dustūr maʿālim al-ḥikam*

Manuscripts

I am aware of four extant manuscripts of the *Dustūr*: a thirteenth-century Sunni Egyptian manuscript in the Chester Beatty Library in Dublin; a second, nearly identical Turkish manuscript from the early twentieth century in a private collection in Baghdad which I could not locate; a third Zaydī Yemeni manuscript from the seventeenth century at Yale University's Beinecke Library; and a fourth Ṭayyibī Indian manuscript from the seventeenth century in the collections of the Institute of Ismaili Studies in London. There is also a Twelver Shiite Iraqi manuscript from the thirteenth century of the *Munājāt ʿAlī*, which is the bulk of the text of the *Dustūr*'s chapter on prayer, in the Metropolitan Museum of Art in New York.

[م] **Egyptian manuscript (611/1214), Chester Beatty Library, Dublin**, catalog number 3026.[46]

This manuscript was copied in 611/1214 in Cairo, Egypt, by the judge ʿIzz al-Quḍāh Abū ʿAbdallāh Muḥammad ibn Abī l-Fatḥ Manṣūr ibn Khalīfah ibn Minhāl, from a manuscript endorsed with the signature of the Zaydī *sharīf* and Egyptian preacher and judge Fakhr al-Dawlah Abū l-Futūḥ Nāṣir ibn al-Ḥasan ibn Ismāʿīl al-Ḥusaynī (d. 563/1168). The latter transmitted the book, having studied it with the grammarian Muḥammad ibn Barakāt ibn Hilāl al-Saʿīdī, (or al-Saʿdī, (d. 525/1131), who himself studied the book with its compiler, al-Quḍāʿī (d. 454/1062).

The manuscript has a distinguished pedigree. It bears the certificates of authorization to transmit from three of its master narrators, all judges (reproduced on pp. 6–8 in the al-ʿAẓm edition), and appears to have been used and collated by several important scholars. In addition to the illustrious chain of transmitters listed above, the audition colophon on the last page states that the copyist, the judge ʿIzz al-Quḍāh, read the text with the judge Abū ʿAbdallāh Muḥammad, son of the judge Raḍī al-Dawlah Abū ʿAlī al-Ḥasan ibn Muḥammad al-ʿĀmirī, who had studied the book with the above mentioned Zaydī *sharīf*, Fakhr al-Dawlah.

The manuscript is complete and written in clear *naskh* script with full vocalization. With a few exceptions, it transcribes the *hamzah*. It has 127 folios and several corrections in the margins.

[ي] **Yemeni manuscript (1079/1668), Yale University's Beinecke Library, New Haven, Conneticut**, catalog number Landberg 471.

This manuscript was copied or patronized in 1079/1668 by a Zaydī jurist named Badr al-Dīn Muḥammad ibn Jaʿfar al-Unsī. In the Beinecke microform, the *Dustūr* is sandwiched between two Zaydī works.[47] It has 72 folios.

The manuscript is complete and written in fair *naskh* script, in red and black ink, with vocalization of letters provided in a few places, and several corrections in the margins. Despite its later provenance than the Egyptian manuscript, the script is more archaic: it is only partially dotted, has no *hamzah*, and uses و instead of ا in words such as حيوة.

[هـ] **Indian manuscript, (eleventh/seventeenth century), Institute of Ismaili Studies, London**, catalog number 190.

The folio following the title page contains an ascription of the book's contents to ʿAlī, beginning "*min kalām amīr al-muḥsinīn wa-amīr al-mu'minīn . . .*" followed by a full page of laudatory epithets of ʿAlī in Arabic with some Persian-Gujarati vocabulary. The manuscript is complete and written in clear and handsome *naskh* script, in red and black ink, with several corrections and lexical explanations on the margins, and spare vocalization. It has 88 folios, some water-stained.

The final folio with the copyist's name and date of transcription is missing, but transcribed on the title page below the title in a different hand is the name Miyān Chānd ibn Miyān Abūjī and (probably a different version of the same name) Miyān Shaykh ibn Miyān Abūjī Chāndjī: Chānd ibn Abūjī (if this is the same Chānd) was one of the three people who, during the reign of the Ṭayyibī Dā'ūdī dāʿī, Sayyidnā Fīr Khān Shujāʿ al-Dīn (r. 1056–65/1646–55, Ahmedabad), broke off to found the Hujūmiyyah sect, later becoming their second dāʿī. Presumably the manuscript was at one time in his possession. In the Institute catalog, Adam Gacek estimates the date of the manuscript to be eleventh/seventeenth century, without stating the basis of the dating. Two ownership seals on the blank folio before the title page bear the name of the Ṭayyibī Dā'ūdī dā'ī Sayyidnā 'Abd al-Qādir [Najm al-Dīn] (r. 1256–302/1840–85, Surat).[48] Several pages are stamped with the later ownership mark of The Ismaili Society, Bombay, which was founded in 1946 under the patronage of the Agha Khan Sultan Muhammad Shah and the academic support of the Russian scholar Wladimir Ivanow.

[ع] **Iraqi manuscript (ca. sixth/thirteenth century), Metropolitan Museum of Art, New York**, accession number 1995.324.

Titled *Munājāt amīr al-mu'minīn 'Alī ibn Abī Ṭālib* (*Prayers of the Commander of the Faithful 'Alī ibn Abī Ṭālib*), this manuscript contains a large portion of chapter 8 of the *Dustūr*: "Prayers and Supplications."[49] The entire manuscript of 8 folios is online at the Museum website: http://www.metmuseum.org/collections/search-the-collections/140010773.

The manuscript is written in clear *naskh* script with full vocalization. The Museum's dating of the manuscript is based on the similarity of the calligraphy of its title and surrounding illuminated scrolls to another manuscript dated and attributed to Mosul. The manuscript lists a chain of transmission of nine authorities, transmitting partly through written texts, going back to the narration of the eleventh Twelver Shi'ite Imām al-Ḥasan al-'Askarī in 260/874 in Samarrā'. This list is distinct from the chain of transmission of the piece provided in the *Dustūr*. The copyist's name and the date of the manuscript's transcription are absent. A colophon gives the name of a medieval reader, but no date.

Previous editions and commentaries

The first edition of the *Dustūr* was published by Jamīl al-'Aẓm in Cairo in 1914 using the Egyptian manuscript, with a commentary by the Azharite shaykh Ibrāhīm al-Daljamūnī. 'Abd al-Zahrā' al-Ḥusaynī published another edition in Beirut in 1981, using primarily the al-'Aẓm edition, supplemented by a Turkish manuscript he found in a private collection in Baghdad, copied in Constantinople in 1909, which he says was nearly identical to al-'Aẓm's edition of the Egyptian manuscript.[50] The al-'Aẓm edition has been reprinted numerous times by various editors, who wrote new introductions and commentaries, and corrected some typographical errors. These editions-reprints include a 1997 Beirut edition by Barakāt Yūsuf Habbūd, with a commentary titled *Bawāriq al-ishārāt wa-l-tawjīhāt limā fī l-Dustūr min al-maṭālib wa-l-maʾāthir wa-l-ʿiẓāt* (*Lightning Flashes of Directives and Explanations regarding the Aims, Benefits, and Recommendations of the Dustūr Compendium*), and a 2003 Damascus edition by Ḥasan al-Samāḥī Suwaydān with the earlier al-Daljamūnī commentary. An online version of the text is also available.[51]

This edition

In formulating a new critical edition of the *Dustūr*, I have relied equally on the Egyptian, Yemeni, and Indian manuscripts. All three appear to be largely accurate, the Egyptian manuscript having been corrected by students over several generations, and the Yemeni and Indian manuscripts also bearing marks of rectification. All three also have some lacunae resulting perhaps from water damage, and—this is true of the Yemeni manuscript in particular—a few clear mistranscriptions as well as missing words or lines.

The manuscripts have distinct pedigrees, the variant readings in the manuscripts indicating dissimilar copyist traditions. However, some of the differences appear to stem from disparities in the earlier, oral transmission, rather than writing errors.[52] In weighing the variants of the three manuscripts, I have factored those in the *Nahj al-balāghah* (*Path of Eloquence*) and works of history, as well as al-Kaydarī's compilation of ʿAlī's *Dīwān* for chapter 9, and the Iraqi manuscript *Munājāt amīr al-muʾminīn* (*Prayers of the Commander of the Faithful*) for chapter 8.

My principal editing choices include the following:

- The three full manuscripts contain a fairly large number of variant words or phrases. I have chosen the reading I thought worked best with regard to the grammar, meaning, rhythm, and rhyme of the piece, indicating substantial variants in the notes.
- I have given preference to any reading supported by two manuscripts against the sole reading of the third; typically, the Egyptian and Indian versus the Yemeni.
- I have not indicated minor differences such as variances in prepositions, conjunctions, orthography, and arrangement of proverbs (for this last, I follow the Egyptian manuscript).
- To make the text more accessible to readers, I have numbered the proverbs and other sections of the text, and inserted paragraphs and

appropriate punctuation. Among the earlier editors, Suwaydān alone numbers the texts; my numbering partially corresponds to his.

- In Chapter 9, I have provided the poetic meters in parentheses.
- The Egyptian and Iraqi manuscripts, and all the previous editions provide full—albeit sometimes differing—vocalization. I vocalize only those parts of the text which may not be obvious to an educated reader of classical Arabic.
- The manuscripts differ in their rendition of pious formulae attached to the name of God and the names of exalted personages in Islam; I have not indicated these differences.
- In his Introduction to the *Dustūr*, al-Quḍāʿī writes that he has included marks within the text identifying the transmitters of individual sayings, and that he has explained these marks at the end of the book. None of the manuscripts retains these marks, and as a result, they do not appear in this edition.

II. Al-Jāḥiẓ, *One Hundred Proverbs* (*Miʾat kalimah*)

The *Miʾat kalimah* does not appear to have survived as a stand-alone text, but multiple copies of commentaries, translations, versifications, and illuminations of the work appear in most major manuscript collections, and several have been published. Some literary works also include the text of the *Miʾat kalimah*. Of these sources, I have relied on the following manuscripts and editions to formulate a critical edition of the stand-alone text:

Manuscripts

[١] **Istanbul manuscript (early tenth/sixteenth century), Topkapi,** B. 122. This manuscript was copied in the early tenth/sixteenth century by Manṣūr ibn Yūsuf al-Malakī al-Ashrafī. It is beautifully calligraphed and illuminated, with a Persian verse rendition by al-Waṭwāṭ, and an Ottoman Turkish commentary. It does not include the Ibn Durayd-Ibn Abī Ṭāhir preface. This is the earliest manuscript I have used. With 98 sayings, it is missing two which occur in all the other sources. It has been reproduced in a facsimile edition by Ananiasz Zajączkowski as *Sto Sentencyj i Apoftegmatów Arabskich Kalifa Alīego w Parafrazie Mamelucko-*

Tureckiej (Warsaw: Państwowe wydawnictwo naukowe, 1968), which I have used.

[ط] **Tokyo manuscript (1158/1745), University of Tokyo**, Arabic-Daiber collection, ms. 136, text no. 2294. This manuscript was copied in 1158/1745 by al-Sayyid Ṣādiq Muḥammad al-ʿUmarī al-Dimashqī. It includes the Ibn Durayd-Ibn Abī Ṭāhir preface, and a brief commentary by an anonymous scholar.

Previous editions

[و] **Al-Waṭwāṭ (d. 578/1182) commentary/versification**, edited by M. Heinrich Leberecht Fleischer (Leipzig: W. Vogel Sohn, 1837). This is an edition of a brief Arabic and Persian commentary with an additional Persian couplet rendition and a Persian introduction by Rashīd al-Dīn ʿAbd al-Jalīl, known as al-Rashīd al-Waṭwāṭ. The commentary is titled *Maṭlūb kull ṭālib min kalām ʿAlī ibn Abī Ṭālib* (*What Every Student Needs, to Understand the Words of ʿAlī ibn Abī Ṭālib*). The Fleischer edition includes a facing-page German translation, and is titled *Ali's hundert Sprüche: arabisch und persisch paraphrasirt von Reschideddin Watwat nebst einem doppelten Anhange arabischer Sprüche*. Al-Waṭwāṭ's introduction includes the line from the Ibn Durayd-Ibn Abī Ṭāhir preface, which has al-Jāḥiẓ saying that each maxim is worth a thousand eloquent sayings of the Arabs.

[ب] **Al-Baḥrānī (d. 679/1280) commentary**, edited by Mīr Jalāl al-Dīn al-Ḥusaynī al-Armawī al-Muḥaddith (Qom: Manshūrāt al-Mudarrisīn fī l-Ḥawzah al-ʿIlmiyyah, 1970). This is an edition of a lengthy Arabic commentary by Kamāl al-Dīn Maytham al-Baḥrānī titled *Sharḥ al-ʿĀlim al-rabbānī Kamāl al-Dīn Maytham ibn ʿAlī ibn Maytham al-Baḥrānī qaddasa sirrahū ʿalā l-Miʾat kalimah li-Amīr al-muʾminīn ʿAlī ibn Abī Ṭālib ʿalayhi l-salām* (*The Commentary of the Divine Scholar Kamāl al-Dīn Maytham ibn ʿAlī ibn Maytham al-Baḥrānī on the One Hundred Proverbs of ʿAlī ibn Abī Ṭālib*). Al-Baḥrānī's introduction includes a paraphrase of the Ibn Durayd-Ibn Abī Ṭāhir preface.

Literary works that include the text of the Mi'at kalimah[53]

[ث] **Al-Thaʿālibī (d. 429/1038)**, *al-Iʿjāz wa-l-ījāz* (*Inimitability and Pithiness*), edited by Ibrāhīm Ṣāliḥ (Damascus: Dār al-Bashāʾir, 2001), pp. 37–38. Al-Thaʿālibī says he includes "the 100 proverbs collected by Abū ʿUthmān ʿAmr ibn Baḥr al-Jāḥiẓ," but he only appears to list 82 of them, and does not include the Ibn Durayd-Ibn Abī Ṭāhir preface.

[خ] **Al-Khwārizmī (d. 568/1172)**, *Kitāb al-Manāqib* (*The Book of Virtues*) (Najaf: al-Maktabah al-Ḥaydariyyah, 1965), pp. 270–73. Abū l-Muʾayyad al-Muwaffaq ibn Aḥmad al-Bakrī al-Makkī al-Ḥanafī al-Khwārizmī cites the al-Jāḥiẓ attribution, lists 104 proverbs, and includes the Ibn Durayd-Ibn Abī Ṭāhir preface.

This edition

I primarily follow the Istanbul manuscript, supplemented closely by the Tokyo manuscript and Fleischer's edition of the al-Waṭwāṭ commentary; I also use al-Armawī's edition of al-Baḥrānī's commentary, Ṣāliḥ's edition of al-Thaʿālibī's *al-Iʿjāz*, and the 1965 Najaf edition of al-Khwārizmī's *Kitāb al-Manāqib*. With some exceptions, all the sources listed above contain the same hundred sayings, and follow the same order. Within the text of the sayings, there are several minor variants, and a few consequential differences which I note. Some details pertaining to my editing choices are as follows:

- I have included the Ibn Durayd-Ibn Abī Ṭāhir preface, using the version provided by the Tokyo manuscript, supplemented by the 1965 Najaf edition of al-Khwārizmī's *Kitāb al-Manāqib*.
- The Istanbul manuscript begins most sayings with "And he also said," which does not occur in the other sources; I have omitted this.
- The Istanbul manuscript lists only 98 sayings; I have added the missing two (no. 73 and no. 97) from Fleischer's edition of the al-Waṭwāṭ commentary and collated them with the Tokyo manuscript.
- There are several nouns which are presented in some sources with the definite article *al-* and in others without (such as no. 15 and no. 16). I have followed the Istanbul manuscript in these, and have not indicated the variants.

III. The Translations

Any literary work in which rhythm and metaphor play a key role poses a challenge to the translator, and ʿAlī's words, even in the original Arabic, have been described as "easy yet impossible" to mimic (*sahl mumtaniʿ*). The language of the Arabic text is for the most part deceptively simple, with straightforward syntax and a commonly used lexicon (common, at least, for ʿAlī's time). Individual words are often unproblematic to translate on their own, but when strung together, the deeper meaning of the sentence is not so easy to convey. The Arabic text is pithy, and maintaining a similar succinctness in translation is difficult. Furthermore, the texts are poetically dense, abounding in culturally specific idioms and historical allusions, whereas English has a wholly different set of associations. A translator has to navigate treacherous waters, for unlike a commentator, she must select just one rendering to convey a host of meanings, a rendering that best articulates the substance of the original yet makes sense to an audience whose cultural background is quite different. On the one hand, it is important to use an idiom that resonates with the English reader. On the other, it is also important to retain raw and graphic expressions, and to translate metaphors literally, rather than interpreting them away into hollow abstractions that dilute the cultural specificity of the original.

Keeping these larger issues in mind, I have striven for sentence to sentence translation, rather than word to word correspondence. Instead of pedantically trying to reproduce the lexical meaning of each word, I have found it is more important to convey the spirit of what is being said in the Arabic. The following list catalogs the choices I have made in the translation to achieve this purpose. Where appropriate, I have:

- added words to unpack the dense Arabic;
- modified syntax and morphology for an idiomatic English rendering;
- changed third person to second person in proverbs;
- replaced pronouns with names for clarity;
- converted passives to actives;
- dropped "He said, . . . I said . . ." phrases introducing individual lines of the question-and-answer pieces in chapter 5;
- translated a single Arabic word differently in different places;

- removed the phrase "another category" that occurs at the head of certain sets of proverbs in chapters 1 and 4, which indicate the groupings' similar grammatical structure (they are retained in the Arabic);
- removed "narrated from ʿAlī" and similar phrases from the chapter titles; and
- presented in smaller font: (a) the chains of transmitters in several chapters, and (b) al-Quḍāʿī's explanation of rare words in chapter 6.

Three other points to note:

- Translations of Qur'anic verses are my own; I have found it preferable to do so in order to maintain the consistency of the translation, as well as to highlight the meaning of the verse in the context of each piece.
- Specialized terminology is a challenge encountered equally by translators of literary and non-literary texts. As any good Saussurian knows, differences in language arise not just from differences in the signifier, but more deeply, from differences in the concepts signified. There is no perfect translation of these culturally specific words, but some renderings come closer to the import of the word in the original culture than others. To this end, I have translated certain technical religious terms differently from their conventional English rendering, to convey better what I believe is the traditional usage of the term in its Islamic context: For example, I translate "Islam" as "commitment to God's will" (rather than "submission" to it); *taqwā* as "piety" or "being conscious of God" (rather than "fear of God"); *zuhd* as "rejection of worldliness" or "indifference to the world" (rather than "rejection of the world" or "asceticism").
- For pronouns referring to the world (*al-dunyā*), I have sometimes used the neutral form "it," and at other times, when the context is clearly playing to the metaphor of the world as temptress, the feminine "she"; the word *al-dunyā* is feminine in Arabic.

Notes to the Introduction

1 Ibn ʿAsākir, *Tārīkh Madīnat Dimashq*, 24: 402.

2 Al-Jahshiyārī, *Kitāb al-Wuzarāʾ*, p. 82. Other accolades include those by al-Sharīf al-Raḍī (*Nahj al-balāghah*, pp. 28–29), Ibn Abī l-Hadīd (*Sharḥ Nahj al-balāghah*, 1:24), Muḥammad ʿAbduh (*Nahj al-balāghah*, p. 23), and Ṭāhir Sayf al-Dīn (*Tadhkirat al-labīb*, pp. 80–81). Eulogies for ʿAlī's wisdom and eloquence abound, many of which have been collected by ʿAbd al-Zahrāʾ in *Maṣādir*, 1:43–47, 87–99, and by editors of compilations of ʿAlī's words.

3 ʿAlī's close companions include Salmān al-Fārisī, ʿAmmār ibn al-Yāsir, Abū Dharr al-Ghifārī, Miqdād ibn al-Aswad al-Kindī, Ḥudhayfah al-Yamān, Mālik al-Ashtar, ʿAbdallāh ibn ʿAbbās, Muḥammad ibn Abī Bakr, and Kumayl ibn Ziyād.

4 This report is found in several sources; this version is from the earliest: al-Qālī, *al-Amālī*, 2:147. Other sources include: al-Masʿūdī, *Murūj al-dhahab* 2:415; Abū Nuʿaym al-Iṣbahānī, *Ḥilyat al-awliyāʾ*, 1:84–85; al-Raḍī, *Nahj al-balāghah*, pp. 641–42; Ibn ʿAsākir, *Tārīkh Madīnat Dimashq*, 24:401; Ibn Ḥamdūn, *al-Tadhkirah*, 4:28; Ibn Abī l-Ḥadīd, *Sharḥ Nahj al-balāghah* 18:225–26; it is also cited in the modern anthology by Ṣafwat, *Jamharat khuṭab al-ʿArab* 2:374.

5 This line is added from the al-Masʿūdī version, *Murūj al-dhahab* 2:415.

6 Lit., "Wisdom spoke from his sides" (*tanṭiqu l-ḥikmatu min nawāḥīhi*), its meaning is not conveyed clearly if translated literally. I have modified the word "sides" to "tongue" here, basing my translation on the variant version of Ibn ʿAsākir (*Tārīkh Madīnat Dimashq*, 24:402): "Wisdom spoke upon his tongue" (*tanṭiqu l-ḥikmatu ʿalā lisānihī*).

7 Al-Masʿūdī, *Murūj al-dhahab* 2:415, adds here: "His smile revealed two rows of strung pearls. He respected the pious and was kind to the poor. He fed the hungry, «orphaned relatives, and the starving destitute.» [Q Balad 90:15–16]. He clothed the naked and consoled the grieving."

8 What is more, just as some of the materials that entered the corpus of teachings attributed to ʿAlī were likely produced afterward, some may even have preceded him. Dimitri Gutas in "Classical Arabic Wisdom Literature: Nature and Scope," and Riad Kassis, in *The Book of Proverbs and Arabic Proverbial Works*, argue that some maxims from the Islamic corpus may actually be older than Islam, arising from a mixture of Biblical and other Near Eastern cultural material.

9 See Carruthers, *The Book of Memory.*

10 See Schoeler, *The Genesis of Literature in Islam,* and *idem, The Oral and the Written in Early Islam.*

11 I have argued this position in more detail elsewhere: see my article, "*Khuṭba*: Evolution of Early Arabic Oration," pp. 187–89, and my forthcoming book, *Classical Arabic Oratory*. See also ʿAbd al-Zahrāʾ, *Maṣādir*, vol. 1. A list of people who transmitted from ʿAlī is provided by Habbūd in the introduction to his edition of the *Dustūr*, p. 20.

12 See ʿAbd al-Zahrāʾ, *Maṣādir*, 1:51.

13 For details of these attributions, see ʿAbd al-Zahrāʾ, *Maṣādir*, 1:51–66.

14 Scholars who recorded ʿAlī's words in synthetic works of history include Ibn Saʿd (d. 230/845), al-Balādhurī (d. 279/892), Ibn al-Aʿtham al-Kūfī (fl. early third/ninth c.), al-Yaʿqūbī (d. 284/897), and al-Ṭabarī (d. 314/923).

15 For a full list, see ʿAbd al-Zahrāʾ, *Maṣādir*, 1:66–86.

16 For example, a few maxims are attributed to ʿAlī in the *Treasury of Virtues*, but credited to the prophet Muḥammad in certain hadith compilations, and a pious sermon from the *Treasury of Virtues* is ascribed in another source to the Khārijite commander Qaṭarī ibn al-Fujāʾah.

17 Cf. the detailed exposition in Richard Lanham, *Analyzing Prose*, pp. 122–39 (ch. 6, "Tacit Persuasion Patterns").

18 Ong, *Orality and Literacy*, p. 34 and *passim.*

19 Ong, *Orality and Literacy*, pp. 34–57.

20 I have explored this confluence in some detail through a close reading of certain key texts of ʿAlī's sermons in a recent article, "The Sermons of ʿAli."

21 "Egyptian" subjects, *per* Ibn Khallikān.

22 Ibn Mākūlā, *Kitāb al-Ikmāl*, 7:115.

23 Al-Silafī, *Mashyakhat al-Rāzī*, 1:241–42.

24 Al-Quḍāʿī's biographers include: al-Ḥabbāl, *Wafayāt qawm min al-Miṣriyyīn*, 1:87; Ibn ʿAṭiyyah, *Fihris Ibn ʿAṭiyyah*, 1:128; Ibn ʿAsākir, *Tārīkh Madīnat Dimashq*, 53:167–70; Ibn Khallikān, *Wafayāt al-aʿyān*, 4:212, 4:523–24; al-Dhahabī, *Tārīkh al-Islām* 30:368–70; al-Yāfiʿī, *Mirʾāt al-jinān*, 3:75; al-Subkī, *Ṭabaqāt al-Shāfiʿiyyah al-Kubrā*, 3:62–63; and Ibn al-ʿImād, *Shadharāt al-dhahab*, 3:293.

25 Al-Quḍāʿī studied hadith with several well-known scholars including Abū Muslim Muḥammad ibn Aḥmad al-Baghdādī, Aḥmad ibn ʿUmar al-Jīzī, and Abū ʿAbdallāh al-Yamanī. He transmitted hadith to men who would become well-known jurists in their own right, including Ibn Mākūlā, Abū Bakr Aḥmad ibn ʿAlī al-Khaṭīb, Abū Saʿd ʿAbd

al-Jalīl al-Sāwī, Muḥammad ibn Barakāt al-Saʿīdī, Sahl ibn Bishr al-Isfarāʾīnī, and Abū ʿAbdallāh al-Rāzī.

26 Ibn ʿAsākir, *Tārīkh Madīnat Dimashq*, 53:168–69.

27 Al-Maqrīzī mentions al-Quḍāʿī's *Khiṭaṭ* in his own *Khiṭaṭ* (1:5) but oddly, does not do so in his biographical entry on al-Quḍāʿī in the *Muqaffā* (5:710–11).

28 Al-Silafī, *Mashyakhat al-Rāzī*, 1:241–42; al-Maqrīzī, *Muqaffā*, 5:710. Habbūd, in his edition of the *Dustūr* (p. 33) and al-Salafī in his introduction to the *Musnad al-Shihāb* (1:9) say al-Quḍāʿī's *Tafsīr* is in 20 volumes, but they do not cite the medieval source for their information.

29 Ibn ʿAṭiyyah, *Fihris*, 1:128, presumably about the number of verses in the Qur'an, in the vein of several other books by that name.

30 The *Durrat al-wāʿiẓīn* is cited by Ḥājjī Khalīfah, *Kashf al-ẓunūn*, 1:745. Habbūd in his edition of the *Dustūr* (p. 33) says it is extant in manuscript form, but does not provide its location.

31 The *Daqāʾiq al-akhbār* is cited by Ismāʿīl Pāshā, *Hadiyyat al-ʿārifīn*, 6:70.

32 Al-Silafī, *Mashyakhah*, 1:242.

33 Suwaydān ed. pp. 13–14, Habbūd, p. 33, al-Salafī, pp. 9–10, citing al-Marāghī, *al-Lubāb fī-sharḥ al-Shihāb*.

34 Ibn ʿAsākir, *Tārīkh Madīnat Dimashq*, 53:169; al-Silafī, *Mashyakhah*, 1:241; al-Dhahabī, *Tārīkh al-Islām* 30:370; al-Maqrīzī, *Muqaffā*, 5:711.

35 See for example 5.7, 8.1.41.

36 Al-Shāfiʿī, *Dīwān*, 5 segments, pp. 58, 73, 89, 113.

37 Al-Thaʿālibī, *al-Iʿjāz wa-l-ījāz*, pp. 37–38.

38 Al-Khwārizmī, *Kitāb al-Manāqib*, pp. 270–73.

39 Ibn al-Ṣabbāgh, *al-Fuṣūl al-muhimmah*, pp. 537–48.

40 Al-Āmidī, *Ghurar al-ḥikam*, p. 2.

41 Pellat, "Nouvel essai d'inventaire de l'oeuvre Ǧāḥiẓienne," p. 131, no. 35.

42 I found three maxims from the *One Hundred Proverbs* in al-Jāḥiẓ, *al-Bayān*: "قيمة كل امرئ ما يحسنه" (1:83, 2:77); "الحكمة ضالة المؤمن" (1:85); and "السعيد من وعظ بغيره" (1:398); the first of these also occurs in his *Risālah fī l-Muʿallimīn* (*Rasāʾil al-Jāḥiẓ*, 3:25) and *Risālah fī Manāqib al-Turk* (ibid., 1:29); a fourth maxim occurs in *Risālah fī l-Jidd wa-l-hazl* "رأي الشيخ أحب إلي من جلد الغلام" (ibid., 1:192); and a fifth (without specific attribution to ʿAlī) in *Risālah fī l-Awṭān wa-l-buldān* "الناس بأزمانهم أشبه منهم بآبائهم" (ibid., 4:79).

43 See the folio from an illuminated manuscript of the *Mi'at kalimah* in the Bavarian State Library, with Arabic original and an anonymous scholar's Persian verses, in *The Wonders of Creation*, pp. 148–49; and another with al-Waṭwāṭ's verses in *ibid.*, pp. 174–75.

44 Al-Baḥrānī also wrote two commentaries on the *Path of Eloquence.*

45 Ockley, *Sentences of Ali,* section A3: "Preface."

46 I would like to acknowledge my debt to Ṭabāṭabā'ī's article, "Ahl al-bayt fī l-maktabah al-'arabiyyah," for the current location of this manuscript in the Chester Beatty library, which al-'Aẓm had seen as part of a private collection. The article also provides useful biographical references for scholars and transmitters associated with the manuscript.

47 The first work in the manuscript is titled *Tafsīr gharīb al-Qur'ān* (*Exegesis of the Rare Words of the Qur'an*) attributed to Zayd ibn 'Alī (d. 122/740, from whom the Zaydī school of Shi'ism takes its name), followed by the *Dustūr,* and the third text, or rather set of texts, is informally titled *Naql mā lafiẓahū* (*A Record of Things He Said,* referring to Zayd again, as noted in the margin).

48 The post title page folio with 'Alī's praise has what appears to be a narrow piece of paper pasted on the right side, covering some of the writing below, which states in verse that the book is "Donated as a religious endowment, *waqf,* to the children of the community, by a servant of 'Alī (or by a man named 'Abd-Alī)," (*waqfun li-wajhi l-wāḥidi l-fardi l-'alī – 'alā banī l-da'wati min 'abdi 'Alī*). Another note on the same piece of paper states "from the first, divinely aided, treasury" (*min al-khazānah al-awwalah al-muwaffaqah*).

49 The Iraqi manuscript contains roughly half of *Dustūr* 8.1, viz. 8.1.1–8.1.3, 8.1.16–8.1.18, 8.1.20–8.1.39, 8.1.67, 8.1.74, and part of 8.1.77. Moreover, it includes 9 short prayers that are not present in the *Dustūr.*

50 'Abd al-Zahrā' (in the Introduction to his edition of the *Dustūr,* p. 9) mentions a work by Abū l-Sa'ādāt As'ad ibn 'Abd al-Qāhir al-Iṣbahānī titled *Majma' al-baḥrayn wa-maṭla' al-sa'ādatayn* that he says brings together al-Quḍā'ī's *Kitāb al-Shihāb* containing the wisdom of the prophet Muḥammad and his *Dustūr* containing the wisdom of 'Alī. This statement appears to be incorrect, since the author says in his introduction (p. 63) that he has based his work on al-Quḍā'ī's *Kitāb al-Shihāb* and on al-Raḍī's compilation of 'Alī's words, the *Nahj al-balāghah.*

There is some confusion among scholars regarding the title of al-Iṣbahānī's compilation. The printed edition of this work (ed. Ṣādiq al-Ishkivarī, Tehran, 1385/1965) is titled *Maṭla' al-ṣabāḥatayn wa-majma' al-faṣāḥatayn* (*The Rising-Place of the Two Mornings, and the Confluence of the Two Eloquences*)—slightly different from the title cited by 'Abd al-Zahrā'. It is possible that there is more than one work by this author drawing on different collections of sayings by 'Alī, and that one draws on the *Nahj al-balāghah* while the other draws on the *Dustūr.* More likely, 'Abd al-Zahrā' was mistaken, and al-Iṣbahānī produced one compilation that scholars referred to by two or more names, which drew not on the *Dustūr* but on the *Nahj al-balāghah.*

51 http://gadir.free.fr/Ar/imamali/kutub2/Destur_Mealimul_Hikem.htm The website does not mention the source for the text, nor the name of an editor; presumably it is copied from the al-ʿAẓm Cairo 1914 edition (it misspells the name of the author in the same way the al-ʿAẓm edition does, viz., al-Quṣāʾī). The text is not vocalized, but the meanings of rare words are provided; there are some typographical errors.

52 The dissimilar letters *n* and *z* in the words نائل in the Egyptian manuscript and زايل in the Yemeni manuscript (*Dustūr* 2.3) derive from copyist error, but variant pairs such as لم يتَّهِمْها in the former and يسكن إليها in the latter (*Dustūr* 2.14.2), or عصرة in the former and ملجأ in the latter (*Dustūr* 8.2), would seem to originate in the distinct oral transmission of each manuscript, their differences rooted in the meaning, rather than the consonantal skeleton, of the words.

53 There is a third book, a late work, that includes the text of the *Miʾat kalimah*, which I have not used for this edition, as it does not add anything we do not already have from the earlier sources, namely, Ibn al-Ṣabbāgh (d. 855/1451), *al-Fuṣūl al-muhimmah*, pp. 537–48. Ibn al-Ṣabbāgh records the text without referring to it by this, or any other, title, but he does cite its attribution to al-Jāḥiẓ. He lists 93 proverbs, but among his list are a few pairs that are presented as a single aphorism in the other works. His introduction includes a line from the Ibn Durayd-Ibn Abī Ṭāhir preface, without naming either individual.

دستور معالم الحِكَم ومأثور مكارم الشِّيَم

من كلام أمير المؤمنين عليّ بن أبي طالب

صلّى الله تعالى عليه وآله وسلّم

من تأليف

القاضي محمّد بن سلامة القُضاعيّ

A Treasury of Virtues

Sayings, Sermons, and Teachings of ʿAlī

compiled by

AL-QĀḌĪ AL-QUḌĀʿĪ

بسم الله الرحمن الرحيم

الحمد لله الذي وسع كلّ شيء علمه ونفذ في كلّ مصنوع قضاؤه وحُكمه وعمّ جميع العباد عفوه وحلمه. الذي يختصّ بالحكمة من يشاء من أوليائه ويختار لها المخلصين من أصفيائه نعمة منه جلّت قدرته وفضلا كبيرا ﴿وَمَن يُؤْتَ ٱلْحِكْمَةَ فَقَدْ أُوتِيَ خَيْرًا كَثِيرًا﴾. فتعالى الله الحكيم الخبير الذي ﴿لَيْسَ كَمِثْلِهِۦ شَىْءٌ ۖ وَهُوَ ٱلسَّمِيعُ ٱلْبَصِيرُ﴾.

وصلّى الله على المخصوص من الحكمة بأفصحها لسانا وأوضحها دلالة وبيانا وأظهرها حجّة وسلطانا محمّد نبيّ الرحمة والمؤيّد بالهداية والعصمة والكاشف لغياهب العمى والظلمة حتّى أشرقت أحكام الإيمان وبسقت أعلام القرآن[1] ونطقت الألسنة مخلصة بتوحيد ٱلرحمٰن و زهقت أباطيل الضلالة والبهتان. وعلى آله الذين ٱصطفاهم لوراثة كتابه وحباهم بالنصيب الأوفى من ثوابه وجعلهم للأمّة هداة وأعلاما وبأحكام دينه قوّاما وحكّاما. وسلّم عليه وعليهم تسليما.

أمّا بعد: فإنّي لمّا جمعت من حديث رسول الله صلّى الله عليه وعلى آله وسلّم ألف كلمة ومائتي كلمة في الوصايا والأمثال والمواعظ والآداب وضمّنتها كتابا وسمّيته بالشّهاب سألني بعض الإخوان أن أجمع من كلام أمير المؤمنين عليّ بن أبي طالب صلوات الله عليه وسلامه نحوا من عدد الكلمات المذكورة وأن أعتمد في ذلك على ما أرويه وأجده في مصنّف من أثق به وأرتضيه وأن أجعله مسرودا محذوف الأسانيد كفعلي في كتاب الشهاب. فٱستخرت الله جلّت قدرته وجمعت من كلامه عليه السلام وبلاغته وحِكمه وعِظاته وآدابه وجواباته وأدعيته ومناجاته والمحفوظ من شعره وتمثيلاته تسعة أبواب منوّعة أنواعا:

١ فالباب الأوّل: فيما رُوي عنه من فوائد حِكمه

٢ والباب الثاني: فيما روي عنه في ذمّه الدنيا وتزهيده فيها

٣ والباب الثالث: فيما روي عنه من المواعظ

٤ والباب الرابع: فيما روي عنه من وصاياه ونواهيه

---

١ هـ: (الفرقان).

In the name of God, the compassionate, the merciful

God be praised! His knowledge encompasses all things, his judgment and rule direct every creature, and his forgiveness and forbearance envelop all his servants. He grants wisdom to whomsoever he wishes among his elect, and he chooses for that wisdom the sincere among his select, as a grace from him and a great favor—for «whosoever is granted wisdom is granted much good.»[1] God is most high, wise, knowing, «there is none like him, he is the listener, the perceiver.»[2]

May God bless the one favored with the most eloquent tongue of wisdom, its clearest proof and exposition, its plainest evidence and authority: Muḥammad, the prophet of mercy, divinely aided by right-guidance and infallibility, who removed the veils of blindness and obscurity, so that the laws of belief shone forth, the banners of the Qur'an became elevated, tongues declared God's oneness, and the falsehoods of error and calumny disintegrated. May he bless Muḥammad's progeny, whom he selected as legatees for his book, and to whom he gifted the largest share of his reward; he made them guides for the community, and judges and upholders of the laws of his religion. May he bestow well-being upon him and upon them.

I collected into a book twelve hundred testaments, maxims, counsels, and directions for refined behavior from the Traditions of the messenger of God, calling it *The Blazing Star* (*al-Shihāb*). Upon its completion, one of my brothers asked me to collect approximately the same number of sayings from the words of the commander of the faithful, ʿAlī ibn Abī Ṭālib. He asked me to rely on texts that I have myself transmitted and those in books written by people I trust, asking that I present them uninterruptedly, omitting the chains of transmission, just as I did in *The Blazing Star*. I accordingly sought God's guidance, and collected materials from ʿAlī's words, eloquent sayings, wise maxims, counsels, directions for refined behavior, answers to questions, prayers, supplications, preserved verse, and allegories. I produced nine chapters divided by genre, as follows:

1 The first chapter on valuable sayings transmitted from him.
2 The second chapter on censure of this world and exhortations to reject worldliness transmitted from him.
3 The third chapter on counsels transmitted from him.
4 The fourth chapter on prescriptions and proscriptions transmitted from him.

٥ والباب الخامس: في المرويّ عنه من أجوبته عن المسائل وسؤالاته

٦ والباب السادس: في المرويّ عنه من غريب كلامه

٧ والباب السابع: في المرويّ عنه من نوادر كلامه وملح ألفاظه

٨ والباب الثامن: في أدعيته ومناجاته

٩ والباب التاسع: فيما انتهى إليّ من شعره

وقد أعلمت عند الكلمة التي أرويها علامة يُستدلّ بها على راويها على ما أبيّنه آخرَ هذا الكتاب وذكرت أسانيد الأخبار الطوال وأعلمت على ما كان منها وِجادة جيما

وأنا أرغب إلى الله تعالى في حسن التوفيق لما يُرضيه والمَعونة على العمل بما يُزلِف لديه وهو حسبي ونعم الوكيل

5 The fifth chapter on questions and answers to questions transmitted from him.
6 The sixth chapter on sayings with unusual words transmitted from him.
7 The seventh chapter on unique sayings and pithy words transmitted from him.
8 The eighth chapter on his prayers and supplications.
9 The ninth chapter on verse composed by him that I have come across.

I have placed next to every text that I transmit a mark indicating its narrator, which I shall explain at the end of the book. I have included the chains of transmission for the long reports, and indicated by the letter J those I have found in texts without continuous aural transmission.[3]

I ask God Most High for direction so that I may do what pleases him, and for aid to undertake this task, a task whose undertaking will bring me closer to him. He is my sufficiency, and he is the best guardian.

الباب الأوّل

فيما روي عنه عليه السلام من فوائد حكمه

خير ما جرّبتَ ما وعظك ١.١

خير أهلك من كفاك ١.٢

خير المقال[١] ما صدّقه الفِعال ١.٣

خير البلاد ما حملك ١.٤

خير الأمور أوساطها ١.٥

لكلّ أمر عاقبة ١.٦

لكلّ حياة أجل ١.٧

لكلّ مُقبِل إدبار ١.٨

لكلّ زمن قوت وأنت قوت الموت ١.٩

التاجر مُخاطر ١.١٠

التثبّت حزم ١.١١

الصاحب مناسِب ١.١٢

القِلّة ذلّة ١.١٣

الإنصاف راحة ١.١٤

اللَّجاج وَقاحة ١.١٥

التواني إضاعة ١.١٦

الحرص محقرة ١.١٧

الزنا مفقرة ١.١٨

---

١ هـ: في المتن (الكلام)، ونسخة في الحاشية (المقال).

Chapter 1

Wise Sayings

The best experience gives good counsel. 1.1

The best kinsman suffices in times of need. 1.2

The best words are backed by deeds. 1.3

The best country is one that sustains you. 1.4

The best affairs are those in the middle. 1.5

Every affair has a consequence. 1.6

Every life has an appointed end. 1.7

Everything that moves forward turns back. 1.8

Everything has its fodder; you are Death's. 1.9

A trader takes risks. 1.10

Constancy is a sign of character. 1.11

Friends are like kin. 1.12

Poverty humiliates. 1.13

Justice comforts. 1.14

The quarrelsome have no shame. 1.15

Delay causes waste. 1.16

Greed debases. 1.17

Fornication begets poverty. 1.18

السخاء قربة ١.١٩

اللؤم غربة ١.٢٠

التذلّل مسكنة ١.٢١

العجز مهانة ١.٢٢

العجز آفة ١.٢٣

العجلة زَلَل ١.٢٤

الإبطاء مَلَل ١.٢٥

الصبر شجاعة ١.٢٦

الجُبن منقصة ١.٢٧

البخل عارٌ ١.٢٨

الكذب ذلّ ١.٢٩

الحزم كِياسة ١.٣٠

الأدب رياسة ١.٣١

الفاحشة كاسمها ١.٣٢

الصدود آية المقت ١.٣٣

كثرة العلل آية البخل[١] ١.٣٤

التجرّم[٢] وجه القطيعة ١.٣٥

العبادة انتظار الفرج ١.٣٦

الفكرة مرآة صافية ١.٣٧

البشاشة مخّ[٣] المودّة ١.٣٨

الصبر جُنّة من الفاقة ١.٣٩

الحرص علامة الفقر ١.٤٠

---

١ ي: (كثرة العلل لآمة).

٢ هـ: (التحرم).

٣ م: (مح).

Generosity attracts affection. 1.19

Depravity isolates. 1.20

Dishonor bankrupts. 1.21

Incapacity is a form of wretchedness. 1.22

Incapacity is a calamity. 1.23

To hasten is to fall. 1.24

Tardiness wearies. 1.25

Forbearance is a form of courage. 1.26

Cowardice is a defect. 1.27

Stinginess is a vice. 1.28

Falsehood is a disgrace. 1.29

Prudence is smart. 1.30

Refinement elevates. 1.31

Wantonness is like its name.[4] 1.32

Obstruction is a sign of hatred. 1.33

Too many excuses are a sign of stinginess. 1.34

False accusations cause discord. 1.35

Waiting on God's succor is a form of worship. 1.36

Thought is a polished mirror. 1.37

Cheerfulness is the marrow of friendship. 1.38

Patience is a shield against destitution. 1.39

Greed is a sign of impoverishment. 1.40

التخلّي جلباب المسكنة ١٠٤١

المودّة قرابة مستفادة ١٠٤٢

الإعجاب ضدّ الصواب ١٠٤٣

الإعتبار مُنذر ناصح ١٠٤٤

الإعتبار يفيدك الرشاد ١٠٤٥

الشُّحّ يجلب المَلامة ١٠٤٦

الصديق من صدق غيبه ١٠٤٧

الهوى شريك العمى ١٠٤٨

عاقبة الكذب الذمّ ١٠٤٩

المِزاح يورث الضغائن ١٠٥٠

الإجتهاد أربح بضاعة ١٠٥١

الإقتصاد يُنمي اليسير ١٠٥٢

الفساد يُبيد الكثير ١٠٥٣

صدر العاقل صندوق سرّه ١٠٥٤

الغريب من ليس له حبيب ١٠٥٥

المُقلّ غريب في بلدته ١٠٥٦

الإحتمال قبر العيوب ١٠٥٧

رأس الدين صحّة اليقين ١٠٥٨

رأس العلم الرفق وآفته الخُرق ١٠٥٩

رأس الأمر معرفة الله تعالى وعموده طاعة الله عزّوجلّ ١٠٦٠

السلامة مع الإستقامة ١٠٦١

العَجَل مع الزلل ١٠٦٢

الدعاء مفتاح الرحمة ١٠٦٣

الصدقة دواء مُنجح ١٠٦٤

To shirk is to wear humiliation's robes. 1.41

Affection is a valuable form of kinship. 1.42

Conceit is the enemy of good judgment. 1.43

A lesson learned counsels best. 1.44

A lesson learned guides you aright. 1.45

Avarice disgusts. 1.46

A friend is true in your absence. 1.47

Desire blinds. 1.48

Falsehoods beget blame. 1.49

Teasing bequeaths malice. 1.50

Effort is the most profitable commodity. 1.51

Frugality increases what little you have. 1.52

Discord destroys prosperity. 1.53

A wise man's heart is a vault for his secrets. 1.54

The real exile is the person who has no-one to love. 1.55

A pauper is an exile in his hometown. 1.56

Forbearance is a tomb for shortcomings. 1.57

Conviction is the pinnacle of religion. 1.58

Compassion is the pinnacle of knowledge; harshness is its scourge. 1.59

Religion is a body; its head is knowledge of God, its spine obedience to him. 1.60

Well-being comes from uprightness. 1.61

Haste will be followed by a fall. 1.62

Supplication is the key which unlocks God's mercy. 1.63

Almsgiving is powerful medicine. 1.64

تمام الإخلاص تجنّب المعاصي ١٠٦٥

الهدى يجلو العمى ١٠٦٦

رسولك ترجمان عقلك ١٠٦٧

مِنك مَن أعتبك ١٠٦٨

العاقل من وعظته التجارب ١٠٦٩

المُخاف شرُّه يُخاف ١٠٧٠

المرء أحفظ لسرّه ١٠٧١

ظلم الضعيف أفحش الظلم ١٠٧٢

العقل حفظ التجارب ١٠٧٣

العفاف زينة الفقر ١٠٧٤

الشكر زينة الغنى ١٠٧٥

الشكر والورع جُنّة ١٠٧٦

الزهد في الدنيا قِصَر الأمل ١٠٧٧

الزهد قربة ١٠٧٨

الحلم سجيّة فاضلة ١٠٧٩

العلم وراثة كريمة ١٠٨٠

الفكرة نور والغفلة ضلالة ١٠٨١

الحقّ مثال والباطل خَبال ١٠٨٢

الحق يُنجي والباطل يُردي ١٠٨٣

دواء كلّ داء كتمانه ١٠٨٤

الآداب حُلل مُجدّدة ١٠٨٥

حسن الخُلق خير قرين ١٠٨٦

التوفيق خير قائد ١٠٨٧

الآداب خير ميراث ١٠٨٨

Repentance is complete when you cease to sin.	1.65
Right guidance banishes blindness.	1.66
The one who carries your message is your intellect's interpreter.	1.67
The one who sets right what you have done wrong is a friend indeed.	1.68
An intelligent man is counseled by experience.	1.69
A feared man is feared for his evil.	1.70
You protect your own secret best.	1.71
Oppressing the weak is the worst oppression.	1.72
Learning from experience is smart.	1.73
Decency adorns poverty.	1.74
Gratitude adorns affluence.	1.75
Gratitude and self-restraint are a shield.	1.76
Rejecting worldliness means desiring little.	1.77
Reject worldliness and you will draw closer to God.	1.78
Forbearance is an illustrious trait.	1.79
Knowledge is a noble legacy.	1.80
Thought is radiance, heedlessness is error.	1.81
Righteousness is exemplary, iniquity unsound.	1.82
Righteousness saves, iniquity destroys.	1.83
The cure for every illness is in its concealment.	1.84
Refined behavior is like new clothing.	1.85
Good character is your best companion.	1.86
Direction from God steers you best.	1.87
Refined behavior is the best legacy.	1.88

إمـام عادل خـير من مطر وابل ١.٨٩

مواصلة المُعدِم خـير من جـافٍ مُكثِر ١.٩٠

سَبُع أكول حَطوم خير من والٍ غَشوم ظَلوم ووال غشوم ظلوم خير من فتنة تدوم ١.٩١

رأي الشيخ خـير من مشهـد الغلام ١.٩٢

كَدَر الجماعة خـير من صفو الفُرقة ١.٩٣

العفـة مع الحرفة خـير لك من سرور مع فجور ١.٩٤

قُرنت الهيبة بالخيبة والحياء بالحِرمـان ١.٩٥

حسن اليأس خـير من الطلب إلى النـاس ١.٩٦

حسن التدبير مع الكَفـاف أكفى لك من الكثـير مع الإسراف ١.٩٧

المعروف أفضل الكنوز وأحصن الحصون ١.٩٨

الفرصـة تمرّ مَرّ السحـاب فٱنتهِزوا فرص الخير ١.٩٩

حفظ ما في يـدك أحبّ اليك من طلب مـا في يد غـيرك ١.١٠٠

تلافيك مـا فرّطت من صمتك أيسر من إدراكك مـا فات من منطقك ١.١٠١

تـذِلّ الأمور للمقادير حتّى يكون الحَتف في التدبير ١.١٠٢

قلّة الثقـة بعزّ[1] الله ذلّة ١.١٠٣

قطيعـة الجاهل تَعـدل صلة العـاقل ١.١٠٤

كفر النعمـة لؤم وصحبـة الجاهل شؤم ١.١٠٥

أَخلِقْ بمن غـدر أن لا يوفى له ١.١٠٦

في القُـنوط التفريـط ١.١٠٧

في الصـمت السلامـة من الندامـة ١.١٠٨

في سعـة الأخلاق كنوز الأرزاق ١.١٠٩

---

١ ي: (عزة). هـ: (نصر).

A just leader is better than abundant rainfall. 1.89

Better the companionship of the poor than the friendship of those who are wealthy but harsh. 1.90

Better a ravenous, devouring wild animal than a violent, tyrannical governor; and better a violent, tyrannical governor than lasting sedition. 1.91

An elder's advice is worth more than a youth's martyrdom. 1.92

Better turbidity in unison than purity in dissension. 1.93

Self-restraint combined with an occupation is better for you than gratification paired with dissoluteness. 1.94

The timid will falter and the meek lose their share. 1.95

Better to accept privation with grace than to solicit others. 1.96

Better good planning coupled with simple fare than plenty coupled with waste. 1.97

Good deeds are the richest treasure and the most impregnable fortress. 1.98

Opportunity passes like a cloud, so seize every opportunity for good. 1.99

Guarding your property is far better than coveting another's. 1.100

Making up for too much silence is easier than retracting what escapes your lips. 1.101

All affairs bow to the fates; sometimes too much planning can lead to death. 1.102

Lack of trust in God's power debases. 1.103

Dissociating from a fool is equal to befriending an intelligent man. 1.104

Ingratitude for God's favors is contemptible, and the company of the ignorant is grievous. 1.105

It is most fitting for a deceiver to be deceived. 1.106

Utter despair is excessive. 1.107

Silence saves you from regret. 1.108

God's sustenance is located in the expanses of noble character. 1.109

في خلاف النفوس رشد ١.١١٠

في التجارب[1] علم مُستأنَف ١.١١١

لقاء أهل الخير عمارة القلوب ١.١١٢

إنّ من الكرم الوفاء بالذمم ١.١١٣

لَبعض إمساكك عن أخيك مع لطف خير لك من بذل[2] مع حَيف ١.١١٤

مِن الكرم لِين الشِّيَم ١.١١٥

من الكرم صلة الرحِم ١.١١٦

من الكرم منع الحُرَم ١.١١٧

من الحزم العزم ١.١١٨

من خير حظّ آمرئ قرين صالح ١.١١٩

من سبب الحرمان التواني ١.١٢٠

من الفساد إضاعة الزاد ١.١٢١

من شرّ ما صحب المرءَ الحسد ١.١٢٢

من التوفيق الوقوف عند الحيرة ١.١٢٣

مرتبة الرجل بحسن عقله ١.١٢٤

عزّ[3] المؤمن غِناه عن الناس ١.١٢٥

المؤمن لا يحيف على من يبغض ١.١٢٦

المؤمن أخو المؤمن فلا يَغُشّه ولا يغتابه ولا يدَع نصرته ١.١٢٧

الحكمة ضالّة المؤمن فآطلب ضالّتك ولو في أهل الشرك ١.١٢٨

الموعظة كهف لمن وعاها ١.١٢٩

التواضع يُرشد إلى السلامة ١.١٣٠

الساعات تَهضِم عمرك ١.١٣١

---

١ ي: (التجارات).

٢ ي: (الكرم).

٣ ي: (غنا).

Resisting the appetite fosters rectitude. 1.110

New experiences rejuvenate knowledge. 1.111

Meeting good people makes the heart blossom. 1.112

The noble fulfill their pledges. 1.113

Better to withhold something from your brother with kindness than to proffer it with severity. 1.114

Gentle character is a sign of nobility. 1.115

Affection toward kin is a sign of nobility. 1.116

Protection of women is a sign of nobility. 1.117

Resolve brings self-control. 1.118

A man's greatest fortune is a virtuous life partner. 1.119

Delay causes deprivation. 1.120

Squandered provisions make for a hard journey. 1.121

Envy is one of man's worst companions. 1.122

Pausing when you are confused is a sign of God's stewardship. 1.123

A man's intelligence determines his rank. 1.124

The measure of a believer's honor is his self-reliance. 1.125

A believer does not oppress his detractor. 1.126

Believers are brothers: they should not cheat, or slander, or hesitate to help one another. 1.127

Believers, wisdom is like your own lost camel; seek it even among the infidels. 1.128

A piece of advice is a sheltering cave for the heedful. 1.129

Humility guides you to safety. 1.130

The passing hours inexorably devour your allotted lifespan. 1.131

الرغبة مفتاح التعب ومطيّة النصَب ١.١٣٢

الشَّرَهُ جامع لمساوئ العيوب ١.١٣٣

الحسد آفة الدين ١.١٣٤

خسر مروءته من ضعفت نفسه ١.١٣٥

أَزرى بنفسه من ٱستشعر الطمع ١.١٣٦

هانت عليه نفسه من أمَّر عليها لسانه ١.١٣٧

رضي بالذلّ مَن كشف ضرّه ١.١٣٨

قد خاطر بنفسه من ٱستغنى برأيه ١.١٣٩

قد يُدرَك بشكر الشاكر ما يَضيع بجُحود الكافر ١.١٤٠

قد يكون اليأس إدراكا إذا كان الطمع هلاكا ١.١٤١

أوحش الوحشة العُجب ١.١٤٢

أكرم الحسب حسن الخلق ١.١٤٣

الحرص داعٍ إلى التقحّم في الذنوب ١.١٤٤

أنفع الكنوز محبّة القلوب ١.١٤٥

الفقر يُخرِس الفَطِن عن حجّته ١.١٤٦

التدبير قبل العمل يؤمِنك من الندم ١.١٤٧

أغنى الغنى ترك المنى ١.١٤٨

أفضل الزهد إخفاء الزهد ١.١٤٩

التواضع يكسوك السلامة ١.١٥٠

أبى الله إلّا خراب الدنيا وعمارة الآخرة ١.١٥١

المَغبون مَن غُبِن نصيبَه من الله عزّ وجلّ ١.١٥٢

الحياء سبب إلى كلّ جميل ١.١٥٣

أوكد سببٍ أخذته سبب بينك وبين الله ١.١٥٤

Desire is the key to fatigue and the steed of exhaustion. 1.132

To gluttony accrue all the worst faults. 1.133

Envy is the bane of religion. 1.134

One whose soul becomes weak loses his virtue. 1.135

One who dons the robe of greed belittles himself. 1.136

One who lets his tongue command him denigrates himself. 1.137

If you reveal your troubles be ready for humiliation. 1.138

He who disdains advice puts his life in danger. 1.139

What is lost by thanklessness may yet be obtained by gratitude. 1.140

Accepting that hopes may not be realized could mean their realization, whereas coveting them could bring destruction. 1.141

Conceit begets loneliness. 1.142

The noblest lineage is good character. 1.143

Greed invites you to rush blindly into sin. 1.144

The best treasure is heartfelt affection. 1.145

Poverty strikes a clever man dumb, preventing him from presenting his arguments. 1.146

Planning before action secures you against regret. 1.147

The greatest wealth is abandonment of desires. 1.148

Rejection of worldliness is best done in secret. 1.149

Humility clothes you in safety. 1.150

God will surely destroy this world and elevate the hereafter. 1.151

The one whose share from God is appropriated is truly cheated. 1.152

Modesty is the road to every kind of favor. 1.153

The sturdiest rope is the one that links you to God. 1.154

أعمال العباد في عاجلهم نُصبَ أعينهم في آجلهم ١.١٥٥

بِرّ الوالدين من أكرم الطبائع ١.١٥٦

لم يهلك من اقتصد ولم يفتقر من زهِد ١.١٥٧

تُنبِئ عن امرئ دِخلتُه ١.١٥٨

شكر كلّ نعمة الورع عن محارم الله ١.١٥٩

إذا كان الرفق خُرقا كان الخرق رفقا ١.١٦٠

إذا قَوِيتَ فاقْوَ على طاعة الله وإذا ضَعُفتَ فاضْعَف عن معصية الله عزّوجلّ ١.١٦١

إذا تَغيّر السلطان تغيّر الزمان ١.١٦٢

إذا كنتَ في إدبار والموت في إقبال فما أسرع المُلتقى ١.١٦٣

إذا ظهر الرِّبا في قوم بُلُوا بالوَباء وإذا مَنعوا الخُمس بلوا بالسنين الجَدبة ١.١٦٤

إذا هُديتَ لقصدك فكن أخشع ما تكون لربّك ١.١٦٥

إذا قارفتَ سيّئة فعاجِل محوَها بالتوبة ١.١٦٦

إن كنت جازعا على ما يَفلِت من يديك فاجزع على ما لم يصل اليك ١.١٦٧

إنّ أغنى الغنى العقل وأكثر الفقر الحمق ١.١٦٨

نِعمَ القرين الرضى ١.١٦٩

نعم الخلق الصبر ١.١٧٠

نعم حظّ المؤمن القنوع ١.١٧١

نعم طارد الهمّ اليقين ١.١٧٢

نعم الخلق التكرّم ١.١٧٣

نعم وزير العلم سمت صالح ١.١٧٤

نعم عَوِين الدِين الصبر ١.١٧٥

Believers' deeds in this world will be presented to them in the hereafter. 1.155

Kindness to one's parents is among the noblest of attributes. 1.156

One who follows the middle road does not perish from want, and one who rejects worldliness is not afflicted with poverty. 1.157

A man's intention reveals his true worth. 1.158

To show gratitude for God's favors, refrain from what he has forbidden. 1.159

If goodness is stupid, then stupidity is good. 1.160

When you become strong, strengthen in your obedience to God, and when you become weak, weaken in your transgressions of the Almighty's prohibitions. 1.161

New ruler, new age. 1.162

How soon the meeting when you are in retreat and death is pressing forward! 1.163

When usury spreads in a society, epidemics will plague them, and when they refuse to pay the tithe, years of drought will afflict them. 1.164

When you are guided to your purpose, humble yourself truly before your lord. 1.165

When you have sinned, be quick to erase it with repentance. 1.166

If you would bewail the loss of what you once had, then bewail also the lack of things you never had. 1.167

Intelligence is the most precious wealth and foolishness the greatest poverty. 1.168

Acceptance is the best companion. 1.169

Forbearance is the best of traits. 1.170

Contentment is a believer's best fortune. 1.171

Conviction is the best repudiator of cares. 1.172

Avoiding shameful acts is the best moral trait. 1.173

Righteous behavior is the best of knowledge's viziers. 1.174

Patience is the best of religion's aides. 1.175

بئس الطعام الحرام ١.١٧٦

بئس القلادة للخيّر العفيف قلادة الدَّين ١.١٧٧

قلّ ما يُنصفك اللسان في نشر قبيح أو إحسان ١.١٧٨

قلّ ما تَصدقك الأُمنية ١.١٧٩

ما كلّ ما تخشى يكون ١.١٨٠

ما أقرب النقمة من أهل البغي ١.١٨١

ما كلّ مفتون يُعاتَب ١.١٨٢

ما خيرُ خيرٍ بعده النار ١.١٨٣

ما شرّ شرّ بعده الجنّة ١.١٨٤

ما خير خير لا يُنال إلّا بشرّ ويسر لا يُنال إلا بعسر ١.١٨٥

ما أقبح القطيعة بعد الصلة والجفاء بعد الإخاء والعداوة بعد المودّة والخيانة لمن ٱئتمنك والغدر لمن ٱستسلم إليك ١.١٨٦

ما أقبح الخضوع عند الحاجة والجفاء عند الغنى[1] ١.١٨٧

ما أهمّني ذنب أُمهلت بعده حتّى أصلّي ركعتين[2] ١.١٨٨

الرزق رزقان رزق تطلبه ورزق يطلبك فإن لم تأته أتاك ١.١٨٩

كم من عاكف على ذنبه تاب في آخر عمره ١.١٩٠

كم من دَنِف قد نجا وصحيح قد هوى ١.١٩١

ألأم اللؤم البغي عند القدرة ١.١٩٢

ويل للباغين من ﴿أَحۡكَمِ ٱلۡحَٰكِمِينَ﴾ ١.١٩٣

لو كان الصبر رجلا لكان رجلا صالحا ١.١٩٤

---

١ هـ: (الغرض).

٢ هـ: (عن العثير).

How vile is forbidden food! 1.176

Debt's shackles on an upright man are the worst ornament. 1.177

The tongue can rarely be discriminating when disseminating put-downs or kindnesses. 1.178

Wishes are seldom realized. 1.179

Not everything you fear will come to pass. 1.180

How close to the treacherous has their punishment drawn! 1.181

Not every deluded person should be chastised. 1.182

How can a good thing be good if it leads to hellfire! 1.183

How can a bad thing be bad if it leads to paradise! 1.184

What is the good of a good thing obtained through evil! Or of ease obtained through hardship! 1.185

How repugnant is severance after attachment, aloofness after association, enmity after friendship, treachery toward the trusting, and duplicity toward the submissive! 1.186

How ugly is feigned humility in times of need, and aloofness in times of affluence! 1.187

I do not fear the consequences of my sins as long as I can pray for forgiveness. 1.188

Sustenance is of two types: sustenance you seek, and sustenance which seeks you. If you do not find it, it will find you. 1.189

How many a persistent sinner repents at the very end of his life! 1.190

How many a mortally ill person recovers, and a healthy man is felled! 1.191

Injustice by those in power is the vilest form of baseness. 1.192

Woe to the unjust from «the wisest of judges!»[5] 1.193

If patience were a man, he would be virtuous. 1.194

إنّ من كنوز البرّ الصبر على الرزايا وكتمان المصائب ١.١٩٥

إنّ من الغِرّة بالله أن يُصِرّ العبد على المعصية ويتمنّى على الله المغفرة ١.١٩٦

إنّ القلوب تَمَلّ كما تملّ الأبدان فٱبتغوا لها طرائف الحكمة ١.١٩٧

إنّ الله تعالى لَيُدخل الفاسق في دينه الجريء على خلقه الجنّة بسخائه ١.١٩٨

إن ٱستطعت أن لا يكون بينك وبين الله ذو نعمة فٱفعل ١.١٩٩

إذا مات العالم ٱنثلم بموته في الإسلام ثُلْمَة لا تُسَدّ إلى يوم القيامة ١.٢٠٠

إذا وصلت إليكم أطراف النعم فلا تُنَفِّروا أقصاها بقلّة الشكر ١.٢٠١

إنّ اليسير من الله أكثر وأعظم من الكثير من خلقه وإن كان كلٌّ منه ١.٢٠٢

ما أنعم الله على عبد نعمة فشكرها بقلبه إلّا ٱستوجب المزيد منها قبل أن يَظهر شكرها على لسانه ١.٢٠٣

ما أضمر أحد شيئًا إلّا ظهر من فَلَتات لسانه وصفحات وجهه ١.٢٠٤

ما أوضح الحقّ لذي عينين ١.٢٠٥

إنّ الرحيل حقّ أحد اليومين ١.٢٠٦

ما أُبالي باليسير رُميت أم بالعسير لأنّ حقّ الله تعالى في العسر الرضى وفي اليسر الشكر ١.٢٠٧

يا بَردها على الكَبِد إذا سُئل العالم عمّا لا يعلم أن يقول الله أعلم ١.٢٠٨

العافية عشرة أجزاء تسعة منها في الصمت إلّا من ذكر الله تعالى وواحدة في ترك مجالسة السفهاء ١.٢٠٩

Among virtue's treasures are forbearance in distress and concealing one's problems. 1.195

One who persists in sinning yet hopes for God's forgiveness is truly deluded. 1.196

Just as bodies tire, minds tire, so seek pearls of wisdom for them. 1.197

God's generosity allows even corruptors of his religion and transgressors against his creatures to enter his garden. 1.198

If you can arrange things so that no benefactor stands between you and God, do so. 1.199

When a learned man dies, his death makes a breach in Islam that will not be filled till judgment day. 1.200

If the fringes of God's favors reach you, do drive away the favors yet to come with a lack of gratitude. 1.201

A little from God is both more and of greater worth than a lot from his creatures. Ultimately, everything comes from him. 1.202

When a person's heart gives thanks for a favor from God, more favors are allotted to him even before his tongue expresses gratitude. 1.203

When you conceal something in your heart, it becomes manifest in the slips of your tongue and the lines of your face. 1.204

How clear is the truth to one who possesses two eyes! 1.205

Death will surely come, if not today, then tomorrow. 1.206

It is the same to me whether hardship is thrown at me or ease, for I owe it to God to accept God's will in times of hardship, and to give thanks to him in times of ease. 1.207

How the heart is gladdened when a learned man, asked about something he does not know, answers "God knows best." 1.208

Well-being has ten parts: nine are obtained by keeping silent in all things except when praising God, and the tenth by refusing the company of fools. 1.209

ما المبتلى وإن آشتدّ بلاؤه بأحقّ بالدعاء من المعافى لأنّه لا يأمن من البلاء ١.٢١٠

الجهاد ثلاثة: أوّل ما يُغلب عليه من الجهاد اليدُ ثمّ اللسان ثمّ القلب فإذا كان القلب لا يعرف معروفا ولا يُنكر منكرا نُكس فجُعل أعلاه أسفلَه ١.٢١١

أربعٌ يُمِتن القلب: الذنب على الذنب ومُلاحاة الأحمق[1] وكثرة مُثافنة النساء والجلوس مع الموتى. قالوا: ومن الموتى يا أمير المؤمنين؟ قال: كلّ عبد مُترَف ١.٢١٢

كفى بالعلم شرفا أنّه يدّعيه من لا يُحسنه ويفرح به إذا نُسب إليه ١.٢١٣

الإيمان أن تؤثر الصدق حيث يضرّك على الكذب حيث ينفعك ١.٢١٤

الداهية من الرجال من كتم سرّه ممّن يحبّ كراهية أن يَشهره عند غضب من المستودَع والصُّلب من آشتدّت عارضته في اليقين وظهر حزمه في التوكّل ١.٢١٥

الخير الذي لا شرّ فيه الشكر مع النعمة والصبر عند النازلة ١.٢١٦

أوّل عِوَض الحليم من حلمه أنّ الناس أنصار له على الجاهل ١.٢١٧

العالم أفضل من الصائم القائم الغازي[2] في سبيل الله تعالى ١.٢١٨

العالم بمنزلة النخلة تنتظر متى يسقط عليك منها شيء ١.٢١٩

العالم بلا عمل كالرامي بلا وَتَر ١.٢٢٠

من كفّارات الذنوب العظام إغاثة الملهوف والتنفيس عن المكروب ١.٢٢١

إذا أقبلت الدنيا على رجل أعارته محاسن غيره وإذا أدبرت عنه سَلبته محاسن نفسه ١.٢٢٢

---

١ ي: (الأعمى).

٢ هـ: (المجاهد).

One who is not in great distress should pray no less than one who is, since he has no security against it. 1.210

Righteous struggle is of three types: the first thing to be overcome in this struggle is the hand, then the tongue, then the heart. Once the heart cannot recognize good or decry evil, it is upended and turned topsy-turvy. 1.211

ʿAlī said: Four things kill the soul: ncessant sinning, arguing with fools, excessive dallying with women, and keeping company with the dead. Who are the dead, commander of the faithful? ʿAlī's companions asked. All those mired in luxury, he answered. 1.212

Suffice this honor for knowledge: he who does not have it claims it, and if he is called learned he is overjoyed. 1.213

A true believer prefers a truth that hurts him over a falsehood that benefits him. 1.214

A shrewd man hides secrets even from loved ones, lest they reveal them in a moment of anger. A strong man is strengthened by his conviction, and his resolution is manifest in his reliance on God. 1.215

Pure goodness, untainted by evil, is this: to be grateful when blessed, and forbearing when afflicted. 1.216

The first reward for a man of restraint is people siding with him against the reckless. 1.217

A learned man is better than one who fasts, prays, and battles in the path of God. 1.218

A learned man is like a date palm; you can expect a date to drop on you at any moment. 1.219

A learned man without good deeds is like an archer without a bow. 1.220

By consoling the heartbroken and comforting the grief-stricken you atone for the gravest sins. 1.221

When the world smiles at someone, it lends him the good qualities of others, and if it turns away from him, it snatches from him his own. 1.222

العالم من عرف أنّ ما يعلم في جنب ما لا يعلم قليل فعَدّ نفسه بذلك جاهلا فآزداد بما عرف من ذلك في طلب العلم آجتهادا. والجاهل من عَدّ نفسه بما جهل في معرفة العلم عالما وكان برأيه مكتفيا ١.٢٢٣

إنّما لك من دنياك ما أصلحت به مثواك ١.٢٢٤

إنّما قلب الحَدَث كالأرض الخالية ما أُلِقي فيها من شيء قَبلته ١.٢٢٥

إنّي لأستحيي من الله تعالى أن يكون ذنب أعظم من عفوي أو جهل أعظم من حلمي أو عورة لا يواريها سِتري أو خَلّة لا يَسدّها جودي ١.٢٢٦

نوع منه:

رُبَّ ساعٍ فيما يضرّه ١.٢٢٧

ربّ مُشيرٍ بما يَضير ١.٢٢٨

ربّ طمع خائب وأمل كاذب ١.٢٢٩

ربّ رجاء يؤول إلى الحرمان و ربّ أرباح تؤول إلى الخسران ١.٢٣٠

ربّ طلب قد جرّ إلى حَرَب ١.٢٣١

ربّ باحث عن حتفه[1] ١.٢٣٢

ربّ هزل قد عاد جِدّا ١.٢٣٣

ربّ بعيد أقرب من قريب ١.٢٣٤

ربّ أمر قد طلبتَه وفيه هلاك دينك لو أتيته ١.٢٣٥

ربّما كان الدواء داء ١.٢٣٦

ربّما أكدى الحريص ١.٢٣٧

ربّما نصح غير ناصح وغشّ غير المتنصّح ١.٢٣٨

ربّما أخطأ البصير قصده وأصاب العميّ رشده ١.٢٣٩

---

١ ي: تضيف (بظلفه).

A learned man realizes that what he knows is little compared to what he does not know, thus he considers himself ignorant, and increases his efforts to seek knowledge. An ignorant man, because he is ignorant of how much he does not know, considers himself learned and contents himself with his own opinion. 1.223

Your greatest assets are the deeds you carry to the grave. 1.224

The heart of a young man is like untilled earth—whatever is planted in it will grow. 1.225

I would be mortified before God if there were a transgression greater than my forgiveness, a fit of anger greater than my forbearance, a shame that my robe could not conceal, or a need that my generosity could not fill. 1.226

Often the very thing you strive for harms you when you get it. 1.227

A counselor can sometimes guide you to harm. 1.228

Ambitions are often unfulfilled, hopes often disappointed. 1.229

A wish often ends in privation, profits often end in loss. 1.230

A pursuit often leads to deprivation. 1.231

A seeker often finds death. 1.232

A joke can turn serious. 1.233

Those far are often closer than those nearby. 1.234

Often a thing you anxiously seek could, when found, destroy your faith. 1.235

Sometimes the cure becomes the disease. 1.236

Coveting does not always mean getting. 1.237

A person who does not intend it often unwittingly counsels, and a well-wisher often unwittingly deceives. 1.238

Sometimes a perceptive man misses the target and a blind man hits the mark. 1.239

ربّما سألتَ الشيء فلم تؤتَه أو أُوتيت خيرا منه عاجلا أو آجلا وصُرف عنك بما هو خير لك ١.٢٤٠

ربّما أُخّر عنك الإجابة ليكون أطول للمسألة وأجزل للعطيّة ١.٢٤١

نوع منه:

مَن أكثر أهجر ١.٢٤٢

من تفكّر أبصر ١.٢٤٣

من ٱشتاق سَلا ١.٢٤٤

من نال ٱستطال ١.٢٤٥

من مَزَح ٱستُخُفّ به ١.٢٤٦

من أكثر من شيء عُرف به ١.٢٤٧

من زنى زُني به ١.٢٤٨

من جفا طغى ١.٢٤٩

من ترك القصد جارَ ١.٢٥٠

من سلّ سيف البغي قُتل به ١.٢٥١

من حفر بئرا وقع فيها ١.٢٥٢

من تهاون بالدين ٱرتطم ١.٢٥٣

من أحسن السؤال عَلِم ومن علم عمل ومن عمل سلم ١.٢٥٤

من كابد الأمور عَطِب ومن ٱقتحم اللُّجَج غرق ١.٢٥٥

من أُعجب برأيه ضلّ ومن ٱستغنى بعلمه زلّ ومن تكبّر على الناس ذلّ ١.٢٥٦

من أَطلق[1] طَرْفه كثر أسفه ١.٢٥٧

من صارع الحقّ صرعه ١.٢٥٨

من تعدّى الحقّ ضاق مذهبه ١.٢٥٩

---

١ هـ: (أكثر).

Sometimes you are not given what you seek, but are given something better, either here or in the hereafter–the better thing turned away what you sought. 1.240

Sometimes an answer to your prayer is delayed so that you ask longer and receive more. 1.241

Whosoever talks too much blathers. 1.242

Whosoever thinks perceives. 1.243

Whosoever yearns too long forgets why. 1.244

Whosoever gets what he wants becomes arrogant. 1.245

Whosoever jokes too much is not taken seriously. 1.246

Whosoever does something often becomes known for it. 1.247

Whosoever commits adultery invites adultery. 1.248

Whosoever is harsh is cruel. 1.249

Whosoever leaves the middle road deviates. 1.250

Whosoever unsheathes the sword of treachery is slain by it. 1.251

Whosoever digs a well risks falling into it. 1.252

Whosoever scorns religion is crushed. 1.253

Whosoever asks good questions learns; whosoever learns performs good deeds; and whosoever performs good deeds is saved. 1.254

Whosoever pitches himself against fate perishes from exhaustion, and whoever jumps into the deeps drowns. 1.255

Whosoever delights in his own opinion will go astray; whoever suffices himself with his own knowledge will slip; and whoever is too arrogant to ask others for advice will be humbled. 1.256

Whosoever gives free rein to his eyes long regrets it. 1.257

Whosoever wrestles truth is knocked out by it. 1.258

Whosoever transgresses the truth finds his path closing in on him. 1.259

من حصّن شهوته صان قدره ١.٢٦٠

من غلب لسانه أَمّره قومُه ١.٢٦١

من ضاق خلقه مَلَّه أهله ١.٢٦٢

من طلب شيئًا ناله أو بعضه ١.٢٦٣

من كثر كلامه كثر خطؤه ومن كثر خطؤه قلّ حياؤه ومن قلّ حياؤه قلّ ورعه ومن قلّ ورعه مات قلبه ومن مات قلبه دخل النار ١.٢٦٤

من حمل ما لا يطيق عجز ١.٢٦٥

من دخل مداخل السوء ٱتُّهِم ١.٢٦٦

من تحرّى الصدق خفّت عليه المؤون ١.٢٦٧

من تشبّه بقوم عُدّ منهم ١.٢٦٨

من ٱقتصر على قدره كان أبقى له ١.٢٦٩

من طلب الكيمياء ٱفتقر ١.٢٧٠

من طلب علم النجوم تكهّن ١.٢٧١

من تفكَّر في ذات الله تعالى تزندق ١.٢٧٢

من رضي زلّة نفسه ٱستعظم زلّة غيره ١.٢٧٣

من رضي عن نفسه كثر الساخط عليه ١.٢٧٤

من خالط العلماء وُقِّر ومن خالط الأنذال حُقِّر ١.٢٧٥

من لم يملك غضبه لم يَكمل عقله[1] ١.٢٧٦

من ٱستقبل وجوه الآراء عرف مواقع الخطأ ١.٢٧٧

من ضيّعه الأقرب أتيح له الأبعد ١.٢٧٨

من جرى في عِنان أمله عثر بأجله ١.٢٧٩

---

١ ي: (من لم يملك عقله لم يملك غضبه).

Whosoever controls his base desires protects his standing. 1.260

Whosoever conquers his tongue, people make him their leader. 1.261

Whosoever's character is harsh, his own family tires of him. 1.262

Whosoever seeks something obtains it or part of it. 1.263

When words multiply, errors multiply; when errors multiply, modesty lessens; when modesty lessens, self-restraint lessens; when self-restraint lessens, the heart dies; and whosoever's heart dies enters hellfire. 1.264

Whosoever carries a burden beyond his strength wearies. 1.265

Whosoever enters places of vice is suspect. 1.266

Whosoever pursues truth cares not about his belly. 1.267

Whosoever seeks to resemble a people is reckoned among them. 1.268

Whosoever limits himself to his capacity abides. 1.269

Whosoever pursues alchemy is impoverished. 1.270

Whosoever pursues astrology turns into a soothsayer. 1.271

Whosoever thinks too deeply about the nature of God Most High loses faith. 1.272

Whosoever is complacent about making slips himself usually overstates the slips of others. 1.273

The smug invite detractors. 1.274

Whosoever associates with the learned is honored, and whosoever associates with the reviled is scorned.[6] 1.275

Whosoever cannot control his anger, his mind is not mature. 1.276

Whosoever solicits others' opinions will recognize potential errors. 1.277

Whosoever is shunned by those close to him will find help from distant strangers. 1.278

Whosoever gallops forward loosening the reins of his hopes will stumble into death. 1.279

من أبصر عيب نفسه شُغل عن عيب غيره ١.٢٨٠

من رضي برزق[1] الله لم يحزن على ما في يد غيره ١.٢٨١

من أكثر من ذكر الموت رضي من الدنيا باليسير ١.٢٨٢

من علم أنّ كلامه من عمله قلّ كلامه إلّا فيما ينفعه[2] ١.٢٨٣

من نظر في عيوب الناس و رضيها لنفسه فذاك الأحمق بعينه ١.٢٨٤

من قلّب الأحوال عرف جواهر الرجال ١.٢٨٥

من تلذّذ بمعصية الله أورثه الله ذلّا ١.٢٨٦

من عرف الأيّام لم يُغفل الإستعداد ١.٢٨٧

من عُرف بالحكمة لاحظته العيون بالوقار ١.٢٨٨

من أصبح والآخرة همُّه ٱستغنى بغير مال وٱستأنس بغير أهل وعزّ بغير عشيرة ١.٢٨٩

من علم مِن أخيه مروءة جميلة فلا يَسمعنّ فيه الأقاويل ١.٢٩٠

من ٱقتصر على بُلغة الكفاف فقد تعجّل الراحة[3] وتبوّأ خفض الدَّعة ١.٢٩١

من تورّط في الأمور غير ناظر في العواقب فقد تعرّض لفادحات النوائب ١.٢٩٢

من سرق من الأرض شِبرا كلّفه الله تعالى يوم القيامة نقله ١.٢٩٣

من كان مطيّته الليل والنهار فإنّه يُسار به وإن كان لا يسير ١.٢٩٤

---

١ م: (بقسم). هـ: سقطت (الله) الآتية.

٢ ي: (يعنيه).

٣ ي: (الرحمة). م: في المتن (الرحمة) مصحّحة في الحاشية (الراحة).

Whosoever perceives his own faults is too preoccupied to see the faults of others. 1.280

Whosoever is happy with the sustenance God has given him will not be saddened if another has more. 1.281

Whosoever contemplates death wants little from this world. 1.282

Whosoever realizes that words are like deeds will speak only when it benefits him. 1.283

Whosoever remarks on the faults of others while tolerating his own is the epitome of a fool. 1.284

Whosoever has confronted many situations recognizes the true essence of men. 1.285

Whosoever takes pleasure in sinning against God, God will bequeath him humiliation. 1.286

Whosoever has seen battle knows to prepare. 1.287

Whosoever becomes known for wisdom will be regarded with respect. 1.288

Whosoever rises daily with the hereafter in mind will be wealthy even without riches, at peace even without family, and strong even without a tribe's backing. 1.289

Whosoever knows his brother to be a decent man should not give ear to rumors about him. 1.290

Whosoever contents himself with basic rations attains tranquility and peace of mind. 1.291

Whosoever rushes precipitously into affairs without thinking of the consequences exposes himself to terrible dangers. 1.292

Whosoever steals a handspan of land, God will make him carry it on his back on judgment day. 1.293

Whosoever's steeds are Day and Night is carried forward even when he does not move. 1.294

من أمن الزمان خانه ومن تعظّم عليه أهانه ومن ترغّم عليه أرغمه ومن لجأ إليه أسلمه ١.٢٩٥

من حسُنت علانيته فنحن لسريرته أرجى ١.٢٩٦

من عزف[١] نفسه عن دنيء المطامع كملت محاسنه ومن كملت محاسنه حُمد والمحمود محبوب ولن يحبّ العباد عبدا إلّا بعد حبّ الله تعالى إيّاه ١.٢٩٧

من هتك حجاب غيره انكشفت عورات بيته ١.٢٩٨

من يثق بك أو يرجو صلتك إذا قطعت صلة قرابتك ١.٢٩٩

نوع منه:

لا شرفَ أعلى من الإسلام ١.٣٠٠

ولا كنز أعزّ من التقوى ١.٣٠١

ولا لباس أجمل من العافية ١.٣٠٢

ولا كنز أغنى من القناعة ١.٣٠٣

ولا مَعقِل أحصن من الورع ١.٣٠٤

ولا شفيع أنجح من التوبة ١.٣٠٥

ولا وِقاية أمنع من السلامة ١.٣٠٦

ولا كنز أغنى من القنوع ١.٣٠٧

ولا مال أذهب للفاقة من الرضا بالقوت ١.٣٠٨

لا خير في مُعين مَهين ١.٣٠٩

لا خير في زلّة[٢] تورث ندما ١.٣١٠

لا خير في الدنيا إلّا لرجلين: رجل أذنب ذنوبا فهو يتدارك ذلك بتوبة و رجل يسارع في الخيرات ١.٣١١

---

١ م: (عزفت). هـ: (عذب)، وفي الحاشية (عذبه عن الشيء أي منعه).

٢ هـ: (لذّة).

Whosoever trusts the age will be deceived by it. Whosoever is arrogant toward it will be reviled by it. Whosoever shows anger at it will be abased by it. And whosoever takes refuge in it will surrender to misfortune. 1.295

Whosoever's behavior is virtuous, we can hope his intentions are also good. 1.296

Whosoever's soul turns away from lowly cravings will find his character perfected. Whosoever's character is perfected will be praised. Whosoever is praised is loved, and God's servants will only love someone if God loves him. 1.297

Whosoever rends the veil of another, the hidden shame of his own home will be revealed. 1.298

Who will trust you, or wish to associate with you, if you cut off ties with your own kin? 1.299

There is no honor higher than Islam. 1.300

There is no treasure more precious than piety. 1.301

There is no garment more beautiful than well-being. 1.302

There is no treasure richer than contentedness. 1.303

There is no refuge more protective than self-restraint. 1.304

There is no intercessor more effective than repentance. 1.305

There is no protection stronger than good health. 1.306

There is no treasure richer than contentment. 1.307

No wealth alleviates poverty faster than satisfaction with one's basic rations. 1.308

There is no good in a contemptible helper. 1.309

There is no good in a deed whose legacy is regret. 1.310

No good is obtained in this world except by two kinds of men: a man who commits a sin but atones for it by repenting, and a man who hastens toward good deeds. 1.311

لا حسب إلّا بتواضع ولا كرم إلّا بتقوى ولا عمل إلّا بنيّة ولا عبادة إلّا باليقين ١.٣١٢

نوع منه:

ليس كلّ طالب يُصيب ولا كلّ غائب يؤوب ١.٣١٣

ليس كلّ من طلب وَجَدَ ولا كلّ من توقّى نجا ١.٣١٤

ليس كلّ من رمى أصاب ١.٣١٥

ليس كلّ عورة تُصاب ١.٣١٦

ليس في البرق اللامع مُستمتَع لمن يخوض في الظلمة ١.٣١٧

ليس مع الفجور نماء ولا مع العدل ظلم ولا مع القتل عدل ولا مع القطيعة غنى ١.٣١٨

ليس مع الإختلاف ائتلاف ١.٣١٩

ليس جزاء من سَرّك أن تَسوءه ١.٣٢٠

ليس الدين بالرأي إنما هو اتّباع ١.٣٢١

Lineage has no value unless it is coupled with humility. Generosity has no value unless it is coupled with piety. Good deeds have no value unless they are coupled with intent. Worship has no value unless it is coupled with conviction. 1.312

Not every seeker gets what he wants and not everyone who leaves returns. 1.313

Not everyone who seeks finds and not everyone who is vigilant escapes. 1.314

Not everyone who shoots hits the mark. 1.315

Not every gap in the fortress can be breached. 1.316

There is no benefit in a bolt of bright lightning for someone who persists in plunging into darkness. 1.317

There can be no prosperity where there is immorality; no oppression where there is justice; no justice where there is murder; no wealth where kin shun one another. 1.318

There can be no friendship where there is discord. 1.319

Do not reward someone who has pleased you by doing him harm. 1.320

Religion is not based on one's personal opinion; rather, it is to adhere. 1.321

الباب الثاني

ما روي عنه عليه السلام في ذمّ الدنيا وتزهيده فيها

٢.١ فمن ذلك قوله عليه السلام:

الدنيا أوّلها عناء وآخرها فناء حلالها حساب[١] وحرامها عذاب من صحّ فيها أَمِن ومن مرض فيها نَدِم ومن ٱستغنى فيها فُتِن ومن ٱفتقر فيها حَزَن ومن ساعاها فاتته ومن قعد عنها أتته ومن نظر إليها أعمته ومن نظر بها بصّرته.

لله ٱمرؤٌ عمل صالحا وقدّم خالصا وٱكتسب مذخورا وٱجتنب محذورا وبنى غرضا وأحرز عِوَضا كابَرَ هواه وكذّب مُناه وجعل الصبر مطيّة نجاته والتقوى عُدّة وفاته.

٢.٢ وقال عليه السلام:

الدنيا دار فناء وعناء وغِيَر وعِبَر:

فمن الفناء أنّ الدهر مُوتِر قوسه مُفوّق نَبْله لا تَطيش سهامه ولا تؤسى جِراحه يرمي الشباب بالهَرَم والصحيح بالسَّقَم والحياة بالموت. شاربٌ لا يَروى[٢] وآكل لا يَشبع.

ومن العناء أنّ المرء يجمع ما لا يأكل ويبني ما لا يسكن ثمّ يخرج إلى الله تعالى بلا بناء نَقَل ولا مال حَمَل.

ومن غيرها أنّها تُلفيك المرحومَ مغبوطا والمغبوط مرحوما ليس بين ذلك إلّا نعيم زال وبؤس نزل.

---

١ هـ: تضيف (ومشيبها عتاب).

٢ ي: (ينقع).

Chapter 2

Censure of this World and Exhortations to Reject Worldliness

ʿAlī said: This world begins in weariness and ends in death. You are accountable for what is lawful in it and punishable for what is unlawful. The healthy are safe and the ailing remorseful. The wealthy are seduced and the poor grieve. It escapes those who try to catch it and comes willingly to those who ignore it. It blinds those who look at it with longing and instructs those who view it with perception. 2.1

How excellent is the man who performs good deeds and undertakes acts of purity, who earns something he can set aside and avoids what he is warned against, who sets a goal for himself and guards his store, who overcomes his desires and gives the lie to his wishes, who makes forbearance the steed of his salvation and piety the provision for his passing!

ʿAlī said: This world is a place of perishing and weariness, of vicissitudes and instruction: 2.2

Perishing is this—Fate stands stretching his bow, loading his arrows. His arrows do not miss and their wounds do not heal. He strikes the young with old age, the healthy with illness, and the living with death. He is a drinker whose thirst is never quenched; an eater who is never satiated.

Weariness is this—A man gathers food he will not eat, and builds edifices he will not inhabit. He leaves this world to go to God, with no edifice to take with him, no property to carry.

Its vicissitudes are these—The world gladdens the deprived and deprives the glad. Between the two is only a pleasure that has ceased or a misfortune that has arrived.

ومن عبرها أنّ المرء يُشرف على أمله فيقطعه دونه أجله فلا أملٌ مدرَك ولا مؤمِّل مدرِك.[1]

فسبحان الله ما أغرّ سرورها وأظمأ رِيّها وأضحى فيأها كأنّ الذي كان من الدنيا لم يكن وكأنّ الذي هو كائن منها قد كان. لا جاءٍ يُرَدّ ولا ماضٍ يُرتجع.

وإنّ الآخرة هي دار القرار ودار المُقام وجنّة ونار. صار أولياء الله إلى الآخرة بالصبر وإلى الأمل بالعمل. جاوروا الله في داره ملوكا خالدين.

٢٠٣

وقال عليه السلام:

الدنيا دار غرور حائل وزخرف زائل وظلّ آفل وسَنَد مائل. تُردي مستزيدها وتضرّ مستفيدها. فكم من واثق بها راكن إليها قد أرهقته إيثاقها وأعلقته أرباقها[2] وأشربته خِناقها وألزمته وثاقها.

٢٠٤

وقال عليه السلام:

إنّ الدنيا قد أدبرت وآذنت بوداع وإنّ الآخرة قد أقبلت وأشرفت باطّلاع. والمضمار اليوم وغدا السِّباق.

٢٠٥

وقال عليه السلام:

طوبى للزاهدين في الدنيا والراغبين في الآخرة. أولئك قوم اتّخذوا أرض الله بساطا وترابها فراشا وماءها طيبا والكتاب شعارا والدعاء دثارا وقرضوا الدنيا قرضا على منهاج المسيح ابن مريم عليه السلام.

---

١ ه: (فلا أمل يدرك ولا مؤمّل يترك).

٢ ي: (قد أرهقته أنياقها وأعلقته أزياقها).

Its lessons are these—A man is about to see his aspirations fulfilled when they are severed by the ending of his life. No aspiration is attained, and no aspirer attains.

God be praised! How deceiving are the pleasures of this world! How parching its drink! How scorching its shade! It is as though what existed in this world never did, and what is about to be already is. None who arrives is turned away and none who leaves can return.

Truly, the hereafter is a place everlasting, a place of permanence, whether paradise or hellfire. God's elect attain paradise in the hereafter through patience, and realize their aspirations through good deeds. They become companions of God in his abode, abiding there as kings forever.

2.3 ʿAlī said: This world is a place of barren deceptions and ephemeral embellishments. It is a fast-disappearing shade and a keeling support. It destroys whomsoever wants more of it, and harms any who try to benefit from it. How many place their trust in it, depend upon it! But it oppresses them with its bonds, binds them with its tethers, overcomes them with its strangling rope, and enmeshes them in its cords.

2.4 ʿAlī said: The world has turned away and declared its farewell. The hereafter is approaching and has almost arrived. Today is the day of training and tomorrow is the race.

2.5 ʿAlī said: Blessed are the people who reject worldliness, who place their desires in the hereafter. They take God's earth as bed, its dust as bedding, its water as perfume, the book as garment, and prayer as robe. They sever all bonds with the world just as the Messiah, the son of Mary did.

٢٠٦ وقال له عليه السلام رجل: صف لنا الدنيا فقال عليه السلام:

وما أصف لك من دار من صحّ فيها زمِن[١] ومن سَقِم فيها ندِم ومن ٱفتقر فيها حزن ومن ٱستغنى فيها فُتن. في حلالها الحساب وفي حرامها النار.[٢]

٢٠٧ وقال عليه السلام:

اعلموا أنّكم ميّتون ومبعوثون من بعد الموت وموقوفون على أعمالكم ومجزيّون بها. فلا تَغُرَّنّكم الحياة الدنيا فإنّها دار بالبلاء محفوفة وبالفناء معروفة وبالغدر موصوفة وكلّ ما فيها إلى زوال وهي بين أهلها دُوَل وسِجال لا تدوم أحوالها ولن يَسلم من شرّ نُزّالها بَيْنا أهلُها منها في رخاء وسرور إذا هم منها في بلاء وغرور. أحوال مختلفة وتارات متصرّفة. العيش فيها مذموم والرخاء فيها لا يدوم وإنّما أهلها فيها أغراض مستهدَفة فترميهم بسهامها وتقصِمهم بِحِمامها. وكلٌّ حَتفُه فيها مقدور وحظّه منها موفور.

وقال عليه السلام:

٢٠٨ الدنيا دار ممرّ إلى[٣] دار مقرّ والناس فيها رجلان: رجل باع نفسه فأوبقها و رجل ٱبتاع نفسه فأعتقها.

٢٠٩ وكتب عليه السلام إلى سلمان الفارسيّ رضوان الله عليه:

أمّا بعد: فإنّ مَثَل الدنيا مثل الحيّة لِيّن مَسُّها قاتل سَمّها يهوي إليها الصبيّ الجاهل ويحذرها اللبيب العاقل. فأعرض عمّا يُعجبك فيها لقلّة ما يَصحبك منها وضَعْ عنك[٤] همومها لما لقيت من فراقها. وكن آنَس ما تكون فيها أحذر ما تكون لها فإنّ صاحبها كلّما ٱطمأنّ منها إلى سرور أشخصه عنه مكروه. والسلام.

---

١ م، هـ: (أمن).

٢ ي: (العقاب). م: (العذاب)، مصحّحة (النار).

٣ ي: (لا).

٤ هـ: تضيف (ثقل).

A man said to ʿAlī, Describe this world to us, and he replied: 2.6

What can I say about a place in which the healthy fall ill and the sick are remorseful, where the poor grieve and the wealthy are seduced, where one is held accountable for what is lawful and where unlawful things lead to the fire?

ʿAlī said: You will die, be resurrected after death, made to stand trial for your deeds, and rewarded or punished for them. Do not let this worldly life seduce you! Truly, the world is girded with calamities. It is known for its impending destruction and characterized by deception. Everything in it moves toward an inexorable end. It passes through the hands of people, turn by turn. Its condition is never stable and its residents never safe from harm. The very moment they wallow in luxuries and pleasures, calamity and deception beset them. Its conditions change and its times vary. Life in it is detestable and luxury in it fleeting. Truly, its people are targets: The world strikes them with its arrows, shattering them with mortal blows. Each person's death is destined, his share of the world allotted. 2.7

ʿAlī said: This world is an abode of transience that leads to an abode of permanence. People in it are of two types: one sells his soul and thereby destroys it; the other buys his soul and thereby frees it. 2.8

ʿAlī wrote to Salmān al-Fārisī: This world is like a snake—she is soft to the touch, but her venom is lethal. The foolish lad rushes toward her, and the intelligent man is wary of her. Turn away from her attractions, for she will be with you only a short time. Shrug off her cares, for you will soon be leaving her. When you are most comfortable in her, beware of her most. For every time the dweller joyfully relaxes in her, an adversity forcefully removes him from her. Go in peace. 2.9

وقال عليه السلام في ذمّ الدنيا: ٢.١٠

٢.١٠.١ احذروا هذه الدنيا الخدّاعة الغرّارة التي قد تزيّنت بحُليّها وفتنت بغُرورها وغرّت بآمالها وتشوّفت[١] لخُطّابها. فأصبحت كالعَروس المجلوّة العيونُ إليها ناظرةٌ والنفوس بها مشغوفة والقلوب إليها تائقة وهي لأزواجها كلّهم قاتلة فلا الباقي بالماضي معتبِر ولا الآخر بسوء أثرها على الأوّل مزدجر ولا اللبيب فيها بالتجارب منتفع. أَبَت القلوب لها إلّا حبّا والنفوس بها إلا ضنّا.

فالناس لها طالبان:

طالب ظَفِر بها فاغترّ فيها ونَسِي التزوّد منها للظعن عنها فقلّ فيها لُبثه حتّى خلت منها يَدُه وزلّت عنها قدمه وجاءته أسرّ ما كان بها منيّته فعظمت ندامته وكثرت حسرته وجلّت مصيبته فاجتمعت عليه سكرات الموت وحسرات الفوت. فغير موصوف ما نزل به.

وآخَر اختُلِج عنها قبل أن يظفر بحاجته ففارقها بغِرّته وأسفه ولم يُدرك ما طلب منها ولم يظفر بما رجا فيها.

فارتحلا جميعا من الدنيا بغير زاد وقَدِما على غير مهاد.

٢.١٠.٢ فاحذروا الدنيا الحذر كلّه فإنّما مَثَلها مثل الحيّة لِيّن مَسُّها قاتل سَمّها. فأعرض عمّا يُعجبك فيها لقلّة ما يصحبك منها وضع عنك ثقل همومها لما تيقّنت من وَشْك زوالها.

وكن أسرّ ما تكون فيها أحذر ما تكون لها فإنّ صاحبها كلّما اطمأنّ منها إلى سرور أشخصه عنها مكروه وكلّما اغتبط منها بإقبال نَغّصه عنها إدبار وكلّما ثنى عليه منها رِجلا طَوت عنه كَشحا. فالسارّ فيها غارّ والنافع فيها ضارّ. وُصل رخاؤها بالبلاء وجُعل بقاؤها إلى الفناء. فرحها مشوب بالحزن وآخر

---

[١] ي: (تشوقت). هـ: (تشوفت)، زيدت فيها نقطة بحبر آخر لتُقرأ (تشوقت).

ʿAlī said, censuring the world: 2.10

2.10.1 Be wary of this deceiving, dishonest world. She appears in her jeweled ornaments, seduces with her deceptions, deceives with her false hopes, and adorns herself for her suitors. She is like a shining bride—eyes following her, souls enamored of her, hearts yearning for her—a bride who will kill every one of her husbands. The new husband does not take heed from the preceding one; the later one is not driven away by her evil marks on the earlier one. Even the intelligent do not benefit from their experiences with her. Hearts cannot but love her. Souls cannot but greedily guard her.

Two types of people seek her:

The first is a seeker who has won her and is totally taken in by her; he forgets to gather provisions from her in preparation for his departure from her. He resides in her for a short time, until he is bereft of her then slips away. When he is happiest in her, death comes to him. His regret is great, his loss heavy, his misfortune immense. The anguished convulsions of death and the remorseful pangs of loss together bear down upon him—the horror of what descends upon him is beyond words.

The other seeker has been wrested from her before he achieves his desire; he is separated from her with only his heedlessness and remorse to accompany him. He neither obtains what he sought from her, nor achieves in her what he had hoped.

Both seekers depart from this world without provisions and arrive in the hereafter unprepared.

2.10.2 Be wary of this world, utterly, absolutely wary. For she is like a snake—soft to the touch, but her venom is lethal. Turn away from her attractions, for she will be with you for only a short while. Shrug off her cares, for you will soon leave her.

When you are most comfortable with her, beware of her the most. For each time her companion contentedly relaxes with her, an adversity forcefully removes him from her. Each time he is joyful at her kind ministrations, she rebuffs him, choking him. Each time she stretches her leg over him, she follows by turning her waist away from him. This world's happiness deceives, her benefit harms. Her caresses are trailed by misfortunes and her life is followed by death. Her joys are mixed with grief, and your final sorrow in her will be a state of debility. Look at her with the eye of one who rejects

غمومها إلى الوَهَن. فأنظر إليها بعين الزاهد المفارق ولا تنظر إليها بعين الصاحب الوامق.

اعلم يا هذا أنّها تُشخص الوادع الساكن وتفجع المغتبِط الآمن. لا يرجع منها ما تولّى فأدبر ولا يُدرى ما هو آت فيُحذَر. أمانيّها كاذبة وآمالها باطلة. صفوها كَدَر وآبن آدم فيها على خَطَر إمّا نعمة زائلة وإمّا بليّة نازلة وإمّا مُعظِمة جائحة وإمّا منيّة قاضية. فلقد كدّرت عليه المعيشة إن عقل وأخبرته عن نفسها إن وعى.

ولو كان خالقها عزّ وجلّ لم يُخبر عنها خبرا ولم يضرب لها مثلا ولم يأمر بالزهد فيها والرغبة عنها لكانت وقائعها وفجائعها قد أنبهت النائم ووعظت الظالم وبصّرت العالم. وكيف وقد جاء عنها من الله عزّ وجلّ زاجر وأتت منه فيها البيّنات والبصائر. فما لها عند الله عزّ وجلّ قدر ولا وزن ولا خَلَق فيما بلغنا خلقا أبغض إليه منها وما نظر إليها مُذ خلقها.

ولقد عُرضت على نبيّنا صلّى الله عليه وعلى آله وسلّم بمفاتيحها وخزائنها لا ينقصه ذلك من حظّه من الآخرة فأبى أن يقبلها لعلمه أنّ الله جلّ ثناؤه أبغض شيئا فأبغضه وصغّر شيئا فصغّره وأن لا يرفع ما وضع الله جلّ ثناؤه وأن لا يكثّر ما أقلّ الله جلّ وعزّ. ٢.١٠.٣

ولو لم يخبرك عن صِغَرها عند الله إلّا أنّ الله جلّ وعزّ أصغرها عن أن يجعل خيرها ثوابا للمطيعين وأن يجعل عقوبتها عقابا للعاصين.

وممّا يدلّك على دناءة الدنيا أنّ الله جلّ ثناؤه زواها عن أوليائه وأحبّائه نظرا وآختيارا وبسطها لأعدائه فتنة وآختبارا فأكرم عنها محمّدا صلّى الله عليه وعلى آله وسلّم حين عصب على بطنه من الجوع.

وحماها موسى نجيّه المكلّمَ وكانت تُرى خضرة البَقْل من صِفاق بطنه من الهُزال وما سأل الله جلّ ثناؤه يوم أوى إلى الظلّ إلّا طعاما يأكله لما جهده من الجوع.[1] ولقد جاءت الرواية عنه عليه السلام أنّه كان أوحي إليه: إذا رأيت الغنى مُقبلا

---

١ هـ: أخّرت جملة (وحماها موسى . . . لما جهده من الجوع) فأتت بعد (... بشعار الصالحين).

worldliness, who is about to be separated from her. Do not look at her with the eye of a companion or lover.

Know, you, that she terrorizes the calm and serene, and afflicts the joyful and secure. The part of her that has turned away does not return, and the part that is coming cannot be known or guarded against. Her hopes are false, her wishes untrue, her pureness turbid. Man is constantly threatened by danger in this world: a good thing ceasing or a calamity arriving, a destructive catastrophe or a final death. She has made his life murky, if he would only understand. She has informed him about herself, if he would only listen.

Even if her creator had not warned us about her, or described her by analogies, or commanded disinterest in her and dislike of her, her own calamities and disasters should have awoken the sleeping, restrained the oppressors, and opened the eyes of the learned. But her base condition is all the more clear when censure of her has come directly from God, and signs and warnings about her have proceeded from him. She has no value or weight with God. From what has been recounted to us, God hates her the most of all his creation. He has not looked at her since he created her.

2.10.3 This world, including all her treasures and the keys to her, were presented to our prophet, without reducing his share of the hereafter one wit, and still he refused to accept her. He knew God hated her, so he too hated her. He knew that God considered her of little worth, so he too considered her of little worth. He did not raise what God had lowered, nor did he aggrandize what God had belittled.

If nothing else were to apprise you of her lowliness in God's eyes, consider this: God made her too low for her virtues to be the reward for the obedient, or for her punishment to be the penalty for the disobedient.

Another indication of her lowliness is that God has by consideration and choice turned her away from his intimates and devotees, and presented her instead to his enemies as a test and a trial. He raised Muḥammad above her lowliness, when he tied a tight belt around his waist from hunger.[7]

He protected his intimate and confidant Moses from her when Moses became so thin that the greenness of the plants he ate showed through the skin of his stomach. The day he took refuge in the shade, he did not ask God for anything except for some food, because he was exhausted by hunger.[8] It is reported that God said to him: If you see wealth approaching, say

فقل: ذنب عُجّلت عقوبته. وإذا رأيت الفقر مقبلا فقل: مرحبا بشعار الصالحين.

وصاحب الروح والكلمة عيسى ٱبن مريم عليهما السلام إذ قال: أُدمي الجوع وشعاري الخوف ولباسي الصوف ودابّتي رجلاي وسراجي بالليل القمر وصِلائي في الشتاء مشارق الشمس وفاكهتي ما أنبتت الأرض للأنعام. أَبيت وليس لي شيء وليس أحد أغنى منّي.

أو سليمان بن داود عليهما السلام وما أوتي من الملك إذ كان يأكل خبز الشعير ويُطعم أهله الحِنطة وإذا جَنّه الليل لبس المُسوح وغلّ يده إلى عنقه وبات باكيا حتى يصبح ويُكثر أن يقول ﴿ رَبِّ إِنِّي ظَلَمْتُ نَفْسِي ﴾ كثيرا ﴿ وَإِلاَّ تَغْفِرْ لِي وَتَرْحَمْنِي أَكُن مِّنَ ٱلْخَاسِرِينَ ﴾ ﴿ لاَّ إِلَٰهَ إِلاَّ أَنتَ سُبْحَانَكَ إِنِّي كُنتُ مِنَ ٱلظَّالِمِينَ ﴾.

فهؤلاء أنبياء الله وأصفياؤه وأولياؤه تنزّهوا عن الدنيا و زهدوا فيما زهّدهم الله جلّ ثناؤه فيه منها وأبغضوا ما أبغض وصغّروا ما صغّر.

ثمّ ٱقتصّ[1] الصالحون آثارهم وسلكوا منهاجهم وأَلطفوا الفِكَر وٱنتفعوا بالعبر وصبروا في هذا العمر القصير عن متاع الغرور الذي يعود إلى الفناء ويصير إلى الحساب. نظروا بعقولهم إلى آخر الدنيا ولم ينظروا إلى أوّلها ونظروا إلى باطن الدنيا ولم ينظروا إلى ظاهرها وفكّروا في مَرارة عاقبتها فلم يَستَهوِهم[2] حلاوة عاجلها ثمّ ألزموا أنفسهم الصبر وأنزلوا الدنيا من أنفسهم كالمِيتة التي لا يَحِلّ لأحد أن يشبع منها إلّا في حال الضرورة إليها وأكلوا منها بقدر ما أبقى لهم النَفَس وأمسك الروح وجعلوها بمنزلة الجِيفة التي ٱشتدّ نَتْنها فكلّ من مرّ بها أمسك على أنفه منها فهم يتبلّغون منها بأدنى البلاغ ولا ينتهون إلى الشِّبَع من النّتن ويتعجّبون من الممتلئ منها شبعا والراضي بها نصيبا.

إخواني والله لهي في العاقبة والآجلة لمن ناصح نفسَه في النظر وأخلص له الفكر أنتن من الجيفة وأكره من الميتة غير أنّ الذي نشأ في دباغ الإهاب لا يجد نتنه ولا ٢.١٠.٤

---

١ ي: (اقتفى).

٢ م: (تستهوتهم). هـ: في المتن (تستفزّهم) وفي الحاشية نسخة (يستهوهم).

this is advance punishment for a sin, and if you see poverty approaching, say welcome, garment of the pious!

The Spirit and Word, Jesus, son of Mary, said: My food is hunger, my garment fear of God, my clothing rough wool, my mount my own two feet, my night-lamp the moon, my heating in winter the rays of the sun, my fruit what the earth has grown for grazing animals. I go to sleep owning nothing, yet no-one is wealthier than I am.

Or consider Solomon, son of David, and the kingdom bestowed upon him. He fed his family the finest wheat, while he himself ate bread made from coarse barley. When night fell, he would put on a coat of rough hair, shackle his hand to his neck, and spend the hours until morning weeping, saying, «O lord, I have sinned»[9]—«if you do not forgive me, if you do not have mercy on me, I will surely be lost.»[10] «There is no god but you, exalted above all else—I am surely a transgressor!»[11]

These, the prophets of God, his chosen and select, distanced themselves from the world, and rejected of her what God urged them to reject. They hated what he hated and considered lowly what he considered lowly.

The pious learned from their example and followed in their footsteps. They focused their reflection and benefited from exemplary lessons. In their short time, they forbore from acquiring ephemeral worldly goods for which they would be held accountable. Not looking at her outward appearance, they pondered her bitter end, and so her redolent gifts failed to tempt them. Their souls steadfastly cleaved to patience. They considered the world carrion, lawful only in desperate situations. They ate only as much as would keep them breathing and keep the soul in the body. They considered the world a carcass of such overpowering stench that a passerby would hold his nose. They consumed little, and because of her stench they refrained from filling their stomachs. They wondered at those who gorged themselves on her meat, rejoicing at their share.

2.10.4 My brothers, by God, for the one who does well by his soul and takes care of it sincerely, this world is now and will always be smellier than a carcass and more detestable than carrion. Only the one who has grown up in a tannery full of untreated hides is not conscious of its stench; its smell does not pain him as it would a passerby or a person who has just come in and sat down. Suffice it for an intelligent man to recognize her for what she is: the fact that when a man dies leaving behind a powerful kingdom, he wishes he

يؤذيه من رائحته ما يؤذي المارّ به والجالس عنده وقد يكفي العاقل من معرفتها علمه فإنّ من مات وخلّف سلطانا عظيما سرّه أنّه عاش فيها سوقة خاملا أو كان فيها مُعافى سليما سرّه أنّه كان فيها مبتلى ضريرا فكفى بهذا على عورتها والرغبة عنها دليلا.

والله لو أنّ الدنيا كانت من أراد منها شيئا وجده حيث تنال يده من غير طلب ولا تعب ولا مؤونة ولا نصب ولا ظعن ولا دَأَب غير أنّ ما أخذ منها من شيء لزمه حقّ الله فيه والشكر عليه وكان مسؤولا عنه مُحاسَبا به لكان يَحِقّ على العاقل أن لا يتناول منها إلّا قوته وبُلغَة يومه حذَر السؤال وخوفا من الحساب وإشفاقا من العجز عن الشكر. فكيف بمن تجشّم في طلبها من خضوع رقبته ووضع خدّه وفرط عَنائه والإغتراب عن أحبّائه وعظيم أخطاره ثمّ لا يدري ما آخر ذلك الظفر أم الخيبة.

وإنّما الدنيا ثلاثة أيّام: يوم مضى بما فيه فليس بعائد ويوم أنت فيه فحَقّ عليك اغتنامه ويوم لا تدري أأنت من أهله ولعلّك راحل فيه. فأمّا أمس فحكيم مؤدِّب وأمّا اليوم فصديق مُوَدِّع وأمّا غد فإنّما في يديك منه الأمل. فإن يكن أمس سبقك بنفسه فقد أبقى في يديك حكمته وإن يكن يومك هذا آنسك بمَقدمه عليك فقد كان طويل الغيبة عنك وهو سريع الرحلة فتزوّد منه وأحسن وداعه. ٢.١٠.٥

وخذ بالثقة في العمل وإيّاك والإغترار بالأمل. ولا تدخل عليك اليوم هَمّ غد يكفي اليوم همّه وغد داخل عليك بشغله. إنّك إن حملت على اليوم همّ غد زدت في حزنك وتعبك وتكلّفت أن تجمع في يومك ما يكفيك أيّاما فعظم الحزن وزاد الشغل واشتدّ التعب وضعف العمل للأمل. ولو أخليت قلبك من الأمل لجدّ ذلك العمل والأمل منك في اليوم قد ضرّك في وجهين: سوّفت به العمل وزدت به في الهمّ والحزن. أوَلا ترى أنّ الدنيا ساعة بين ساعتين؟ ساعة مضت وساعة بقيت وساعة أنت فيها. فأمّا الماضية والباقية فلست تجد لرخائهما لذّة ولا لشدّتهما ألما. فأنزِل الساعة الماضية والساعة التي أنت فيها منزلة الضيفين نَزَلا بك فظعن

had lived as an ordinary, anonymous person; or that when he dies sound and healthy, he wishes that he had been afflicted with chronic illness instead. Suffice this as proof of her shame and despicable nature.

By God, if the world were such that whosoever wanted something from her found it, his hand just taking it without seeking it out, without fatigue, or trouble, or weariness, or travel, or striving; except that for whatever he took of her, he would have to pay God's dues, offer gratitude, and be held accountable—even then it would be incumbent upon an intelligent man to take from her only his basic needs, his daily food, apprehensive of being asked about it, for fear of the accounting, and in dread of falling short in gratitude. How much more so for the one who, in seeking her, has to bear the pain of bowing his neck, of lowering his cheek to the dirt, of crushing toil, of separation from loved ones, and of grave dangers—all the while not knowing whether the end will bring success or failure!

2.10.5 The world consists of three days: the day that has passed, taking all that was in it, never to return; the day you are in now, which you must take advantage of; and the day which offers no security since you could die in it. Yesterday is a wise teacher and today is a friend about to take leave. As for tomorrow, all you can do is hope. If yesterday is beyond you, its wisdom nevertheless remains with you. If today has given you comfort by its arrival, it was long absent from you and will soon leave, so take provisions from it and bid it a fond farewell.

Place your trust in good deeds and beware of being deceived by false hopes. Do not let today bring on the cares of tomorrow. Let today's cares suffice; tomorrow will bring its own worries. If you add the cares of tomorrow to today's burden, you will increase your grief and tiredness, and pointlessly strive to gather something today to last you for many days, days that you may not have. Your grief will be great, your work doubled, and your fatigue considerable. Your resolve to do good deeds will be weakened by false hope. If you were to empty your heart of false hope, it would urge you once again to perform good deeds. Your false hope in today has hurt you in two ways: you have put off doing good deeds because of it, and your cares and grief have increased from it. Do you not see that the world is but an hour between two others? An hour that has passed, an hour that remains, and an hour in which you live? In the past and future hours, you find neither pleasure in luxury, nor pain in hardship. Regard the past hour and the one in which you

الراحل عنك بذمّه إيّاك وحلّ النازل بك بالتجربة لك فإحسانك إلى الثاوي يمحو إساءتك إلى الماضي. فأدرك ما أضعت بإعتابك فيما ٱستقبلت وٱحذر أن تجمع عليك شهادتهما فيوبقاك.

٢.١٠.٦ ولو أنّ مقبورا من الأموات قيل له: هذه الدنيا أوّلها إلى آخرها تُخلّفها لولدك الذين لم يكن لك همّ غيرهم أو يومٌ نردّه إليك فتعمل فيه لنفسك لٱختار يوما يستعتب فيه من سيّئ ما أسلف على جميع الدنيا يورثها ولده خَلْفه. فما يمنعك أيّها المغترّ المضطرّ المؤتنف أن تعمل على مَهَل قبل حلول الأجل. وما يجعل المقبور أشدّ تعظيما لما في يديك منك. ألا تسعى في تحرير رقبتك وفكاك رِقّك ووِقاء نفسك من النار التي عليها ملائكة غِلاظ شِداد.

٢.١١ وقال عليه السلام:

أيّها الناس ٱنظروا إلى الدنيا نظر الزاهدين فيها الماقتين لها. فما خُلق ٱمرؤ عَبَثا فيلهو ولا أُهمل سُدى فيلغو وما دنياه التي تَزيّنه بخَلَف من الآخرة التي قبّحها سوء النظر إليها وما الخسيس الذي ظَفِر به من الدنيا[١] على سُهمته. لا يُرجَع بما تولّى منها فأدبر ولا يُدرى ما هو آت منها فيُنتظر. فٱعتبروا وٱنظروا إدبار ما قد أدبر وحضور ما قد حضر فكأنّ ما هو كائن لم يكن وكأنّ ما هو آتٍ قد نزل.

٢.١٢ وقال عليه السلام:

انظروا إلى الدنيا نظر الزاهدين فيها[٢] فإنّها والله عن قليل تُزيل الثاوي الساكن وتَفجع المُترَف الآمِن. لا يرجع ما تولّى عنها فأدبر ولا يُدرى ما هو آت منها فيُنتظر.

---

١ م، ي: (الآخرة).

٢ هـ: تضيف (الماقتين لها).

live now as visiting guests. The departing guest has gone, blaming you. The one who is with you now is testing you. Your kindness to the resident guest will wash away your ungraciousness to the departed one. Make up for your ill treatment of the departed guest by pleasing the one who follows. Let not the testimony of both come against you, for together they will destroy you.

2.10.6 If a dead man in his grave were told: Choose: You can leave for your children—for whom you cared above all else—everything in this world, every last bit of its wealth. Or you can have back one day of your life to spend performing good deeds for your soul's salvation. He would choose the one day to make up for his evil deeds over the legacy of all the world's riches bequeathed to his children. What prevents you, O deceived one, O powerless one, O shameful one, from performing good deeds now, when you still have time, before your end is upon you? Why is the man in the grave quicker to recognize the value of what you have in your hands than you? Will you not strive to remove your yoke, to break your bonds, and to protect your soul from a fire guarded by harsh, rough angels?

2.11 ʿAlī said: O people! Look at the world with the eyes of those who have little interest in her and detest her. Man was not created to spend his time in play, nor given reprieve to speak nonsense. The world he finds so beautiful is no substitute for the hereafter he finds so ugly. The vile stuff he gains from the world is no replacement for a share of the hereafter. The part of the world which turns away and leaves does not return, and there is no guarantee that the part which appears to be coming will arrive. Take heed! Notice the turning away of what has turned away, and the coming of what has come. It is as though what is never was, and what is coming has already occurred.

2.12 ʿAlī said: Look at the world with the eyes of those who have little interest in her. She will, by God, very soon displace her tenant, and afflict the complacent and secure. The part of her which turns away and leaves does not return, and the part of her which appears to be coming does not always arrive, such that it can be guaranteed. Her happiness is mixed with grief, and the last stage of your life in her is spent in growing weakness and incapacity. Do not

سرورها مَشوب بالحزن وآخر الحياة فيها إلى الضعف والوَهَن. فلا يَغُرّنّكم كثرة ما يُعجبكم منها لقلّة ما يَصحبكم منها.

رحم الله عبدا تفكّر فاعتبر واعتبر فأبصر إدبار ما قد أدبر وحضور ما قد حضر. وكأنّ ما هو كائن من الدنيا عن قليل لم يكن وكأنّ ما هو كائن من الآخرة لم يزل. وكلّ ما هو آت قريب.

وقال عليه السلام: ٢.١٣

أوصيكم عباد الله بتقوى الله جلّ وعزّ واغتنام ما استطعتم عملا به من طاعة الله جلّ وعزّ في هذه الأيام الخالية لجليل ما يُشفي عليكم به الفوت[1] بعد الموت. وبالرفض لهذه الدنيا التاركة لكم وإن لم تكونوا تحبّون تركها والمُبلية لكم وإن كنتم تحبّون تجديدها. فإنّما مَثَلكم ومثلها كرَكْب سلكوا سبيلا فكأنّهم قد قطعوه وأَمّوا عَلَما فكأن قد بلغوه. وكم عسى الجاري إلى الغاية أن يجري حتّى يبلغها. وكم عسى أن يكون بقاء من له يوم لا يَعدوه. ومن ورائه طالب حثيث يَحدوه في الدنيا حتّى يفارقها.

فلا تتنافسوا في الدنيا وفخرها ولا تُعجبوا بزينتها ولا تَجزعوا من ضرّائها وبؤسها فإنّ عزّ الدنيا وفخرها إلى انقطاع وإنّ زينتها ونعيمها إلى زوال وإنّ ضرّاءها وبؤسها إلى نَفاد وكلّ مدّة فيها إلى منتهى وكلّ حيّ فيها إلى فناء.

أوَ ليس لكم في آثار الأوّلين وفي آبائكم الماضين معتبَر وتبصرة إن كنتم تعقلون. ألم تَروا إلى الماضين منكم لا يرجعون وإلى الخَلَف الباقي منكم لا يبقون. قال الله عزّ وجلّ ﴿وَحَرَامٌ عَلَىٰ قَرْيَةٍ أَهْلَكْنَاهَا أَنَّهُمْ لَا يَرْجِعُونَ﴾[2] وقال عزّ وجلّ ﴿كُلُّ نَفْسٍ ذَائِقَةُ ٱلْمَوْتِ وَإِنَّمَا تُوَفَّوْنَ أُجُورَكُمْ يَوْمَ ٱلْقِيَامَةِ فَمَن زُحْزِحَ عَنِ ٱلنَّارِ وَأُدْخِلَ ٱلْجَنَّةَ فَقَدْ فَازَ وَمَا ٱلْحَيَاةُ ٱلدُّنْيَا إِلَّا مَتَاعُ ٱلْغُرُورِ﴾.

أَلَستم تَرون أهل الدنيا يُمسون ويُصبحون على أحوال شتّى: ميّت يُبكى وآخر يُعزّى

١ ي: (ما يبقى عليكم به الفوز).

٢ تضيف المخطوطات (الآية والتي بعدها).

be deceived by the abundance of her wonders, for she will only accompany you for a short while.

May God have mercy on the person who reflects and takes heed; who, taking heed, recognizes the turning away of what turns away, and the coming of what comes. In a short while, it will be as though this world never was, and as though the hereafter has already occurred. All that will come is at hand!

2.13

ʿAlī said: I counsel you, servants of God, to be conscious of him; and to seize the opportunity—as often as you are able—to perform deeds in obedience to him in your remaining days. To miss such an opportunity will bring great pain when you die. I counsel you to reject the world which will reject you despite your dislike of leaving her, and cause your decay despite your wish for renewal. You and she are like a band of travelers who, traversing a path, seem already to have crossed it, who, heading for a mountain, seem already to have reached it. How very likely it is that someone who runs toward a goal will soon attain it! How very likely it is that the life of someone alive today will not continue beyond it! For behind him is an assiduous seeker who drives him forward in the world until he makes him leave her.

Do not compete for the world or her glories. Do not be taken by her beauty or shaken by her injuries and sorrows. For her might and pride will be cut off, her beauty and delights will cease, and her injuries and sorrows will end. Each period of time in her will conclude. Each living being in her will perish.

Does the evidence of earlier peoples and the example of your forefathers not alert and enlighten you? If you would only understand! Have you not seen that those among you who pass away do not return? And that you, their remaining heirs, will not remain forever? As God Almighty has said: «It is forbidden to the village that we have destroyed—they will not return.» And the Almighty said: «Every soul will taste death. Indeed, you will be given your fair recompense on judgment day: One who has been snatched away from hellfire and given entry to paradise will have won. This worldly life is but a cargo of deception.»[12]

Do you not see the people of this world, evening and morn, in disparate states? A dead man lamented, another man consoled; one felled and afflicted,

وصريع مُبتلى وعائد يَعود وآخر بنفسه يجود وطالب والموت يطلبه وغافل وليس بمغفول عنه. وعلى أثر الماضي منّا يمضي الباقي.

فلله الحمد ﴿رَبِّ ٱلسَّمَٰوَٰتِ ٱلسَّبۡعِ وَرَبِّ ٱلۡعَرۡشِ ٱلۡعَظِيمِ﴾ الذي يبقى ويفنى ما سواه وإليه موئل الخلق[1] ومَرجع الأمور.

وقال عليه السلام: ٢.١٤

٢.١٤.١ أمّا بعد: فإنّي أحذّركم الدنيا فإنّها حُلوة خَضِرة حُفّت بالشهوات وراعت بالقليل وتحبّبت بالعاجلة وعُمّرت بالآمال وتزيّنت بالغرور فلا تدوم حَبرتها ولا تؤمَن فجائعها. غرّارة ضرّارة خاتلة زائلة نافدة بائدة أكّالة غوّالة. لا تَعدو إذا هي تناهت إلى أمنية أهل الرغبة فيها والرضى بها أن تكون كما قال الله جلّ وعزّ ﴿كَمَآءٍ أَنزَلۡنَٰهُ مِنَ ٱلسَّمَآءِ فَٱخۡتَلَطَ بِهِۦ نَبَاتُ ٱلۡأَرۡضِ فَأَصۡبَحَ هَشِيمٗا تَذۡرُوهُ ٱلرِّيَٰحُۗ وَكَانَ ٱللَّهُ عَلَىٰ كُلِّ شَيۡءٖ مُّقۡتَدِرًا﴾ مع أنّ آمرأ لم يكن فيها في حبرة إلّا أعقبته منها بعد بعَبرة ولم يَلقَ من سرّائها بطنا إلّا أعقبته من ضرّائها ظهرا ولم تَطُلّه فيها ديمة رخاء إلّا هتنت عليه منها مُزنة بلاء وحَريّ إذا أصبحت لك مُهتزّة أن تمسي لك متنكّرة وإن جانب منها آعذوذب لآمرئ وآحلولى أمَرّ منها جانب فأَوبا وإن لبس إنسان من غَضارتها رَغَبا أرهقته من بَوائقها تعبا ولم يُمس آمرؤ منها في جَناح أمن إلّا أصبح في جوف[2] خوف. غرّارة غُرور ما فيها فانية فانٍ مَن عليها. لا خير في شيء من زادها إلّا التقوى. من أقلّ منها آستكثر ممّا يوبقه ومن آستكثر منها لم تَدُم له وزالت عنه.

كم من واثق بها فجعته وذي طمأنينة إليها صرعته وذي خُدَع فيها قد خدعته وكم من ذي أُبّهة فيها قد صيّرته حقيرا وذي نَخْوة فيها قد ردّته خائفا فقيرا وكم من ذي تاج قد أكبّته لليدين والفم.

سلطانها دُوَل وعيشها رَنِق وعذبها أُجاج وحُلوها صَبِر وغذائها سِمام[3] وأسبابها

١ م: (الحق).

٢ هـ: (على قوادم).

٣ هـ: (مرّ).

one who visits the sick, and another who gives up the ghost; a seeker sought by death, and a heedless man who goes not unheeded. Those who remain among us follow upon the traces of those who have passed.

To God belongs all praise, «lord of the seven heavens and lord of the great throne,»[13] who remains when all else perishes. All creatures find refuge in God and all things return to him.

2.14

ʿAlī said:

2.14.1

I warn you of the world, sweet and green, surrounded by delights, inspiring awe with her trifles, beloved for her favors, furnished with hopes, ornamented by deceit. Her joys do not remain and her calamities cannot be secured against. Deceiver, harmer, trickster, departer, vanisher, perisher, gorger, devourer! When she fulfills the wish of those who desire her and are happy with her, she never fails to become as God has said: «like water that we have sent down from the sky; the plants of the earth mix with it; then they become dry and crushed, scattered by the winds. God is able to do all things.»[14] What is more, when a man finds gladness in the world, it is always followed by tears. When he derives joy from her in his belly, he is always injured by her in his back. A raindrop of her ease does not gently caress him without a cloudburst of her calamities pouring down upon him. If she is in good spirits towards him in the morning, she will change for the worse in the evening. If one part of her becomes sweet and sugary for him, another becomes bitter and sickens him. If he dons a garment of her prosperity in hope, her catastrophes oppress him with fatigue. A man does not spend the evening under the wing of security without waking up in the belly of fear. Deceiver, everything in her is deceit. Perisher, all in her will perish. The only good thing among the supplies she offers is piety. Whosoever gathers a little of her wants more, then she destroys him. Whosoever gathers more of her will lose that abundance, and it will soon dissipate.

She afflicts with loss those who trust her, fells those who put confidence in her, and tricks the trickmaster. She reduces grandees to abjectness, turns high spirited men into nervous beggars, and flings crowned heads into the dirt.

Her rule swings from one to another. Her life is murky, her water brackish, her sweetness bitter, her food poisonous, her subsistence decayed, her fruits sour. Those living in her are targets for death, the healthy are targets for sickness, and the protected are targets for cruelty. Her kingdom will be

رِمام وقطافها سَلَع. حيّها بعرض موت وصحيحها بعرض سقم ومنيعها بعرض اهتضام. وملكها مسلوب وعزيزها مغلوب وضيفها منكوب وجارها محروب. مع أنّ وراء ذلك سكرات الموت وزفراته وهَول المُطّلَع والوقوف بين يدي الحَكَم ﴿ لِيَجْزِيَ ٱلَّذِينَ أَسَٰٓـُٔواْ بِمَا عَمِلُواْ وَيَجْزِيَ ٱلَّذِينَ أَحْسَنُواْ بِٱلْحُسْنَى ﴾.

٢.١٤.٢ ألستم[1] في مساكن من كان قبلكم كانوا أطول منكم أعمارا وأبقى منكم آثارا وأعدّ منكم عديدا وأكثف منكم جنودا وأشدّ منكم عُنودا[2] تعبّدوا للدنيا أيّ تعبّد وآثروها أيّ إيثار ثمّ ظعنوا عنها بالصغار. فهل بلغكم أنّ الدنيا سخت لهم نفسا بفدية أو عَدَت عنهم فيما قد أهلكتهم به بخَطْب بل أوهنتهم بالقوارع وضعضعتهم بالنوائب وعقرتهم بالمناحر وأعانت عليهم رَيب المَنون.

فقد رأيتم تنكّرها لمن دانَ لها وآثرها وأخلد إليها حين ظعنوا عنها لفراق الأبد وإلى آخر زوال. هل زوّدتهم إلا الشَّغَب[3] أو أحلّتهم إلّا الضَّنْك أو نوّرت لهم إلّا الظلمة أو أعقبتهم إلّا النار. أفهذه تؤثرون أم عليها تَحرصون أم إليها تطمئنّون. يقول الله عزّ وجلّ ﴿ مَن كَانَ يُرِيدُ ٱلْحَيَوٰةَ ٱلدُّنْيَا وَزِينَتَهَا نُوَفِّ إِلَيْهِمْ أَعْمَٰلَهُمْ فِيهَا وَهُمْ فِيهَا لَا يُبْخَسُونَ ۞ أُوْلَٰٓئِكَ ٱلَّذِينَ لَيْسَ لَهُمْ فِي ٱلْءَاخِرَةِ إِلَّا ٱلنَّارُ وَحَبِطَ مَا صَنَعُواْ فِيهَا وَبَٰطِلٌ مَّا كَانُواْ يَعْمَلُونَ ﴾ فبئست الدار لمن لم يتّهمها[4] ولم يكن فيها على وَجَل منها. اذكروا عند تصرّفها بكم[5] سرعة انقضائها عنكم ووَشْك زوالها وضعف مجالها.

ألم تَحذُكم على مثال من كان قبلكم وحَذَت من قبلكم على مثال من كان قبلهم جيل بعد جيل وأمّة بعد أمّة وقرن بعد قرن وخَلَف بعد خلف. فلا هي تستحيي من العار ولا تنتهي من المُندبات ولا تخجل من الغدر.

اعلموا وأنتم تعلمون أنّكم تاركوها لا بدّ وإنّما هي كما نعت الله جلّ وعزّ ﴿ لَعِبٌ وَلَهْوٌ وَزِينَةٌ وَتَفَاخُرٌ بَيْنَكُمْ وَتَكَاثُرٌ فِي ٱلْأَمْوَٰلِ وَٱلْأَوْلَٰدِ ﴾.

١ ي: (ونظرتم).
٢ ي: (عتودا).
٣ ي: (السغب). هـ: (التعب) وفي الحاشية نسخة (الشغب).
٤ ي: (يسكن إليها).
٥ ي: (عند مسيركم).

snatched away, the mighty will be brought down, guests will be ill-treated, and protégés looted. All this—and afterward the anguished pangs and deep sighs of death, the dread of the overlook into the terrors of hell, and the summoning before the judge, «so that he recompense those who did evil with what they did, and those who performed good deeds with good.»[15]

2.14.2 Do you not reside in the dwellings of those who lived before you? They were longer lived than you, had longer lasting monuments than you, were more numerous than you, had more abundant armies than you, and were more obstinate than you in opposing the truth. They worshiped the world devotedly and gave her complete precedence, then departed from her in humiliation. Have you heard tell that the world offered to let their souls go for a ransom? Or passed them over among those she destroyed? No, indeed! She weakened them with calamities, shook them with troubles, and killed them by slitting their throats. She gave strength to the blows of death that fell on them.

You have seen the world's disavowal of those who kowtowed to her, of those who gave her precedence and took comfort in her, when they separated from her eternally, departing to their final end. Did she supply them with anything other than wickedness, give them a residence other than a narrow home, give them light other than a murky gloom, or take them to anywhere but the fire? Do you give this precedence? Is this what you covet? Or take comfort from? God says: «As for those who prefer this worldly life and its ornaments, we will recompense their deeds in her; they will not be given a deficient measure. They are the ones for whom there is naught in the hereafter save the fire. All that they wrought will be in vain, and all they did will be of no value.»[16] What a terrible abode for those who do not accuse her, are not wary of her. When she turns toward you, remember the speed with which she will turn away, how close her end, and how weak her compass.

Has the world not torn you to pieces just as she tore those who came before you? And did she not tear them to pieces just as she tore those who came before them—generation upon generation, community upon community, age upon age, descendant upon descendant? She is not ashamed of dishonor, does not cease to afflict, nor shy away from deception.

You should know—and you do know—that you will leave the world. She is, as God has described, nothing «but sport and diversion, beautiful ornaments, a cause for boasting among you, and for rivalry for the most wealth and offspring.»[17]

٢.١٤.٣ فاتّعظوا فيها بالذين كانوا يَبنون بكلّ رِيع آية يعبثون ويتّخذون مصانع لعلّهم يخلدون وبالذين ﴿قَالُوا۟ مَنْ أَشَدُّ مِنَّا قُوَّةً﴾.

واتّعِظوا بمن رأيتم من إخوانكم كيف حُملوا إلى قبورهم لا يُدعَون ركبانا وأُنزلوا لا يدعون ضِيفانا وجعل لهم من الضريح[1] أجنانا ومن التراب أكفانا ومن الرُّفات جيرانا.

فهم جِيرة لا يجيبون داعيا ولا يمنعون ضَيما ولا ينالون مَندَبة ولا يعرفون[2] سيّئا ولا حسنا ولا يشهدون زُورا. إن جِيدوا لم يفرحوا وإن قُحِطوا لم يَقنُطوا. جميع وهم آحاد وجِيرة وهم أبعاد ومُتنادُون[3] لا يتزاورون ولا يَزورون. حلماء قد بادت أضغانهم جهلاء قد ذهبت أحقادهم. لا يُخشى فجعهم ولا يرجى دفعهم. وهم كمن لم يكن وكما قال جلّ ثناؤه ﴿فَتِلْكَ مَسَاكِنُهُمْ لَمْ تُسْكَن مِّنۢ بَعْدِهِمْ إِلَّا قَلِيلًا وَكُنَّا نَحْنُ ٱلْوَارِثِينَ﴾.

٢.١٤.٤ إنّ الدنيا وَهِلٌ مَطلبها رَنِق مشربها رَدِغ مَشرَعها غُرور مَاثل[4] ووشيج قاتل وسِناد مائل يونِق مُطرِفُها ويُعجب مُونِقُها[5] وتُردي مستزيدها وتَصرع مستفيدها بإنفاد لذّتها وموبقات شهوتها وأَسْرنافِها. قنصت بأحبُلها وقصدت بأسهمها فتأثُل لِهَناتها وتُعلّل بهِباتها[6] ليالي عمره وأيّام حياته.

قد عَلِقته وِهاق المنيّة فأردته بمَرائرها قائدة له بحتوفها[7] إلى ضَنْك المَضجَع ووحشة المَرجع ومُجاوَرة الأموات ومعاينة المحلّ وثواب العمل.

ثمّ ضُرب على آذانهم فِنات الدهور فهم لا يرجعون. قد ٱرتُهنت الرقاب بسالف الإكتساب وأحصيت الآثار[8] لفصل الخطاب ﴿وَقَدْ خَابَ مَنْ حَمَلَ ظُلْمًا﴾.

١ هـ: (الصفيح).
٢ هـ: (يقترفون).
٣ هـ: (متدانون). ي: (متنادون).
٤ هـ: (حائل).
٥ هـ: (يونق منظرها ويوبق مخبوها).
٦ ي: (فتأمل لهباتها وتعلل بهناتها).
٧ هـ: (بخنوقها).
٨ ي: (الأنساب).

Take warning from those who built on every height a monument for their amusement, who built for themselves mighty castles, hoping to live forever,[18] and those «who said: is anyone mightier than us?»[19] 2.14.3

Take warning from your brothers whom you have seen die. They were borne to their graves, but cannot be called riders. They were given places to alight, but cannot be called guests. They were given tombs as coverings, earth as shrouds, and dried bones as neighbors, neighbors who do not answer the one who calls out to them, who do not protect from harm, who do not benefit from the laments chanted for them, who do not recognize bad or good, who do not give any more false testimony. If they get rain they do not rejoice. If they have drought they do not despair. They are all together, yet each one is alone. They are neighbors, yet distant from one another. They are in the same assembly, yet no-one visits them, nor do they visit anyone—mature leaders whose enmities have dissipated, rash youths whose hatreds have disappeared. Their blows are no longer feared. Their protection is no longer sought. They are as those who never were. And as God has said: «Those are their abodes, uninhabited after them except for a short time. We, yes we, will inherit.»[20]

The world's claim is weak, her drink murky, and the path to her waterhole thick with mud. She is deception personified, her ashwood spears are ready to strike, and any support she provides is unsteady. Her silk robes dazzle, and her beauty amazes. But she kills the one who seeks excess of her, and prostrates the one who would benefit from her, by the unavoidable cessation of her pleasures, by her destructive desires, and by imprisoning whomsoever would break loose from her grip. She traps him with her snares, her arrows aimed at him, capturing him with paltry favors, teasing with trivial gifts, every night of his existence and all the days of his life. 2.14.4

Then the rope of death trusses him up and its cords strangle him, leading him in paroxysms to a narrow bed and a fearful place of return, to the company of the lifeless, to the witnessing of his new home, and the recompense for his deeds.

Then time shuts up his ears and he dies. He will not return. He will have to pay—his neck bound with the twine of sins he has earned, all traces accounted for in time for the verdict. «He who bears the burden of evil deeds has indeed failed.»[21]

الباب الثالث

فيما روي عنه عليه السلام من المواعظ

٣.١ فمن ذلك قوله عليه السلام:

٣.١.١ إنّكم مخلوقون ٱقتدارا ومربوبون ٱقتسارا ومضمّنون أجداثا وكائنون رُفاتا ومبعوثون أفرادا ومَدينون حسابا.

فرحم الله عبدا ٱقترف فٱعترف ووَجِل فعمل وحاذر فبادر وعُمّر فٱعتبر وحُذّر فٱزدجر وأجاب فأناب وراجَ فتاب وٱقتدى فٱحتذى. فباحث طلبا ونجا هربا وأفاد ذخيرة وأطاب سريرة وتأهّب للمعاد وٱستظهر بالزاد ليوم رحيله ووجه سبيله وحال حاجته ومَوطِن فاقته فقدّم أمامه لدار مُقامه.

فمهِّدوا لأنفسكم في سلامة الأبدان. فهل يَنتظر أهل غضارة الشباب إلّا حَواني الهَرَم وأهل بَضاضة الصحّة إلّا نوازل السقم وأهل مدّة البقاء إلّا مفاجأة الفناء وٱقتراب الفوت ودنوّ الموت وأَزَف الإنتقال وإشفاء الزوال وحَفز[٩] الأنين ورَشْح الجبين وٱمتداد العِرنين وعَلَز القلق وفَيظ الرمَق وألَم المَضَض وغَصَص الجَرَض.

اعلموا عباد الله أنّكم وما أنتم فيه من هذه الدنيا على سبيل من قد مضى ممّن كان أطول منكم أعمارا وأشدّ منكم بطشا وأعمر ديارا وأبعد آثارا. فأصبحت أصواتهم هامدة خامدة من بعد طول تقلّبها وأجسادهم بالية وديارهم خالية وآثارهم عافية. قد

---

٩ ي: (خفق).

Chapter 3

Counsel

ʿAlī said: 3.1

3.1.1 You have been created by God's power and are ruled by his might. You will be placed in the grave and turn to dry bones. Every one of you will be resurrected alone and held accountable for your deeds.

May God have mercy on the man who, having sinned, confesses. Fearful of punishment in the hereafter, he performs good deeds. Dreading it, he hastens to the straight path. Having been given a long life, he takes heed. Warned, he is driven back from error. Answering, he comes back to God. When he wavers, he repents. When he emulates, he takes good people as an example. He hastens to seek knowledge. He flees from error and is saved. He gives away entire treasures. He purifies his heart. He prepares for the return, gathering provisions for his day of departure when he will set forth on his path, for his moment of need and for his time of want. He assembles supplies beforehand to take to his final abode.

Prime your souls while your bodies are sound. Think: Do people fresh and youthful wait for anything but the humbling ravages of age? People of glowing health for anything but the hard blows of sickness? People still on earth for anything but the arrival of sudden annihilation? And the drawing nigh of death? And the approach of the passing? And the looming closeness of the end? And the piercing moans? And the sweating brow? And the dilating nostrils? And the insomnia of anxiety? And the snuffing out of the last spark of life? And the pain of burning grief? And the choke of the death rattle?

Servants of God! You, and all things with you in this world, are on the path of those who have gone before—people who lived longer than you, who were stronger in battle, and who had more prosperous homes and longer lasting monuments. After a long run of power, their voices have become extinguished, their bodies decayed, their homes emptied, their monuments effaced. In exchange for fortified palaces and lavish thrones and cushions,

ٱستَبدلوا بالقصور المشيّدة والسرر والنمارق الممهّدة الصخور والأحجار المسنّدة في القبور اللاطية المُلحَدة التي قد بيّن الخراب فنائها وشيّد التراب بناءها.

٣.١.٢ فمحلّها مقترب وساكنها مغترب بين أهل عمارة موحشين وأهل محلّة متشاغلين[1] لا يستأنسون بالعمران ولا يَتواصلون كتواصل الجيران والإخوان على ما بينهم من قرب الجوار ودنوّ الدار.

وكيف يكون بينهم تواصل وقد طحنهم بكلكله البِلى وأكلهم الجنادل والثرى فأصبحوا بعد الحياة أمواتا وبعد غضارة العيش رُفاتا. فُجع بهم الأحباب وسكنوا التراب وظعنوا فليس لهم إياب. هَيهات هيهات ﴿كَلَّآ إِنَّهَا كَلِمَةٌ هُوَ قَآئِلُهَا وَمِن وَرَآئِهِم بَرْزَخٌ إِلَىٰ يَوْمِ يُبْعَثُونَ﴾.

وكأن قد صرتم إلى ما صاروا إليه من البلى والوحدة في دار الموت وٱرتُهنتم في ذلك المَضجَع وضمّكم ذلك المستودَع. فكيف بكم لو قد تناهت الأمور وبُعثرت القبور ﴿وَحُصِّلَ مَا فِي ٱلصُّدُورِ﴾ ووُقفتم للتحصيل بين يدي الملك الجليل فطارت القلوب لإشفاقها من سالف الذنوب وهُتكت عنكم الحجب والأستار وظهرت منكم العيوب والأسرار. هنالك تُجزى كلّ نفس ما أسلفت. إنّ الله يقول ﴿لِيَجْزِيَ ٱلَّذِينَ أَسَـٰٓـُٔوا۟ بِمَا عَمِلُوا۟ وَيَجْزِيَ ٱلَّذِينَ أَحْسَنُوا۟ بِٱلْحُسْنَى﴾.

اغتنموا أيّام الصحّة قبل السقم والشبيبة قبل الهرم وبادروا بالتوبة قبل الندم. ولا تَحملنّكم المُهلة على طول الغفلة فإنّ الأجل يهدم الأمل والأيّام موكّلة بتنغيص[2] المدّة وتفريق الأحبّة.

فبادِروا رحمكم الله بالتوبة قبل حضور النَّوبة وبَرّزوا[3] للغيبة التي لا تُنتظر معها الأَوبة وٱستعينوا على بعد المسافة بطول المخافة.

---

١ ه: (بين أهل محلّة موحشين وأهل فراغ متشاغلين).

٢ م: (بتنقيص).

٣ م: (تزوّدوا).

they have been given rocks and stones propped up in the crushing shelter of dug out graves. Ruination has revealed the annihilation of their palaces, and dust has covered their towering edifices.

3.1.2 The grave is at hand. Its resident is like a stranger. He is with those who live together in one domicile and yet are lonely, who stay in one locale yet are too preoccupied to be concerned about each other. They have neither the comfort of a prosperous home, nor do they associate as neighbors and brothers. All this, despite their physical closeness and the proximity of their dwellings.

How could there be association between them, when decay has crushed them, and stones and earth have eaten them up? When after being alive, they have become dead bodies? After having had fresh life, they are now dry bones? Their loved ones are shocked by their death, a death that has sent them to live in the dust, departed, never to return. Woe! Woe! «No indeed, it is but a word that he speaks, while behind them is a barrier till the day they are resurrected.»[22]

It is as though you have arrived at their destination: At the place of decay, solitary in the abode of the dead. It is as though you have already been yielded as collateral to that bed, and that depository has already enveloped you. How do you think it will be with you, when all affairs reach their end? When the contents of graves are scattered forth?[23] When «what is in people's breasts is reaped»?[24] When you are made to stand in front of the mighty judge for your hearts to be reaped? Hearts will flutter from their dread of punishment for past sins. Veils and curtains will be rent. Faults and secrets will be revealed. In that place, each soul will be recompensed for what it has presented.[25] God says: «He will recompense evil with its like, and good with good.»[26]

Take advantage of your days of health before the arrival of days of illness, of youth before the onset of old age. Hasten to repent before the time of regret. Do not let this respite prompt you to ride the back of lasting heedlessness, for the end of your life will destroy your hopes. The passing days are charged with disrupting your time span and with separating you from loved ones.

Hasten to repent—may God have mercy on you! before the arrival of the calamity. Outpace your fellow men in preparation for that disappearance from which there is no return. Seek help in traveling the great distance through a sustained fear of God's punishment.

فكم من غافل وثق بغفلته وتعلّل بمهلته فأمّل بعيدا وبنى مشيدا فنُقص بقرب[1] أجله بُعد أمله وفاجأته منيّته بٱنقطاع أمنيّته فصار بعد العزّ والمنعة والشرف والرفعة مرتهَنا بموبقات عمله. قد غاب فما رجع وندم فما ٱنتفع وشقي بما جمع في يومه وسعد به غيره في غده وبقي مرتهنا بكسب يده ذاهلا عن أهله وولده لا يغني عنه ما ترك فتيلا ولا يجد إلى مَناص سبيلا.

فعلام عباد الله المُنعرَج والدَّلَج وإلى أين المفرّ والمهرب وهذا الموت في الطلب يَخترم الأوّل فالأوّل لا يتحنّن على ضعيف ولا يُعرِّج على شريف والجديدان يَحُثّان الأجل تحثيثا ويسوقانه سَوقا حثيثا. وكلّ ما هو آت فقريب ومن وراء ذلك العجب العجيب. فأعدّوا الجواب ليوم الحساب وأكثروا الزاد ليوم المعاد.

عصمنا الله وإيّاكم بطاعته وأعاننا وإيّاكم على ما يُقرِّب إليه ويُزلِف لديه فإنّما نحن به وله.

٣.٢ إنّ الله وَقّت لكم الآجال وضرب لكم الأمثال وألبسكم الرياش وأرفغ لكم المعاش وآثركم بالنعم السوابغ وتقدّم إليكم بالحجج البوالغ وأوسع لكم في الرفد الرافغ.[2] فشمّروا فقد أحاط بكم الإحصاء وٱرتُهن لكم الجزاء.

٣.٣ القلوب قاسية عن حظّها لاهية عن رشدها سالكة في غير مِضمارها كأنّ المَعنيّ سواها.

---

١ م: (ببتّ).

٢ ي: (الواسع).

How many a heedless person was complacent in his heedlessness, making excuses in his time of respite, hoping long hopes, building strong edifices? The approaching end of his lifespan truncated his long hopes. His death took him by surprise, severing his desires. After having might, power, honor, and standing, he became pawned to his destructive deeds. He left and will not return. He regretted but to no avail. He was reduced to misery by the things he accumulated in his day—and which another enjoyed on the morrow—and he became mortgaged to the earnings of his hands, distracted even from wife and children. What he left behind did not benefit him even a date pit's worth. He found no path of escape.

Servants of God! Why do you race through the winding dunes from the first fall of night? Where will you flee, when death is here, stalking you, snatching up one person after another, not pitying the weak, nor having mercy on the noble? The recurring alternation of day and night urges on your lifespan and drives it forward inexorably. What is to come is at hand. After that, you will see the wonder of wonders. Make ready your answer for the day of reckoning and make plenty of preparations for the day of return.

May God protect us—and you—by aiding us to obey him. May he help us—and you—to do what will bring us closer to him. We come from him, and we belong to him.

3.2 God has decreed your life spans. He has given you instruction through parables. He has clothed you in splendid garments. He has elevated your mode of living. He has graced you with perfect favors. He has come to you with convincing arguments. He has bestowed on you gifts of happiness and ease. So tuck up your garments and make haste! The reckoning will begird you, and the recompense for your deeds is pledged.

3.3 Hardened hearts cannot absorb their full share of God's mercy. Distracted by worldly pleasures, they ignore their better judgment. They race in the wrong track, as though someone else were implicated.

٣.٤ اتّقوا اللّٰه تقيّة مَن شمّر تجريدا وجدّ تشميرا وآنكمش في مَهَل وأشفق في وجل[١] ونظر في كرّة الموئل وعاقبة الصبر ومَغبّة المرجع. وكفى باللّٰه منتقما ونصيرا وكفى بالجنّة ثوابا ونوالا وكفى بالنار عقابا ونكالا وكفى بكتاب اللّٰه حجيجا وخصيما.

٣.٥ رحم اللّٰه عبدا آستشعر الحزن وتجلبب الخوف وأضمر اليقين وعَري من الشكّ في توهّم الزوال فهو منه على بال فزهر مصباح الهدى في قلبه وقرّب به على نفسه البعيد وهوّن الشديد. فخرج من صفة العمى ومشاركة الموتى وصار من مفاتيح الهدى ومغاليق أبواب الردى وآستفتح بما فتح به العالِم أبوابه وخاض بحاره وقطع غِماره ووضحت له سبله ومناره وآستمسك من العُرى بأوثقها وآستعصم من الجبال بأمتنها. كشّاف غَمرات فتّاح مُبهَمات دافع معضلات دليل مُضِلّات[٢] لا يدع للخير مطلبا إلّا أمّه ولا مَظِنّة إلّا قصدها.

١ ي: (عجل).

٢ ي: سقطت (دليل مضلّات). هـ: (معضلات).

Be conscious of God. Roll up your sleeves and apply yourselves. Strip yourself of worldly connections. Accelerate your pace. Speed up your preparations in your time of respite. Be fearful. Ponder the return to the refuge, the end result of patience, and the final homecoming. Surely God suffices as avenger and giver of victory. Surely the garden suffices as reward and gift. Surely the fire suffices as punishment and chastisement. Surely the book of God suffices as interlocutor and adversary. 3.4

May God have mercy on the man who wears the garment of grief and dons the robe of fear. Who, being a man of conviction, divests himself of doubt and patiently awaits the approaching end of his life on earth. Mindful of this end, his heart shines forth as a lamp of guidance. With its light, he brings the far close, and finds difficulties easier to bear. He escapes from the grip of blindness and from association with the dead, and becomes himself a key for the door of guidance and a lock for the door of perdition. He seeks to open the door of guidance as scholars have done, plunging into its sea and venturing through its depths. Its paths and beacons shine bright for him. Grasping the sturdiest of handles, taking refuge in the strongest of mountains, he removes misfortunes, elucidates ambiguities, repulses calamities, and guides others through the wilderness. He pursues every repository of good, seeking it wherever it may be found. 3.5

الباب الرابع

فيما روي عنه عليه السلام من وصاياه ونواهيه

أَحْسِن كما تُحِبّ أن يُحسَن إليك ٤.١.١

أنصف من نفسك قبل أن يُنتصف منك ٤.١.٢

أطلب فإنّه يأتيك ما قُسم لك ٤.١.٣

ساهِل الدهر ما ذَلّ قعودُه ٤.١.٤

بادر الفرصة قبل أن تكون غُصّة ٤.١.٥

أدّب نفسك بما كرهته لغيرك ٤.١.٦

أصلح مثواك وٱبتَعْ آخرتك بدنياك ٤.١.٧

لِنْ لمن خالطك[1] فإنّه يوشِك أن يلين لك ٤.١.٨

اجعل نفسك ميزانا فيما بينك وبين غيرك ٤.١.٩

أَحِبَّ لغيرك ما تحبّ لنفسك وٱكْره له ما تكره لها ٤.١.١٠

اِستقبح من نفسك ما تستقبح من غيرك ٤.١.١١

خذ الفضل وأحسن البذل وقل للناس حسنا ٤.١.١٢

دَعْ عنك أظنّ وأحسب وأرى ٤.١.١٣

دع القول فيما لا تعرف والخطاب فيما لا تكلَّف ٤.١.١٤

اِرْضَ من الناس لك ما ترضى لهم به منك ٤.١.١٥

أَلِحّ بالمسألة تُفتح لك أبواب الرحمة ٤.١.١٦

أنفق في حقّ[2] ولا تكن خازنا لغيرك ٤.١.١٧

---

١ ي: (غالظك). هـ: (يخالطك).

٢ ي: (حياتك).

Chapter 4

Prescriptions and Proscriptions

Be good to others just as you would have others be good to you. 4.1.1

Show justice before justice is meted out to you. 4.1.2

Seek your share and your destiny will come to you. 4.1.3

Fate is a camel. Loosen its reins as long as it is docile. 4.1.4

Seize opportunities before they dissipate. 4.1.5

Discipline yourself to not do what you dislike in others. 4.1.6

Adorn your final dwelling place and trade this world for the hereafter. 4.1.7

Be kind to one who associates with you; perhaps then he will be kind to you. 4.1.8

How you wish to be treated should be the measure of how you treat others. 4.1.9

Choose for others what you would choose for yourself, and dislike for them what you dislike for yourself. 4.1.10

Consider ugly in yourself what you consider ugly in others. 4.1.11

Strive for excellence, give generously, and speak kindly to people. 4.1.12

Avoid saying "I guess," "I suppose," and "I reckon." 4.1.13

Avoid talking about things you do not know, or addressing people regarding things which are not your concern. 4.1.14

Accept from others what you require of them. 4.1.15

Do not stop asking God—the gates of his mercy will open for you. 4.1.16

Spend righteously; do not hoard your wealth for others. 4.1.17

أَخِّرِ الشرّ فإنّك إذا شئت تعجّلته ٤.١.١٨

احتمل أخاك على ما فيه ٤.١.١٩

استعتب من رجوت إعتابه[١] ٤.١.٢٠

أطع أخاك وإن عصاك وصِلْه وإن جفاك ٤.١.٢١

اقبل عذر من اعتذر إليك ٤.١.٢٢

خَفِ الله في سرّك يكفيك ما يضرّك ٤.١.٢٣

ذَكِّ قلبك بالأدب كما تذكّي النار بالحطب ٤.١.٢٤

تباعد من السلطان ولا تأمن من خُدَع الشيطان ٤.١.٢٥

تخيّر لنفسك من كل خُلُقٍ أحسنه فإنّ الخير عادة ٤.١.٢٦

اقطع عنك دابرات[٢] الهموم بعزائم الصبر ٤.١.٢٧

أَقِمِ الحدود في القريب يجتنبها البعيد ٤.١.٢٨

قارن أهل الخير تكن منهم وباين أهل الشرّ تَبِن عنهم ٤.١.٢٩

اِمحَض أخاك النصيحة حسنة كانت أو قبيحة ٤.١.٣٠

ساعد أخاك على كلّ حال وزُل معه حيث زال ٤.١.٣١

خُضِ الغمرات إلى الحقّ ٤.١.٣٢

كن من الدنيا على قُلعة ٤.١.٣٣

عوّد نفسك السماح ٤.١.٣٤

تخيّر لوِردك ٤.١.٣٥

اقبل العفو من الناس ٤.١.٣٦

احذر التلوّن في الدين ٤.١.٣٧

عظّم من يكرمك ٤.١.٣٨

اُعفُ عمّن ظلمك ٤.١.٣٩

---

١ ي: (عتابه).

٢ ي: (واردات).

Impede evil, else you may speed its onset. 4.1.18

Accept your brother, whatever his faults. 4.1.19

Show kindness to those whom you wish to please. 4.1.20

Obey your brother even if he disobeys you, and keep your bonds with him even if he would cut them. 4.1.21

Accept the apology of one who apologizes. 4.1.22

Fear God, and he will suffice you against harm. 4.1.23

Nourish your heart with refined behavior as you would stoke a fire with kindling. 4.1.24

Stay away from power, and do not become complacent against Satan's deceits. 4.1.25

Always choose the best of qualities for your soul—being good is a cultivated habit. 4.1.26

Cut off the traces of care with the resolve of forbearance. 4.1.27

Enforce punishments on those close to you when they transgress, and the public will stay away from crime. 4.1.28

Associate with good people and you will be one of them. Stay away from evil people and you will be differentiated from them. 4.1.29

Give your brother sincere advice, whether palatable or unpleasant. 4.1.30

Help your brother in any circumstance; go with him where he goes. 4.1.31

Plumb the depths to find truth. 4.1.32

Live in this world as though on a journey. 4.1.33

Train your soul to be generous. 4.1.34

Choose carefully where you water your camels. 4.1.35

Accept people's apologies. 4.1.36

Beware of fickleness in religion. 4.1.37

Honor those who are generous to you. 4.1.38

Forgive those who are cruel to you. 4.1.39

أكرم من أهانك ٤.١.٤٠

أحسن إلى من أساء إليك وكافئ مَن أحسن إليك ٤.١.٤١

ادع لمن أعطاك ٤.١.٤٢

أُشكر الله على ما أولاك وٱحمده على ما أبلاك ٤.١.٤٣

احمل[1] لمن أدلّ عليك وٱقبل عذر من ٱعتذر إليك ٤.١.٤٤

خذ العفو من الناس ولا تبلغ من أحد ما يكرهه ٤.١.٤٥

تعفّف عن أموال الناس وٱستشعر منها اليأس ٤.١.٤٦

غلّس بالفجر تَلْقَ الله تعالى أبيض الوجه ٤.١.٤٧

تَفَقَّهْ في الدين وعَوِّد نفسك الصبر على المكروه ٤.١.٤٨

أخلص في المسألة لربّك فإنّ بيده العطاء والحرمان ٤.١.٤٩

أَلجئ نفسك في الأمور كلّها إلى إلٰهك فإنّك تُلجئها إلى كهف حريز ومانع عزيز ٤.١.٥٠

اغتنم من ٱستقرضك في حال غناك وٱجعل قضائك في يوم عسرتك ٤.١.٥١

خذ من الدنيا ما أتاك وتَوَلَّ عمّا تولّى عنك فإن أنت لم تفعل فأجمل في الطلب ٤.١.٥٢

أكرم نفسك عن كلّ دنيئة وإن ساقتك إلى الرغب فإنّك لن تعتاض بما تبذل من نفسك عوضا ٤.١.٥٣

اعرف الحقّ لمن عرّفه لك رفيعا كان أو وضيعا ٤.١.٥٤

اطرَح عنك واردات الهموم بعزائم الصبر وحسن اليقين ٤.١.٥٥

---

[1] ي: (احتمل). م: مصحّحة في الحاشية (أجمل).

Be generous even to those who belittle you. 4.1.40

Be good to those who treat you unkindly, and recompense those who treat you well. 4.1.41

Pray for those who are generous to you. 4.1.42

Thank God for the gifts he bestows upon you, and praise him for the trials he tests you with. 4.1.43

Be patient with those who are cruel to you, and accept apologies from those who proffer them. 4.1.44

Accept apologies. Do not do to anyone something he finds objectionable. 4.1.45

Do not covet another's property—don the garment of contentedness. 4.1.46

Pray the dawn prayer while the night is still dark and you will meet God with a shining face.[27] 4.1.47

Learn the rules of religious practice, and train yourself to be patient when faced with difficulties. 4.1.48

Beseech God with all your heart, for he has the power to give or refuse. 4.1.49

Commit yourself to God in all your affairs—in him you have a sheltering cavern and a mighty protector. 4.1.50

Take advantage of the opportunity to lend when you have wealth, and fix repayment for your day of need. 4.1.51

Take what comes to you of this world, and turn away from what turns away from you. If you cannot bring yourself to do so, then at least be moderate in your ventures. 4.1.52

Honor your soul by protecting it from base things, even if they lead to your heart's desire. Remember, you shall not get back what you expend of it. 4.1.53

Acknowledge your indebtedness to one who guides you to the truth, whether he is high-placed or lowly. 4.1.54

Cast off the fevers of anxiety with patient resolve and beautiful conviction. 4.1.55

أحسن العفو فإنّ العفو مع العدل أشدّ من الضرب لمن كان له عقل ٤.١.٥٦

استعن بالله عزّ وجلّ على أمرك فإنّه أكفى معين ٤.١.٥٧

ابذل لصديقك كلّ المودّة ولا تبذل له كلّ الطمأنينة وأعطه كلّ المواساة ولا تُفضِ إليه بكلّ الأسرار ٤.١.٥٨

احذر دمعة المؤمن في السحَر فإنّها تقصف من دمعها وتُطفئ بحور النيران عمّن دعا بها ٤.١.٥٩

ارفق بالبهائم ولا توقّف عليها أحمالها ولا تُسقى بلُجُمها ولا تُحمّل فوق طاقتها ٤.١.٦٠

أمسك عن طريق إذا خِفت ضلالة فإنّ الكفّ عنه حين الضلال خير من ركوب الأهوال ٤.١.٦١

مُرْ بالمعروف تكن من أهله وأنكر المنكر بلسانك ويدك وباين من فعله بجهدك ٤.١.٦٢

ابذل لصديقك مالك ولمعرفتك معونتك وللعامّة التحيّة والسلام ٤.١.٦٣

احمل نفسك عن أخيك عند صُرمه على الصلة وعند صدوده على لطف المسألة وعند جموده على البذل وعند تباعده على الدنوّ وعند شدّته على اللين وعند تجرّيه على الإعذار حتّى كأنّك عبد وكأنّه ذو نعمة ٤.١.٦٤

لتكن مسألتك فيما يَعنيك ممّا يبقى عليك جماله ولا يبقى عليك وباله لا ما لا يبقى لك ولا تبقى له فإنّه يوشك أن ترى عاقبة أمرك محسنا أو مسيئا أو يعفو العفوّ الكريم ٤.١.٦٥

نوع منه:

لا تخُن من ائتمنك وإن خانك ٤.١.٦٦

لا تُذِع سرّ من أذاع سرّك ٤.١.٦٧

Be forgiving. Reproving forgiveness hurts an intelligent man more than a beating. 4.1.56

Seek help from God in all your affairs. He is the most sufficient helper. 4.1.57

Give a friend full affection but not blind trust. Help him, but do not tell him every secret. 4.1.58

Beware the tears of the believer when he prays at dawn, for they crush the person who has occasioned them and douse the sea of fire engulfing the supplicant. 4.1.59

Be gentle with your horses and camels. Do not keep them standing while loaded. Do not make them drink with their bits in their mouths. Do not load them beyond their capacity. 4.1.60

Stay back from a course if you fear you will stray. Staying back when unsure is better than riding the ominous swells of the sea. 4.1.61

Command good and you shall be good. Forbid evil with your tongue and your hand. Strive to differentiate yourself from those who do evil. 4.1.62

Give your brother your wealth, give your acquaintance your support, and give the public greetings and peace. 4.1.63

Maintain the bonds of kinship with your brother even when he is bent on cutting them. Perform kindnesses for him even when he shuns you. Be generous to him even when he hardens and is close-fisted. Stay close to him even when he distances himself. Be kind to him even when he is harsh. Placate him even when he is cruel. Behave toward him as though you were a slave and he a generous benefactor. 4.1.64

Ask only for things that befit you, whose beautiful goodness will benefit you, the burden of whose evil outcome will not weigh you down. Do not ask for things that will not remain for you or you for them. The time has drawn nigh when you will see the consequences of your deeds, good or bad. Perhaps the generous forgiver will forgive 4.1.65

Do not cheat a person who has given you something in trust, even if he cheats you. 4.1.66

Do not reveal another's secrets, even if he reveals yours. 4.1.67

لا تَصرم أخاك على ارتياب ولا تقطعه دون الإستعتاب ٤.١.٦٨

لا تيأس من[1] الذنب وباب التوبة مفتوح ٤.١.٦٩

لا تظلم كما لا تحبّ أن تظلم ٤.١.٧٠

لا تقل ما لا تعلم بل لا تقل كلّما علمت ٤.١.٧١

لا تُكثر العَتْب في غير ذنب ٤.١.٧٢

لا تُضيِّع الفرائض وتتّكل على النوافل ٤.١.٧٣

لا تعمل بالخديعة فإنّها خلق لئيم ٤.١.٧٤

لا تدع أن تنصح أهلك فإنّك عنهم مسئول ٤.١.٧٥

لا تكن كحاطب الليل وغثاء السيل ٤.١.٧٦

لا تكن عبد غيرك وقد جعلك الله حرًا ٤.١.٧٧

لا تكثر العتاب فإنّه يورث الضغينة ويحرّك البِغضة ٤.١.٧٨

لا تَقضِ وأنت غضبان ولا من النوم سكران ٤.١.٧٩

لا تُحضر مجلسك من لا يشبهك ٤.١.٨٠

لا تُهن من يكرمك ٤.١.٨١

لا تُعوِّد نفسك الضحك فإنّه يذهب بالبهاء ويُجرئ الخصوم على الإعتداء ٤.١.٨٢

لا تَولّ أهل السُخط ولا تُسخط أهل الرضا ٤.١.٨٣

لا تشاقق مؤمنا فتُلحَ كما يُلحى القضيب من لِحائه ولا تأخذ الناس بالإحَن فليس أخو الدين ذا إحن ٤.١.٨٤

---

١ ي: تصيف (غفران).

Do not shun your brother over a suspicion or cut him off without asking for an explanation. 4.1.68

Do not despair if you have sinned, for the door of repentance is open. 4.1.69

Do not oppress others, just as you would not have others oppress you. 4.1.70

Do not speak about things you do not know; indeed, do not speak about everything you do know. 4.1.71

Do not rebuke a person too much for something that is not a sin. 4.1.72

Do not squander mandatory religious obligations, while relying on your performance of supererogatory ones. 4.1.73

Do not make trickery the basis of your dealings; it is a vile trait. 4.1.74

Never leave off counseling your family; you are responsible for them. 4.1.75

Do not speak heedlessly, like someone gathering firewood in the dark, or like scum on surging waves. 4.1.76

Do not become the slave of another when God has made you free. 4.1.77

Do not censure too much, for it bequeaths hatred. 4.1.78

Do not judge when you are angry or intoxicated by sleep. 4.1.79

Do not allow someone who is not like you into your company. 4.1.80

Do not scorn someone who honors you. 4.1.81

Do not make it your custom to laugh loudly, for it lessens your poise and emboldens your antagonist. 4.1.82

Do not befriend ingrates or shun the obliging. 4.1.83

Do not quarrel with a believer or you will be stripped just as a branch is stripped of its bark. Do not hate people; a man of faith does not hate. 4.1.84

لا تتّخذنّ عدوّ صديقك صديقا فتعادي صديقك ٤.١.٨٥

لا تستريبنّ بثقة رجاء ٤.١.٨٦

لا تطلبنّ مُجازاة أخيك وإن حثا التراب بفيك ٤.١.٨٧

لا تضيعنّ حقّ أخيك اتّكالا على ما بينك وبينه فإنّه ليس بأخ من أضعتَ حقّه ٤.١.٨٨

لا تكوننّ على الإساءة أقوى منك على الإحسان ولا على البخل أقوى منك على البذل ولا على التقصير أقوى منك على الفضل ٤.١.٨٩

لا تكوننّ ممّن لا ينتفع من العظة إلّا بما لزمه فآلمه فإنّ العاقل يتّعظ بالأدب والبهائم لا تتّعظ إلّا بالضرب ٤.١.٩٠

لا تكوننّ كمن يعجز عن شكر ما أوتي ويبتغي الزيادة فيما بقي ٤.١.٩١

لا تكفرنّ ذا نعمة فإنّ كفر النعمة مِن ألأم الكفر ٤.١.٩٢

لا يغلبنّ عليك سوء الظنّ فإنّه لا يدع بينك وبين خليلك صلحا ٤.١.٩٣

لا يكن أهلك أشقى الناس بك ولا ترغبنّ فيمن زهد فيك ٤.١.٩٤

لا يكوننّ أخوك أقوى على قطيعتك منك على صلته ٤.١.٩٥

لا يكبر عليك ظلم من ظلمك فإنّه إنّما يسعى في مضرّته ونفعك ٤.١.٩٦

لا يكون الصديق صديقا حتّى يحفظ صديقه في غيبه ويحفظه عند نكبته ويحفظه بعد وفاته في مُخلَّفيه وتَرِكته ٤.١.٩٧

لا يُقنطنّك إن أبطأت عليك الإجابة فإنّ العطيّة على قدر المسألة ٤.١.٩٨

لا يُعدمنّك من شفيق سوء ظنّ ٤.١.٩٩

Do not befriend your friend's enemy, for you would be spurning your friend. 4.1.85

Do not doubt an upright man. 4.1.86

Do not seek to even the score with your brother even if he pours dirt into your mouth. 4.1.87

Do not squander your brother's rights, taking the bond between you for granted. If you squander his rights he is no longer your brother. 4.1.88

Do not be more capable of meanness than kindness, of miserliness than generosity, of negligence than munificence. 4.1.89

Do not heed counsel only when it dogs you and causes you pain. A rational person takes counsel from rebuke; only cattle are counseled by the whip. 4.1.90

Do not be incapable of expressing gratitude for gifts, even as you seek more. 4.1.91

Do not be ungrateful to someone who does you a favor—that is the lowest form of ingratitude. 4.1.92

Do not keep doubting others. Doubt does not leave space for reconciliation between you and your friend. 4.1.93

Do not let your family members be the ones who get the least share of you. Do not place your desires in someone who is indifferent to you. 4.1.94

Do not let your brother be more capable of cutting himself off from you than you of associating with him. 4.1.95

Do not let the oppressor's oppression trouble you unduly. Know that he harms himself and benefits you. 4.1.96

A friend is not a friend unless he protects his friend in his absence and when he is in trouble, and unless he protects his friend's children and his inheritance after he dies. 4.1.97

Do not despair if the answer is slow in coming. The gift will be commensurate to the petition. 4.1.98

Do not let unwarranted distrust deprive you of a compassionate friend. 4.1.99

لا يُزهدنّك في المعروف كفر مَن كفره فقد يشكرك عليه من لم يستمتع منه بشيء ٤.١.١٠٠

لا تُمارِ سفيها ولا فقيها أمّا الفقيه فتُحرَم خيره وأمّا السفيه فيحزنك شرّه ٤.١.١٠١

نمط منه:

إيّاك أن تجمح بك مطيّة اللجاج ٤.١.١٠٢

إيّاك أن توجِف بك مطايا الطمع ٤.١.١٠٣

إيّاك أن تعتذر من ذنب تجد إلى تركه سبيلا فإنّ أحسن حالك في الإعتذار أن تبلغ منزلة السلامة من الذنوب ٤.١.١٠٤

إيّاك والملالة فإنّها من السخف والنذالة ٤.١.١٠٥

إيّاك والإتّكال على المنى فإنّها بضائع النَّوكى وتُثبّط عن الآخرة والدنيا ٤.١.١٠٦

إيّاك والوقوف عمّا عرفته فإنّ كل ناظر مسئول عن عمله وقوله وإرادته ٤.١.١٠٧

إيّاك ومصادقة الأحمق فإنّه يريد أن ينفعك فيضرّك. إيّاك ومصادقة الكذّاب فإنّه يقرّب عليك البعيد ويبعّد عليك القريب. إيّاك ومصادقة البخيل فإنّه يقعد بك عند أحوَج ما تكون إليه. إيّاك ومصادقة الفاجر فإنّه يبيعك بالتافِه.[١] ٤.١.١٠٨

إيّاك ومقارنة مَن رهِبته على دينك وعِرضك ٤.١.١٠٩

إيّاك ومشاورة النساء فإنّ رأيهنّ إلى أَفَن وعزمهنّ إلى وهن ٤.١.١١٠

إيّاك وقبول تُحَف الخصوم ٤.١.١١١

إيّاكم وكفر النعم فتحلّ بكم النقم ٤.١.١١٢

---

١ م: (في نَفاقه) مشكّلة بالفتحة على النون، مصحّحة في الحاشية (بالتافه). ي: (من نِفاقه بالتافه) مشكّلة بالكسرة على النون.

Do not let someone's ingratitude stop you from doing good. The one who reaps no benefit from your generosity thanks you. 4.1.100

Do not quarrel with a fool or a sage. If you quarrel with a sage, you will be deprived of the good he does. If you quarrel with a fool, his evil will grieve you. 4.1.101

Beware lest belligerence's steeds bolt with you. 4.1.102

Beware lest ambition's steeds take off with you. 4.1.103

Beware of making excuses for a sin you could have refrained from committing. Your best apology is not to sin. 4.1.104

Beware lest you weary of life. That is weak-minded and contemptible. 4.1.105

Beware of putting faith in worldly hopes. They are the property of fools, and they hold you back in this world and the next. 4.1.106

Beware of holding back from doing what you know is right. Every person who has been given a reprieve will be held accountable for his deeds, words, and intentions. 4.1.107

Beware of befriending a fool, for he wants to benefit you but harms you instead. Beware of befriending a liar, for he brings near to you the distant and makes distant from you the near. Beware of befriending a miser, for he holds back from helping you when you most need him. And beware of befriending a depraved person, for he will sell you for a trifle. 4.1.108

Beware of associating with people who would harm your religion or your honor. 4.1.109

Beware of seeking advice from women, for their opinion can weaken and their resolve waver. 4.1.110

Beware of accepting gifts from adversaries. 4.1.111

Beware lest your ingratitude for God's favors causes his punishments to alight upon you. 4.1.112

نوع منه: ٤.١.١١٣

لا تكن ممّن يرجو الآخرة بغير عمل ويرجو التوبة بطول الأمل ويقول في الدنيا قول الزاهدين ويعمل فيها عمل الراغبين إنْ أُعطي منها لم يَشبع وإن مُنع منها لم يقنع. يعجز عن شكر ما أوتي ويبتغي الزيادة فيما بقي وينهى ولا ينتهي ويأمر بما لا يأتي. يحبّ الصالحين ولا يعمل بعملهم ويُبغض الطالحين وهو منهم ويكره الموت لكثرة ذنوبه ويقيم على ما يكره الموت له. إن سقم ظلّ نادما وإن صحّ قام لاهيا يُعجَب بنفسه إذا عوفي ويَقنِط إذا ٱبتُلي. تغلبه نفسه على ما يظنّ ولا يغلبها على ما يستيقن. لا يثق من الرزق بما ضُمن له ولا يعمل من العمل بما فرض عليه إن ٱستغنى بَطِر وإن ٱفتقر قنط ووهن. فهو من الذنب والنعمة مُوقَر يبتغي الزيادة ولا يشكر يتكلّف من الناس ما لم يؤمر ويضيع من نفسه ما هو أكثر. يبالغ إذا سأل ويقصّر إذا عمل يخشى الموت ولا يبادر الفوت يستكثر من معصية غيره ما يستقلّ أكثر منه من نفسه ويستكثر من طاعته ما يحقره من غيره وهو على الناس طاعن ولنفسه مُداهن ولَلغو مع الأغنياء أحبّ إليه من الذكر مع الفقراء. يحكم على غيره لنفسه ولا يحكم عليها لغيره وهو يُطاع ويَعصي ويستوفي ولا يوفي.

٤.٢ أخبرنا أبو محمّد عبد الرحمٰن بن عمر المعدَّل قال: أخبرنا أبو الطاهر محمّد بن عبد الغنيّ قال: أخبرنا أبو طالب الخشّاب قال: أخبرنا أبو عبد الله بن يزيد قال: أخبرنا أحمد بن محمّد البغداديّ قال:

يروى عن الحسن بن عليّ بن أبي طالب صلوات الله تعالى عليهما قال: أوصاني أبي عليه السلام قبل موته بثلاثين خصلة. قال: يا بُنَيّ إن أنت عملت بها في الدنيا سلّمك الله من شرّ الدنيا والآخرة. قال: قلت: وما هي يا أَبَهْ؟

4.1.113 Do not be one of those who expect the hereafter without work, or who anticipate forgiveness through lengthy aspirations. They speak of rejecting the world, but reveal their desire for it in the way they behave. When worldly possessions are withheld from them they are discontent, yet when given them they are not satisfied. Incapable of gratitude for God's gifts, they want more. They forbid others from evil, but do not themselves desist. They command others to do what they themselves do not. They love good people but do not behave like them. They detest the wicked but resemble them. They fear death because they have sinned for long, yet continue to do the very things that make them fearful. If they become ill they repent, but once healthy they frolic. When they are fit they are full of themselves, but when tested they despair. Their ego compels them to follow its inclinations; they do not compel it to follow their conviction. They do not trust in the sustenance guaranteed them nor undertake the duties mandated of them. If they gain wealth they turn insolent, if they become poor they despair and weaken. They carry the twin burdens of sins and favors. They keep asking for more yet do not give thanks. Sycophants, they do for others what is not required, while squandering their own precious souls. They make grand requests yet fall short in their deeds. They fear death yet are slow to atone in the time they have. They consider others' sins excessive yet regard as insignificant the many more transgressions they themselves commit. They aggrandize their own deeds of obedience yet think similar acts contemptible in others. They calumniate others and flatter themselves. Idle talk with the rich is dearer to them than worshiping God with the poor. They judge others but not themselves. They expect others to obey them, yet they disobey. They expect full measure but do not pay equally.

4.2 Abū Muḥammad ʿAbd al-Raḥmān ibn ʿUmar al-Muʿaddal reported to us, saying: Abū l-Ṭāhir Muḥammad ibn ʿAbd al-Ghanī reported to us, saying: Abū Ṭālib al-Khashshāb reported to us, saying: Abū ʿAbd Allāh ibn Yazīd reported to us, saying: Aḥmad ibn Muḥammad al-Baghdādī reported to us, saying:

Al-Ḥasan, son of ʿAlī ibn Abī Ṭālib, said: My father counseled me before his death about thirty character traits, saying: Dear son, if you inculcate these qualities in your life in this world, God will protect you from the evils of this world and of the hereafter. What are they, father? I asked, and he replied as follows:

فقال: احذر من الأمور ثلاثا وخَفْ من ثلاث وآرْجُ ثلاثا ووافق ثلاثا وآستحي من ثلاث وآفزع إلى ثلاث وشُحَّ على ثلاث وتخلّص إلى ثلاث وآهرب من ثلاث وجانب ثلاثا يجمع الله لك بذلك حسن السيرة في الدنيا والآخرة.

فأمّا الذي أمرتك أن تحذرها فآحذر الكبر والغضب والطمع. فأمّا الكبر فإنّه خصلة من خصال الأشرار والكبرياء رداء الله عزّوجلّ ومن أسكن الله قلبه مثقال حبّة من كبر أورده النار. والغضب يسفِه الحليم ويُطيش العالم ويُفقَد معه العقل ويظهر معه الجهل. والطمع فَخٌّ من فِخاخ إبليس وشَرَك من عظيم آحتباله يصيد به العلماء والعقلاء وأهل المعرفة وذوي البصائر.

قال: قلت: صدقت يا أبه فأخبرني عن قولك خف ثلاثا.

قال: نعم يا بنيّ. خف الله وخف من لا يخاف الله وخف لسانك فإنّه عدوّك على دينك يؤمنك الله جميع ما خِفته.

قال: قلت: صدقت يا أبه فأخبرني عن قولك وآرج ثلاثا.

قال: يا بنيّ آرج عفو الله عن ذنوبك وَآرج محاسن عملك وآرج شفاعة نبيّك صلّى الله عليه وعلى آله وسلّم.

قال: قلت: صدقت يا أبه فأخبرني عن قولك وافق ثلاثا.

قال: نعم. وافق كتاب الله تبارك وتعالى ووافق سنّة نبيّك صلّى الله عليه وعلى آله وسلّم ووافق ما يوافق الحقّ والكتاب.

قلت: صدقت يا أبه فأخبرني عن قولك آستحي من ثلاث.

قال: نعم يا بنيّ. استحي من مطالعة الله إيّاك وأنت مقيم على ما يكره وآستحي من الحفظة الكرام الكاتبين وآستحي من صالحي المؤمنين.

قلت: صدقت يا أبه. فأخبرني عن قولك: وآفزع إلى ثلاث.

قال: نعم. آفزع إلى الله تعالى في ملمّات أمورك وآفزع إلى التوبة في مساوي عملك وآفزع إلى أهل العلم والأدب عند هفوات جهلك.

قلت: صدقت يا أبه فأخبرني عن قولك شحّ على ثلاث.

Be wary of three things, fear three, hope for three, abide by three, be ashamed of three, take refuge in three, be niggardly with three, focus on three, flee from three, and stay away from three—if you do, God will fashion for you a good character in this world and in the hereafter.

Be wary of pride, anger, and greed. Pride is one of the traits of evil people, and is a garment worthy of the Almighty alone; even a tiny grain of pride placed in someone's heart by God will lead him into hellfire. Anger makes the mature imprudent and the learned unsteady, suppresses reason and exposes ignorance. And greed is one of Satan's traps, one of his terrible snares; he uses it to ensnare the learned, the intelligent, the knowledgeable, and the discerning.

You have spoken truly, father. Now explain to me your words, "Fear three."

Very well, my son. Fear God, fear anyone who doesn't fear God, and fear your tongue, for it is an enemy to your faith. If you fear these three, God will protect you from everything you fear.

You have spoken truly, father. Now explain to me your words, "Hope for three."

My son, hope for God's forgiveness for your sins, hope for a beautiful reward from him for your deeds, and hope for your prophet's intercession.

You have spoken truly, father. Now explain to me your words, "Abide by three."

Abide by the book of God, abide by the practice of your prophet, and abide by whatever accords with truth and the book of God.

You have spoken truly, father. Now explain to me your words, "Be ashamed of three."

Very well, my son. Be ashamed to have God see you all the time doing things he dislikes; be ashamed to have the noble and protecting scribal angels see you thus; and be ashamed to have the pious believers see you.

You have spoken truly, father. Now explain to me your words, "Take refuge in three."

Very well. Take refuge in God if calamities befall you; take refuge in repentance from your bad deeds; and take refuge in people of knowledge and refinement from the slips you make due to ignorance.

You have spoken truly, father. Now explain to me your words, "Be niggardly with three."

قال: نعم. شحّ على عمرك أن تُفنيه ممّا هو عليك لا لك وشحّ على دينك ولا تبذله للغضب وشحّ على كلامك إلّا ما كان لك ولا عليك.

قلت: صدقت يا أبه فأخبرني عن قولك تخلّص إلى ثلاث.

قال: نعم يا بنيّ. تخلّص إلى معرفتك نفسك وإظهار عيوبها ومَقتك إيّاها وتخلّص إلى تقوى الله ثمّ تخلّص إلى إخمال نفسك وإخفاء ذكرك.

قلت: صدقت يا أبه فأخبرني عن قولك وٱهرب من ثلاث.

قال: نعم يا بنيّ. اهرب من الكذب وٱهرب من الظالم وإن كان ولدك أو والدك وٱهرب من مَواطن الإمتحان التي يُحتاج فيها إلى صبرك.

قلت: صدقت يا أبه فأخبرني عن قولك جانب ثلاثا.

قال: نعم يا بنيّ. جانب هواك وأهل الأهواء وجانب الشرّ وأهل الشرّ وجانب الحمقى وإن كانوا متقرّبين أو مَشيَخة مختصّين.

والسلام.

٤٠٣ أخبرني محمّد بن منصور بن عبد الله عن أبي عبد الله التستريّ إجازة قال: أخبرنا أبو الفضل محمّد بن عمر بن محمّد الكوكبيّ الأديب قال: حدّثنا سليمان بن أحمد بن أيّوب قال: حدّثنا محمّد بن عثمان بن أبي شيبة قال: حدّثنا ضرار بن صُرَد قال: حدّثنا عاصم بن حُميد قال: حدّثنا ثابت بن أبي صفِيّة عن أبيّ حمزة الثُّمالي عن عبد الرحمٰن بن جُندُب عن كميل بن زياد قال:

أخذ أمير المؤمنين عليّ بن أبي طالب صلوات الله تعالى عليه بيدي فأخرجني إلى ناحية الجبّان فلمّا أَصحرَ تنفّس الصعداء ثمّ قال:

يا كميل إنّ هذه القلوب أوعية فخيرها أوعاها للعلم. احفظ عنّي ما أقول لك.

الناس ثلاثة: عالم ربّانيّ ومتعلّم على سبيل نجاة وهَمَج رَعاع أتباع كلّ ناعق غاوٍ يميلون مع كلّ ريح لم يستضيئوا بنور العلم ولم يَلجؤوا إلى ركن وثيق.

Very well. Be niggardly with your life, lest you waste it doing what works against you rather than for you; be niggardly with your religion, lest you give it up to anger; and be niggardly with your words, except for those which work for you and not against you.

You have spoken truly, father. Now explain to me your words, "Focus on three."

Very well, my son. Focus on knowing your appetitive soul, exposing its faults, and hating it; focus on piety; and focus on humbling yourself and concealing your eminence.

You have spoken truly, father. Now explain to me your words, "Flee from three."

Very well, my son. Flee from untruth, flee from an oppressor even if he is your son or father, and flee from places of trial where your forbearance might be tested.

You have spoken truly, father. Now explain to me your words, "Stay away from three."

Very well, my son. Stay away from following your desires, and from people who follow their desires; stay away from evil and its people; and stay away from fools, even if they court your friendship or are old and favored.

Go in peace.

4.3

Muḥammad ibn Manṣūr ibn ʿAbd Allāh reported to me, from Abū ʿAbd Allāh al-Tustarī, with a certificate to transmit, saying: Abū l-Faḍl Muḥammad ibn ʿUmar ibn Muḥammad al-Kawkabī the litterateur reported to us, saying: Sulaymān ibn Aḥmad ibn Ayyūb reported to us, saying: Muḥammad ibn ʿUthmān ibn Abī Shaybah reported to us, saying: Ḍirār ibn Ṣurad reported to us, saying: ʿĀṣim ibn Ḥumayd reported to us, saying: Thābit ibn Abī Ṣafiyyah reported to us, from Abū Ḥamzah al-Thumālī, from ʿAbd al-Raḥmān ibn Jundub, from Kumayl ibn Ziyād, who said:

The commander of the faithful, ʿAlī ibn Abī Ṭālib, took my hand and led me toward the wilderness. When he reached the desert, he sighed deeply, and said: Truly, Kumayl, hearts are like vessels, and the best are those that best store knowledge. Take heed of what I am going to tell you:[28]

There are three types of people: a person with divine learning; an apprentice who walks the path of salvation; and ignorant rabble—followers of every deceiving bleater, who sway with every wind, seeking neither illumination from the light of knowledge, nor support from a sturdy column.

يا كميل العلم خير من المال. العلم يحرسك وأنت تحرس المال والمال تنقصه النفقة والعلم يَزكو على الإنفاق.

يا كميل معرفة العلم دين يُدان به. به يكسب الإنسان الطاعة[1] لربّه عزّ وجلّ في حياته وجميل الأُحدوثة بعد وفاته ومنفعة المال تزول بزواله والعلم حاكم والمال محكوم عليه.

يا كميل مات خزّان المال وهم أحياء والعلماء باقون ما بقي الدهر أعيانهم مفقودة وأمثالهم في القلوب موجودة.

ها إنّ هاهنا لَعلما جمّا—وأشار عليه السلام إلى صدره—لو أصبت له حملة.

اللّهمّ بلى. أصبت لَقِنا غير مأمون يستعمل آلة الدين في الدنيا ويستظهر بحجج الله على أوليائه وبنعمه على كتابه. أو مُنقادا لحملة الحقّ لا بصيرة له في إحيائه ينقدح الشكّ في قلبه بأوّل عارض من شبهة. اللّهمّ لا ذا ولا ذاك. أو منهوما باللذّات سَلِس القياد للشهوات أو مُغرَما بجمع الأموال والإدّخار. ليسا من رعاة الدين أقرب شَبَها بهما الأنعام السائمة. كذلك يموت العلم بموت حملته.

اللّهمّ بَلى. لن تخلو الأرض مِن قائم لله بحجّة إمّا ظاهرٍ مشهور وإمّا خائف مغمور كيلا تَبطل حجج الله وبيّناته. وكم وأين. اولئك الأقلّون عددا الأعظمون عند الله قدرا. بهم يحفظ الله حججه حتّى يودعوها نظراءهم ويزرعوها في قلوب أشباههم. هَجَم بهم العلم على حقيقة الإيمان فباشروا رَوح اليقين وٱستسهلوا ما ٱستوعر منه المترَفون وأنسوا بما ٱستوحش منه الجاهلون وصحبوا الدنيا بأبدان أرواحها معلّقة بالمحلّ الأعلى. أولئك خلفاء الله في أرضه الدعاة إلى دينه. هاه شوقا إلى رؤيتهم.

وأستغفر الله لي ولك يا كميل. إذا شئت فقم.

---

١ م، ي: (محبّة العالم دين يدان به يكسبه العلم الطاعة ...).

Knowledge is better than wealth: Knowledge protects you, whereas you have to protect wealth. Wealth decreases with spending, whereas knowledge increases with it.

Knowledge is a faith to be followed. It helps you practice obedience to your lord in your lifetime, and leaves a beautiful legacy of remembrance after your death; whereas the benefits of wealth cease with its ceasing. And knowledge rules, while wealth is ruled over.

Those who hoard wealth are dead even as they live, whereas the learned remain as long as the world remains—their persons may be lost, but their teachings live on in people's hearts.

Truly, abundant knowledge is housed here (signaling to his breast), if only I could find a bearer for it!

But no, by God! I encounter sharp students who are not trustworthy, who use the instrument of religion for worldly benefit, who attempt to use God's own proofs to gain victory over his select, and his own favors to gainsay his book. I encounter others who have been guided to the bearers of truth, but have no real perception with which to revivify it; doubt is kindled in their hearts by the first appearance of misgivings. By God, neither is to be countenanced! There is a third type, enamored of carnal pleasures, easily led to the fulfilling of desires. Or yet another, captivated by the hoarding and collecting of wealth. Neither is mindful of religion. They are the closest thing to cattle. This is how knowledge dies, by the death of its bearers.

No, by God! There will always be men on this earth who uphold God's proof—whether visible and well-known or fearful and hidden—for God's proof can never be invalidated. How many, and where? They are few in number, but great in God's regard. Through them God protects his proof, until they entrust it to others like them, sowing it in the hearts of their peers. Knowledge has brought them to real belief, enabling them to touch the spirit of certainty, and to deem easy what the profligate find difficult, to find comfort in what the ignorant find miserable. They live in this world in bodies whose spirits are linked to the highest abode. They are God's vicegerents on his earth, calling to his religion. Ah! Would that I could see them!

I seek God's forgiveness for me and for you, Kumayl. You may take your leave now.

٤٠٤ وصيّته عليه السلام لمّا ضربه ٱبن ملجم لعنه الله تعالى.

لمّا ضُرب أمير المؤمنين عليه السلام ٱجتمع إليه أهل بيته وجماعة من خاصّة أصحابه فقال:

الحمد لله الذي وقّت الآجال وقدّر أرزاق العباد وجعل لكلّ شيء قدرا ولم يُفرّط في الكتاب من شيء فقال ﴿أَيْنَمَا تَكُونُوا يُدْرِككُّمُ ٱلْمَوْتُ وَلَوْ كُنتُمْ فِي بُرُوجٍ مُّشَيَّدَةٍ﴾ وقال عزّ وجلّ ﴿قُل لَّوْ كُنتُمْ فِي بُيُوتِكُمْ لَبَرَزَ ٱلَّذِينَ كُتِبَ عَلَيْهِمُ ٱلْقَتْلُ إِلَىٰ مَضَاجِعِهِمْ﴾ وقال عزّ وجلّ لنبيّه صلّى الله عليه وآله وسلّم ﴿وَأْمُرْ بِٱلْمَعْرُوفِ وَٱنْهَ عَنِ ٱلْمُنكَرِ وَٱصْبِرْ عَلَىٰ مَآ أَصَابَكَ إِنَّ ذَٰلِكَ مِنْ عَزْمِ ٱلْأُمُورِ﴾.

لقد خبّرني حبيب الله وخِيَرته من خلقه وهو الصادق المصدوق عن يومي هذا وعهد إليّ فيه فقال:

يا عليّ كيف بك إذا بقيت في حُثالة من الناس تدعو فلا تُجاب وتَنصَح[1] عن الدين فلا تُعان وقد مال أصحابك وشَنِف لك نصحاؤك فكان الذي معك أشدّ عليك من عدوّك إذا ٱستنهضتهم صدّوا معرضين وإذا ٱستحثثتهم[2] أدبروا نافرين. يتمنّون فقدك لما يرون من قيامك بأمر الله عزّ وجلّ وظَلْفك[3] إيّاهم عن الدنيا فمنهم من قد حَسَمت طمعه فهو كاظم على غيظه ومنهم من قتلت أسرته فهو ثائر متربّص بك ريب المنون وصروف النوائب وكلّهم نَغِل الصدر ملتهب الغيظ. فلا تزال فيهم كذلك حتّى يقتلوك مكرا ويُرهِقوك شرّا. وسيُسمّونك بأسماء قد سمّوني بها فقالوا كاهن وقالوا ساحر وقالوا كذّاب مُفترٍ فٱصبر فإنّ لك فيّ أُسوة وبذلك أمر الله إذ يقول ﴿لَّقَدْ كَانَ لَكُمْ فِي رَسُولِ ٱللَّهِ أُسْوَةٌ حَسَنَةٌ﴾.

يا عليّ إنّ الله عزّ وجلّ أمرني أن أُدنيك ولا أُقصيك وأن أعلّمك ولا أُهملك وأن أُقرّبك ولا أجفوك.

---

١ م، ي: (تنصح).

٢ م: كذا في المتن، مصحّحة (استحثثتهم). ي: (استحثثتهم).

٣ م: (صرفك).

ʿAlī's testament, delivered after the cursed Ibn Muljam struck him the death blow: 4.4

When the commander of the faithful was struck the death blow, his family and close companions gathered around him, and he said to them:

Praise God, who fixed the span of lives, destined the sustenance his servants receive, ordained a destiny for all things, and omitted nothing from the book. He said: «Wherever you may be, death will find you, even if you take shelter in fortified towers.»[29] He also said: «Say: Even if you had been sheltering in your homes, those who were destined to be slain would have gone forth to the places where they were to lie down in death.»[30] And he said to his prophet: «Command good, forbid evil, and bear patiently the troubles that assail you. Truly, this is part of resoluteness in tackling affairs.»[31]

The beloved of God,[32] God's chosen from among his creatures, the epitome of truthfulness whose veracity we all accept, informed me about this day. He entrusted me with a testament regarding it, saying:

ʿAlī, I wonder how it will be with you when you remain alone among the dregs of humanity. You will call out and none will answer. You will defend the faith and none will come to your aid. Your companions will incline toward another, your advisors will become your adversaries, those with you causing you more harm than your enemy. If you urge them to fight, they will block your attempts and avert their faces. If you exhort them to battle, they will turn their backs and hasten away. Secretly they will wish you gone, all because you undertake God's command and deter them from worldliness. Among them will be one whose ambition you have forestalled, who suppresses his rage and bides his time. And another whose family you have slain in battle, who awaits his vengeance and hopes that fate's vicissitudes and calamities' onslaughts will dispatch you on his behalf. Each will hold malice in his breast, inflamed by wrath. You will remain with them in this state, until, in the end, they will crush you with evil and slay you through deceit. They will call you the names they used on me: soothsayer, magician, fraud, liar. Bear all this patiently, for you have a model to follow in the person of God's messenger. This is what God commanded when he said: «In the person of God's messenger you have a worthy model to follow.»[33]

God has commanded me to bring you close, ʿAlī, and not keep you distant, to teach you and not disregard you, to keep you near and not be harsh with you.

فهذه وصيّته إليّ وعهده إليّ.

ثمّ إنّي أوصيكم أيّها النَفَر الذين قاموا بأمر الله وذبّوا عن الدين وجدّوا في طلب حقوق الأرامل والمساكين أوصيكم بعدي بالتقوى وأحذّركم الدنيا والإغترار بزِبرِجها و زخرفها فإنّها متاع الغرور وجانبوا سبيل مَن ركن إليها وطمست الغفلة على قلوبهم حتّى أتاهم من الله ما لم يكونوا يحتسبون وأُخذوا بغتة وهم لا يشعرون.

وقد كان قبلكم قوم خلفوا أنبيائهم بآتّباع آثارهم فإن تمسّكتم بهديهم وآقتديتم بسنّتهم لم تضلّوا. إنّ نبيّ الله صلّى الله عليه وعلى آله وسلّم خلّف فيكم كتاب الله وأهل بيته فعندهم[1] علم ما تأتون وما تتّقون وهم الطريق الواضح والنور اللائح وأركان الأرض القوّامون بالقسط بنورهم يُستضاء وبهديهم يقتدى. من شجرة كَرُم مَنبِتها فثبت أصلها وبسق فرعها وطاب جناها نبتت في مستقرّ الحرم وسُقيت ماء الكرم وصفت من الأقذاء والأدناس وتُخُيّرت من أطيب مواليد الناس. فلا تزولوا عنهم فتفرّقوا ولا تحرفوا عنهم فتمزّقوا وآلزموهم تهتدوا وترشدوا وآخلفوا رسول الله صلّى الله عليه وعلى آله وسلّم فيهم بأحسن الخلافة فقد أخبركم أنّهما لن يفترقا حتّى يَرِدا عليّ الحَوض أعني كتاب الله وذريّته.

أستودعكم الله الذي لا تضيع ودائعه.

بلّغكم الله ما تأملون ووقاكم ما تحذرون.

اقرؤا على أهل مودّتي السلام والخَلَف وخلف الخلف.

حفظكم الله وحفظ فيكم نبيّكم.

والسلام.

---

١ ي: (فعلّمهم).

This was the prophet's counsel to me and the testament he entrusted to me.

Now I offer my counsel to you, O you who have undertaken God's command, fought to defend the faith, and worked assiduously to secure the rights of the widowed and the needy. I counsel you to maintain your piety after I am gone. I warn you against the world and her adornments and splendors, for they are the cargo of deception. Shun the path of those who relied on the world, whose hearts were so blinded by heedlessness that they lost all mindfulness of the hereafter; God sent them something they had not reckoned with, and seized them suddenly in their blithe oblivion.[34]

There have been people before you who remained true to their prophets and followed in their footsteps. If you embrace their guidance and pursue their practice you will not go astray. Indeed, God's prophet has given you God's book and his own family to lead you after him. They have knowledge concerning what you should or should not do. They are the clear path, the shining light, the supports of the earth, and its just rulers. It is their light from which illumination is sought, and it is their guidance that is to be followed. They come from a tree whose origin is noble, whose roots are firm, whose branches are lofty, and whose fruit is sweet—grown in the solid earth of the holy sanctuary, irrigated by the water of nobility, cleansed of pollution and filth, and selected from the purest of families. Do not turn aside from them or you will be flung asunder. Do not move away from them or you will be torn to pieces. Cleave to them and you will gain guidance and direction. Adhere to the wishes of God's messenger regarding them. For he informed you that "the two will not separate until they come to me at the celestial pool"—I mean God's book and the prophet's progeny.

I entrust you to God, who never abuses trust.

May God give you what you hope for, and protect you from what you fear.

Convey my greetings of peace to those who bear love for me, to their children, and to their children's children.

May God safeguard you, and may he safeguard your prophet in you.

Go in peace.

وصيّته عليه السلام للحسن عليه السلام لمّا ضربه ٱبن ملجم لعنه الله أيضا. ٤.٥

ولمّا ضربه ٱبن ملجم لعنه الله تعالى دخل عليه الحسن عليه السلام وهو باك فقال: ما يُبكيك يا بنيّ. فقال له: مالي لا أبكي وأنت في أوّل يوم من أيّام الآخرة وآخر يوم من أيّام الدنيا.

فقال له: يا بنيّ ٱحفظ عنّي أربعا وأربعا لا يضرّك ما عملت بهنّ شيء.

قلت: وما هنّ يا أَبَتِ؟[1]

قال: إنّ أغنى الغنى العقل وأكبر الفقر الحمق وأوحش الوحشة العُجب وأكرم الحسب حسن الخُلق.

قلت: يا أبت هذه أربع فأعطني الأربع الأُخَر.

قال: يا بنيّ وإيّاك ومصادقة الأحمق فإنّه يريد أن ينفعك فيضرّك. وإيّاك ومصادقة الكذّاب فإنّه يقرّب عليك البعيد ويبعّد عليك القريب. وإيّاك ومصادقة البخيل فإنّه يقعد بك عند أَحوَج ما تكون إليه. وإيّاك ومصادقة الفاجر فإنّه يَبيعك بالتافِه.[2]

أخبرني أبو عبد الله محمّد بن منصور التستريّ فيما أجازه لي قال: أخبرنا الحسن بن محمّد بن سعيد بن حمدان قال: حدّثنا أحمد بن محمّد بن الفضل النحويّ قال: حدّثنا[3] محمّد بن إبراهيم بن قريش الحكيميّ قال: حدّثنا عبد العزيز بن أَبان قال: حدّثنا سهل بن شعيب النَّهميّ عن عبد الأعلى عن نوف[4] البِكاليّ قال: ٤.٦

رأيت عليّ بن أبي طالب عليه السلام ليلة النصف من شعبان قد أكثر الخروج والنظر إلى السماء فقال: أنائم أنت يا نوف؟ قال: قلت: بل رامقٌ أرمُقُ أمير المؤمنين بعيني. ٤.٦.١

فقال: يا نوف طوبى للزاهدين في الدنيا والراغبين في الآخرة. فإنّ أولئك قوم ٱتّخذوا أرض الله بِساطا وترابها فراشا وماءها طيبا والقرآن شعارا والدعاء دثارا

---

١ م، ي: هنا وفي باقي الخبر (أبه).

٢ م، ي: (في نفاقه).

٣ هـ: تضيف (أبو عبد الله).

٤ هـ: تضيف (بن فضالة).

4.5 ʿAlī's counsel to al-Ḥasan, after the cursed Ibn Muljam struck him the death blow:

When Ibn Muljam had struck ʿAlī the death blow, al-Ḥasan came to him weeping, and ʿAlī asked him: What makes you weep, my son?

How can I not weep, al-Ḥasan replied, when you are in the first day of the hereafter, and the last day of this world?

My son, ʿAlī said to him, remember four things, and four more things. As long as you act upon them, nothing will harm you.

What are they, father? al-Ḥasan asked.

ʿAlī replied: The best wealth is intelligence, the greatest poverty is foolishness, the loneliest alienation comes from conceit, and the noblest ancestry is good moral behavior.

Father, said al-Ḥasan, that makes four; what are the other four?

Dear son, ʿAlī replied, beware of befriending a fool, for he wants to benefit you but harms you instead. Beware of befriending a liar, for he brings near to you the distant and makes distant from you the near. Beware of befriending a miser, for he holds back from helping you when you most need him. And beware of befriending a depraved person, for he will sell you for a trifle.

4.6 Abū ʿAbd Allāh Muḥammad ibn Manṣūr al-Tustarī reported, in one of the reports that he authorized me to transmit, saying: al-Ḥasan ibn Muḥammad ibn Saʿīd ibn Ḥamdān informed me, saying: Aḥmad ibn Muḥammad ibn al-Faḍl the grammarian narrated to us, saying: Muḥammad ibn Ibrāhīm ibn Quraysh al-Ḥukaymī narrated to us, saying: ʿAbd al-ʿAzīz ibn Abān narrated to us, saying: Sahl ibn Shuʿayb al-Nahmī narrated to us, from ʿAbd al-Aʿlā, from Nawf al-Bikālī,[35] who said:

4.6.1 I saw ʿAlī ibn Abī Ṭālib on the eve of the fifteenth of Shaʿbān.[36] He gazed long at the stars, then said to me: Nawf, are you asleep? No, commander of the faithful, I replied, I see you. He then declared:

Blessed are those who reject worldliness and focus their desire on the hereafter. They take God's earth for a carpet, its dust for a bed, its water for perfume, the Qur'an as their garment, and prayer as their robe. They cut their bonds with the world in the manner of the Messiah, son of Mary. God revealed to his servant, the Messiah: "Command the children of Israel that

ثمّ قرضوا الدنيا قرضا على منهاج المسيح ٱبن مريم عليهما السلام. فإنّ الله عزّوجلّ أوحى إلى عبده المسيح أن مُرْ بني إسرائيل أن لا يدخلوا بيتا من بيوتي إلّا بقلوب طاهرة وأبصار خاشعة وأيدٍ نقيّة فإنّي لا أستجيب لأحد منهم دعوة لأحد من خلقي قِبَله مَظلِمة.

يا نوف لا تكوننّ شاعرا ولا عشّارا ولا شُرطيّا ولا عَريفا ولا صاحب كُوبة ولا صاحب عَرطبة فإنّ نبيّ الله داود عليه السلام خرج في مثل هذه الليلة فقال: ما من عبد يدعو الله عزّوجلّ إلّا ٱستجاب دعوته في هذه الساعة إلّا أن يكون شاعرا أو عشّارا أو شرطيّا أو عريفا أو صاحب كوبة أو صاحب عرطبة.

٤.٦.٢ أوصيكم عباد الله بتقوى الله والتنافس في الحظّ النفيس والإشفاق من اليوم العبوس والجدّ في خلاص النفوس والسعي في فكاكها قبل هلاكها والأخذ لها قبل الأخذ منها.

اغتنموا أيّام الصحّة قبل السقم والشبيبة قبل الهرم وبادروا بالتوبة قبل الندم ولا تحملنّكم المهلة على طول الغفلة فإنّ الأجل يهدم الأمل والأيّام موكّلة بتنغيص[1] المدّة وتفريق الأحبّة. فبادروا رحمكم الله بالتوبة قبل حضور النوبة وبَرِّزوا[2] للغيبة التي لا تُنتظر معها الأوبة وٱستعينوا على بعد المسافة بطول المخافة. فكم من غافل وثق بغفلته وتعلّل بمهلته فأمّل بعيدا وبنى مشيدا فنُغص بقرب أجله بُعد أمله وفاجأته منيّته بٱنقطاع أمنيّته فصار بعد العزّ والمنعة والشرف والرفعة مرتهنا بموبقات عمله قد غاب فما رجع وندم فما ٱنتفع وشقي بما جمع في يومه وسعد به غيره في غده وبقي مرتهنا بكسب يده ذاهلا عن أهله وولده لا يغني عنه ما ترك فتيلا ولا يجد إلى مناص سبيلا.

٤.٦.٣ فعلامَ عباد الله المُنعرَج والدَّلَج وإلى أين المفرّ والمهرَب وهذا الموت في الطلب يخترم الأوّل فالأوّل لا يتحنّن على ضعيف ولا يعرّج على شريف والجديدان يحثّان الأجل تحثيثا ويسوقانه سَوقا حثيثا. وكلّ ما هو آتٍ قريب ومن وراء ذلك العجب

١ م: (بتنقيص).
٢ م: (تزوّدوا).

they should not enter any of my houses except with pure hearts, eyes cast down, and unsullied hands. I do not answer the prayer of any who has rendered an injustice to one of my creatures."

Nawf, do not be a poet, tax collector, policeman, appraiser, drummer, or lute player. God's prophet, David, stepped outside on just such a night, and said: The prayer of any who prays to God in this hour will be answered, unless he is a poet, tax collector, policeman, appraiser, drummer, or lute player.

4.6.2 Servants of God! I counsel you to piety, to compete for that precious portion of God's reward, to fear the ominous day of judgment, and to work hard for the salvation of your souls—laboring to free them before they perish, and gathering good deeds unto them before they are taken away.

Take advantage of your days of health before illness besets you, and of youth before the arrival of old age. Hasten to repent before the onset of regret. Do not let the respite you have been granted lull you into prolonged heedlessness. The end of a man's life span destroys hope. The passing days are charged with disrupting your time span, and separating you from loved ones. Hasten to repent—may God have mercy on you!—before your turn arrives. Outpace your fellows in preparing for that disappearance from which there is no return. Rely on your substantial fear of God in covering the protracted distance. Many a heedless person, complacent in heedlessness and dallying in his time of respite, has cast hopes far afield and built towering fortresses. His prolonged hopes are interrupted by the approaching end of his life. His death takes him by surprise and cuts short his aspirations. After might and strength, honor and elevation, he becomes mortgaged to his pernicious deeds. He disappears and does not return, regrets too late and loses all he had gathered in his day. Another will enjoy it on the morrow, while he remains mortgaged to the earnings of his own labors, distracted from wife and children, not a single twisted thread of what he left behind helping him, finding no way to escape.

4.6.3 Servants of God! To what end all this restless movement through winding dunes and dark night? Where will you flee or escape, when death is here in pursuit, snatching up one soul after another, neither pitying the weak, nor showing mercy to the noble? The ever-renewing night and day urge your life on, and drive it forward in haste. All that is going to come is at hand. After

العجيب. فأعدّوا الجواب ليوم الحساب وأكثروا الزاد ليوم المعاد.

عصمنا الله وإيّاكم بطاعته وأعاننا وإيّاكم على ما يقرّب إليه ويُزلِف لديه فإنّما نحن به وله.

أوصيكم عباد الله بتقوى الله فإنّ تقوى الله منجاة من كلّ هلكة وعصمة من كلّ ضلالة وبتقوى الله فاز الفائزون وظفر الراغبون ونجا الهاربون وأدرك الطالبون وبتركها خسر المبطلون و ﴿إِنَّ ٱللَّهَ مَعَ ٱلَّذِينَ ٱتَّقَوا۟ وَّٱلَّذِينَ هُم مُّحْسِنُونَ﴾. ٱللَّهَ ٱللَّهَ عباد الله قبل جفوف الأقلام وتصرّم الأيّام ولزوم الآثام وقبل الدعوة بالحسرة والويل والشقوة ونزول عذاب الله بغتة أو جهرة.

أوصيكم عباد الله بتقوى الله الذي ضرب لكم الأمثال ووقّت لكم الآجال وفتق لكم أسماعا لتعي ما عناها وأبصارا لتجلو عن عشاها[1] وأفئدة لتفهم ما دهاها. لم يخلقكم عبثا ولم يهملكم[2] سُدى ولم يضرب عنكم الذكر صفحا. بل أكرمكم بالنعم السوابغ وقطع عذركم بالحجج البوالغ ورفدكم بأحسن الروافد وأعمّ الزوائد وأحاط بكم الإحصاء وأرصد لكم الجزاء في السرّاء والضرّاء.

فٱتّقوا الله عباد الله وجِدّوا في الطلب وبادروا بالعمل قبل حلول الأجل. اقطعوا التُّهمات وٱحذروا هادم اللذّات. تجهّزوا رحمكم الله فقد نودي فيكم بالرحيل وأقِلّوا العُرجة على الدنيا وٱنقلبوا بصالح ما بحضرتكم من الزاد. فإنّ أمامكم عَقَبة كَؤودا ومنازل مَخوفة مجهولة لا بدّ من الممرّ عليها والوقوف عندها فإمّا رحمة من الله جلّ وعزّ فنجوتم من فظاعتها وشدّة مُختبَرها وكراهة منظرها وإمّا مهلكة ليس بعدها ٱنجبار.[3]

---

١ ه: (غشاها).

٢ م: كذا في المتن، مصحّحة (يمهلكم).

٣ ي: (انحياز).

that you will see the wonder of wonders. Prepare your answer for the day of accounting. Make ready your provisions for the day of return.

May God protect us by our obedience to him. May he help us to do what will bring us close to him, and draw us nigh unto him. We come from him, and belong to him.

Servants of God, I counsel you to piety. Piety is salvation from every adversity and protection from every error. It is through piety that winners have won, aspirers have attained victory, fleers have been saved, and seekers have attained. It is by abandoning piety that the negligent have lost. «Truly, God is with those who practice piety, and those who perform good deeds.»[37] Fear God, yes, fear God, servants of God, before pens run dry, before days dwindle, before the time comes when you answer for your sins, before the time when you cry out from regret, and before the time of perdition and wretchedness, before the sudden and plain arrival of God's punishment!

I counsel you, servants of God, to piety, in consciousness of the one who has devised parables and appointed life spans for you, who has sharpened your ears to heed what is relevant, your eyes to see brightly, and your hearts to comprehend what astounds them. He has not created you in vain, nor given you an indefinite reprieve, nor kept the remembrance from you. Rather, he has generously bestowed upon you perfect favors, pared your excuses with cutting proofs, and gifted you the most beautiful gifts, and a vast supply of provisions. He has encompassed you in his reckoning, and prepared a recompense for the actions you take in times of happiness and sorrow.

O servants of God, be conscious of him. Be earnest in your seeking. Make haste to perform good deeds before your life span ends. Stop doing things which invite suspicion. Fear the destroyer of pleasures. Gather up your provisions—may God have mercy on you!—for the call has come to depart. Minimize your inclination toward the world, so that you leave it with goodly provisions from your present. Truly, there is a tough climb before you, and fearsome and unknown waystations you must pass and where you must alight. You will attain either God's mercy—in which case you will have been saved from their hideousness and challenges—or a calamity from which there is no recovery.

٤٠٧ وصيّته عليه السلام لآبن عبّاس.

قال آبن عبّاس رضي الله تعالى عنهما: ما آنتفعتُ بشيء بعد النبيّ صلّى الله عليه وعلى آله وسلّم آنتفاعي بكلمات كتبهنّ إليّ أمير المؤمنين عليّ بن أبي طالب عليه السلام. قال: كتب إليّ:

بسم الله الرحمٰن الرحيم

أمّا بعد: فإنّ المرء يفرح بإدراك ما لم يكن لِيَفوته ويغتمّ لفوت ما لم يكن ليدركه. فإذا آتاك الله من الدنيا شيئا فلا تُكثرنّ به فرحا وإذا منعك منها فلا تكثرنّ عليه حزنا. وليكن همّك لما بعد الموت.

والسلام.

4.7

'Alī's counsel to Ibn 'Abbās:

Ibn 'Abbās said: After the passing of the prophet, I benefited from nothing as much as I did from the following words the commander of the faithful, 'Alī ibn Abī Ṭālib, wrote to me:

In the name of God, the compassionate, the merciful.

A man is gladdened by obtaining a thing he was not going to lose and saddened by the loss of a thing he was not going to obtain. If something of this world comes to you from God do not exult excessively. If he keeps something from you, do not grieve too much. Save your worries for what comes after death.

Go in peace.

الباب الخامس

في المرويّ عنه من أجوبته عن المسائل وسؤالاته عليه السلام

أمّا بعد: ٥.١

أيُّها الناس إذا سأل سائل فليعقل وإذا سئل فليتثبّت فوالله لقد نزلت بكم نوازل البلاء وحقائق الأمور لفشل كثير من المسؤولين وإطراق كثير من السائلين.

قال النبيّ صلّى الله عليه وعلى آله وسلّم لعليّ عليه السلام: ٥.٢
ما أوّل نعمة أنعمها الله تعالى عليك؟

قال: أن خلقني ذكرا ولم يخلقني أنثى.

قال: ثمّ ماذا؟

قال: أن هداني للإسلام وعرّفنيه ومَنّ عليّ بك يا رسول الله.

قال: ثمّ ماذا؟

قال: ﴿وَإِن تَعُدُّوا۟ نِعْمَةَ ٱللَّهِ لَا تُحْصُوهَا﴾.

وإنّ عليّاً عليه السلام سأل ابنه الحسن عليه السلام عن أشياء من المروءة ٥.٣
فقال: يا بنيّ ما السداد؟

قال: يا أبت السداد دفع المنكر بالمعروف.

Chapter 5

ʿAlī's Questions with Answers, and ʿAlī's Answers to Questions

O people! If one of you asks a question, let him be scrupulous in asking. If one of you is asked a question, let him be conscientious in answering. By God, calamitous events and momentous affairs have descended upon you because of the failure of many who are asked, and the submissive acceptance of many who do the asking. 5.1

The prophet asked ʿAlī: 5.2

What is the first favor God bestowed upon you?

That he made me male not female, ʿAlī replied.

Then what?

That he guided me to Islam, and allowed me to recognize its true value, and that in his kindness he gave me you as a guide, O messenger of God.

Then what?

«If you count God's bounty you will be not be able to tally it.»[38]

ʿAlī asked his son al-Ḥasan the following questions about the perfection of human qualities, and al-Ḥasan responded 5.3

Dear son, what is well-directed action?

Well-directed action is repaying wrong with good, father, he replied.

قال: فما الشرف؟

قال: اصطناع العشيرة وحمل الجريرة.

قال: فما المروءة؟

قال: العفاف والصلاح إصلاح المال.

قال: فما الرقّة؟[1]

قال: النظر في اليسير ومنع الحقير.

قال: فما اللؤم؟

قال: احتقار المرء نفسه وبذله عِرسه من اللؤم.

قال: فما السماحة؟

قال: البذل من العسر واليسر.

قال: فما الشُّحّ؟

قال: أن ترى ما أنفقتَه تَلَفا.

قال: فما الإخاء؟

قال: المُواساة[2] في الشدّة والرخاء.

قال: فما الجُبن؟

قال: الجرأة على الصديق والنكول عن العدوّ.

قال: فما الغنيمة؟

قال: الترغيب في التقوى والزهادة في الدنيا هي الغنيمة الباردة.

قال: فما الحلم؟

قال: كَظم الغيظ ومِلك النفس.

قال: فما الغنى؟

قال: رضى النفس بما قسم الله جلّ وعزّ وإن قلّ وإنّما الغنى غنى النفس.

---

١ هـ: (الرأفة).

٢ م: كذا في المتن، وفي الحاشية نسخة (المساعدة). ي: سقطت (المواساة). هـ: (المساعدة).

And what is honor?

Being generous to your kin and enduring injustice.

What is good character?

Virtue. And probity is rectitude with regard to property.

What is refinement?

Compassion in little things and protecting the vulnerable.

What is blameworthiness?

Contempt for yourself and neglect of your bride's honor are blameworthy.

What is generosity?

Giving generously in times of hardship and ease.

What is stinginess?

Believing what you have spent to be a waste.

What is brotherly behavior?

Helping your brother both in times of adversity and security.

What is cowardice?

Being spirited against your friend and cowardly with your enemy.

What is booty?

Consciousness of God and indifference to the world—that is booty easily won.

What is forbearance?

Suppressing rage and controlling desire.

What is wealth?

Accepting what God has ordained for you, even if it is little. True wealth is the wealth of the soul.

قال: فما الفقر؟

قال: شَرَه النفس في كلّ شيء.

قال: فما المَنَعة؟

قال: سداد النفس ومنازعة عزّ اليأس.

قال: فما الذلّ؟

قال: الفزع عند المصدوقة.

قال: فما العِيّ؟

قال: العَبَث باللحية وكثرة التبزّق.

قال: فما الجرأة؟

قال: موافقة الإخوان.

قال: فما الكلفة؟

قال: كلامك فيما لا يعنيك.

قال: فما المجد؟

قال: أن تعطي في الغرم وتعفو عن الجرم.

قال فما العقل؟

قال: حفظ القلب كلّما ٱسترعيته.

قال: فما الخُرق؟

قال: مُعازّتك إمامك و رفعك عليه كلامك.

قال: فما السناء؟

قال: إيثار الجميل وترك القبيح.

قال: فما الحزم؟

قال: طول الأناة والرفق بالولاة والاحتراس من الناس بسوء الظنّ وهو الحزم.

What is poverty?

The appetitive soul's gluttony.

What is might?

The soul's well-directed action, and its combating the power of despair.

What is shame?

Being frightened by the truth.

What are the signs of faltering?

Playing with your beard and spitting excessively.

Whence comes boldness?

Brotherly harmony.

What is unnecessary and painful?

Speaking about things that do not concern you.

What is nobility?

Paying your dues and forgiving acts of injustice.

What is intelligence?

Your heart keeping safe everything with which you have entrusted it.

What is schism?

Striving to oust your leader and raising your voice at him.

What is loftiness?

Choosing goodness and avoiding meanness.

What is resolution?

Long deliberation, calmness in dealing with governors, and caution when dealing with people, by expecting the worst. This is resolution.

قال: فما الشرف؟

قال: موافقة الإخوان وحفظ الجيران.

قال: فما السَّفَه؟

قال: ٱتبّاع الدُّناة ومصاحبة الغُواة.

قال: فما الغفلة؟

قال: تركك المسجد وطاعتك المفسد.

قال: فما الحرمان؟

قال: تركك حظّك وقد عُرض عليك.

قال: فما السيّد؟

قال: الأحمق في ماله المُتهاوِن عن عِرضه يُشتَم فلا يجيب المحترم بأمر عشيرته هو السيّد.

٥.٤ سئل عليه السلام: من العالم؟

فقال: من ٱجتنب المحارم.

قيل: فمن العاقل؟

قال: من رفض الباطل.

قيل: فمن السيّد؟

قال: من فَعاله جيّد.

قيل: فمن السعيد؟

قال: من خشي الوعيد.

قيل: فمن الكريم؟

قال: من نفع العديم.

What is honor?

Brotherly harmony and protecting neighbors.

What is foolishness?

Following immoral people and keeping company with reprobates.

What is heedlessness?

Forsaking the mosque and submitting to malefactors.

What is deprivation?

Giving up your destined share when it has been presented to you.

Who is a real leader?

Whosoever is feckless about his own property, cares not about his own glory, refrains from cursing back when insulted, and is resolute in his clan's affairs. That is a real leader.

Alī was asked:[39] 5.4

Who is knowledgeable?

The one who stays away from forbidden things, he replied.

Who is intelligent?

The one who rejects falsehood.

Who is a leader?

The one whose actions are good.

Who is happy?

The one who fears the promised reckoning.

Who is generous?

The one who gives to the needy.

قيل: فمن الشريف؟

قال: من أنصف الضعيف.

قيل: فمن الغِرّ؟

قال: من عُرف بالكبر.

قيل: فمن الغُمر؟

قال: من وثق بالعمر.

قيل: فمن الهالك؟

قال: من دُفع إلى مالك.

٥٠٥ قام إليه عليه السلام زيد بن صوحان العبديّ رحمه الله تعالى فقال: يا أمير المؤمنين أيّ سلطان أغلب وأقوى؟

قال: الهوى.

قال: فأيّ ذلّ أذلّ؟

قال: الحرص على الدنيا.

قال: فأيّ فقد أشدّ؟

قال: الكفر بعد الإيمان.

قال: فأيّ دعوة أضلّ؟

قال: الداعي بما لا يكون.

قال: فأيّ عمل أفضل؟

قال: التقوى.

قال: فأيّ عمل أنجح؟

قال: طلب ما عند الله.

Who is noble?

The one who shows justice to the weak.

Who is immature?

The one known for his arrogance.

Who is naive?

The one who trusts in his own longevity.

Who is condemned?

The one who is consigned to the angel Malik's care.[40]

Zayd ibn Ṣūḥān al-ʿAbdī came to ʿAlī, asking: 5.5

O commander of the faithful, what kind of sovereignty is the most overwhelming and powerful?

Base desire, he replied.

Which vileness is vilest, he asked.

Greed for worldly things, he replied.

Which is the most painful loss?

Becoming a disbeliever and losing one's faith.

Which supplication goes astray?

The one for something that can never be.

Which act is the most meritorious?

Consciousness of God.

Which act brings the most success?

The quest for God's reward.

قال: وأيّ صاحب أشرّ؟

قال: المزيّن لك معصية الله.

قال: فأيّ الخلق أقوى؟

قال: الحليم.

قال: فأيّ الخلق أشقى؟

قال: من باع دينه برضى غيره.

قال: فأيّ الخلق أشحّ؟

قال: من أخذ المال من غير حلّه فجعله في غير حقّه.

قال: فأيّ الناس أكيس؟

قال: من أبصر رشده من غيّه فمال إلى رشده.

قال: فمن أحلم الناس؟

قال: الذي لا يغضب.

قال: فأيّ الناس أثبت رأيا؟

قال: من لم يَغُرّه الناس من نفسه ولم تغرّه الدنيا بشُنوفها.

قال: فأيّ الناس أحمق؟

قال: المغترّ بالدنيا وهو يرى ما فيها وتقلّب أحوالها.

قال: فأيّ الناس أشدّ حسرة؟

قال: الذي حُرم الدنيا والآخرة ﴿ذَٰلِكَ هُوَ ٱلۡخُسۡرَانُ ٱلۡمُبِينُ﴾.

قال: فأيّ الخلق أعمى؟

قال: الذي عمل لغير الله ويطلب بعمله الثواب من الله تعالى.

Who is the worst friend?

The one who tempts you into sin.

Who is the strongest of people?

The one who controls his anger.

Who is the nastiest wretch?

The one who sells his faith to please another.

Who is the most miserly?

The one who misappropriates property and uses it for unlawful ends.

Who is the smartest?

An errant man who sees the right path and turns toward it.

Who is the most mature?

The one who never flies into a rage.

Who is the most steadfast?

The one whom people cannot deceive and who does not yield to the temptations of this bejeweled world.

Who is the biggest fool?

The one who is seduced by this world, even though he sees what is in her and observes her fickle state.

Who will have the most grievous regrets?

The one who is deprived of this world and the hereafter. «That is truly the most manifest loss.»[41]

Who is the most blind?

The one who performs acts to please someone other than God, yet expects a reward from God.

قال: فأيّ القنوع أفضل؟

قال: القانع بما أعطاه الله عزّوجلّ.

قال: فأيّ المصائب أشدّ؟

قال: المصيبة في الدِّين.

قال: فأيّ الأعمال أحبّ إلى الله عزّوجلّ؟

قال: ٱنتظار الفَرَج.

قال: فأيّ الناس خير عند الله؟

قال: أَخوَفهُم لله وأصبرهم على التقوى وأزهدهم في الدنيا.

قال: فأيّ الكلام أفضل عند الله؟

قال: كثرة ذكر الله والتضرّع إليه ودعاؤه.

قال: فأيّ القول أصدق؟

قال: شهادة أن لا الله إلّا الله.

قال: فأيّ الإيمان أفضل عند الله؟

قال: التسليم والورع.

قال: فأيّ الناس أكرم؟

قال: من صدق في المَواطِن وكفّ لسانه عن المحارم وأمر بالمعروف ونهى عن المنكر.

٥٠٦ قال عليه الصلاة والسلام: سَلوني قبل أن تَفقدوني فإنّ بين كَتِفيّ علماً جمّاً خبّرني به حبيبي رسول الله صلّى الله عليه وعلى آله وسلّم.

فقام إليه صعصعة بن صوحان فقال له: يا أمير المؤمنين متى يخرج الدجّال؟

فقال له: ٱقعد يا صعصعة فقد علم الله جلّ ثناؤه مقامك ولكن له علامات وهَنات وأشياء يتلو بعضها بعضا حَذْوَ النعل بالنعل تكون في حول واحد فإن شئت نبّأتك بعلاماته.

What is the best form of contentment?

That of one who is satisfied with what God has given him.

Which is the severest calamity?

That which shakes your faith.

Which act does God like best?

Patient waiting for deliverance.

Who is the most virtuous person in God's sight?

The one who fears God, cultivates patience and piety, and rejects worldliness.

Which words are the most meritorious in God's sight?

Words spoken in remembrance of God, in supplication to him, and in prayer.

What is the truest assertion?

The testimony that "There is no god but God."

What kind of belief does God like best?

One that encompasses acceptance and restraint.

Who is the noblest of men?

The one who fights gallantly in battle, holds back his tongue from uttering falsehoods, commands good, and forbids wickedness.

5.6 ʿAlī said: Ask before I am lost to you. Truly, my heart holds abundant knowledge—knowledge that my beloved, the messenger of God, imparted to me.

Ṣaʿṣaʿah ibn Ṣūḥān rose, saying, commander of the faithful, when will al-Dajjāl the antichrist appear?

Sit back down, Ṣaʿṣaʿah, ʿAlī replied, God knows your capacity.[42] There are signs and events and happenings announcing the antichrist's coming, which will occur in close succession in the course of a single year—as surely as one shoe follows the other. If you wish, I can inform you about those signs.

فقال: عن ذلك سألتك يا أمير المؤمنين.

قال له: ٱعقِد بيدك يا صعصعة: إذا أمات الناس الصلاة وأضاعوا الأمانة وٱستحلّوا الكذب وأكلوا الربا وأخذوا الرُّشا وشيّدوا البناء وٱتّبعوا الأهواء وباعوا الدين بالدنيا وٱستخفّوا بالدماء. وكان الحلم ضعفا والظلم فخرا والأمراء فَجَرة ووزراؤهم وأمناؤهم خَوَنة وقرّاؤهم فَسَقة. ويظهر الجور ويكثر الطلاق وموت الفُجاءة وحُلّيت المصاحف وزخرفت المساجد وطوّلت المنابر وخرّبت القلوب ونقضت العهود وٱستعملت المَعازِف وشربت الخمور وفشا الزنا وٱئتُمِن الخائن وخُوّن الأمين وشاركت المرأة زوجها في التجارة حرصا على الدنيا وركب ذوات الفروج السروج. والسلام للمعرفة والشاهد من غير أن يستشهَد ولبسوا جلود الضأن على قلوب الذئاب. قلوبهم يومئذ أمَرّ من الصبِر وأنتن من الجيفة. فالنجاءَ النجاء والوحا الوحا والجِدّ الجدّ. نعم المسكن يومئذ بيت المقدس.

فقام إليه الأصبغ بن نُباتة فقال: يا أمير المؤمنين وما الدجّال؟

فقال له: يا أصبغ ألا إنّ الدجّال صيفيّ بن عائذ. الشقيّ من صدّقه والسعيد من كذّبه. يُقتَل على عَقَبة بالشام يقال لها عقبة فِيق في الساعة الثالثة[1] من النهار على يدي المسيح عيسى ٱبن مريم عليهما السلام. ألا ومن بعد ذلك ﴿ٱلطَّآمَّةُ ٱلۡكُبۡرَىٰ﴾ طلوع الشمس من المغرب تطلع مُكوَّرة. فيومئذ ﴿لَا يَنفَعُ نَفۡسًا إِيمَٰنُهَا لَمۡ تَكُنۡ ءَامَنَتۡ مِن قَبۡلُ أَوۡ كَسَبَتۡ فِيٓ إِيمَٰنِهَا خَيۡرًا﴾. فيومئذ لا توبة تُقبَل ولا عمل يَصعد ولا رزق يَنزل.

ثمّ قال عليه السلام: عهد إليّ حبيبي رسول الله صلّى الله عليه وعلى آله وسلّم ألّا أُخبر بما يكون بعد ذلك.

---

[1] هـ: (الثانية).

Yes, that is what I was asking about, commander of the faithful, replied Ṣaʿṣaʿah.

ʿAlī then expounded: Keep count of the following on your fingers, Ṣaʿṣaʿah: When people stop praying, when they squander trust, when they consider falsehood lawful, practice usury, and take bribes. When they build fortified structures, follow their whims, sell their faith for worldly things, and regard killing as unobjectionable. When they consider restraint weakness, and oppression a source of pride. When rulers become immoral, their viziers and counselors fraudulent, their Qur'an readers debauched. When injustice becomes manifest, and divorce and sudden death common. When copies of the Qur'an are decorated, mosques ornamented, and pulpits raised high, but hearts are in ruin, promises broken, lutes played, wine consumed, and adultery widespread. When the fraudster is trusted and the honest man is viewed with suspicion. When women participate in trade with their husbands, greedy for more, and females sit astride their saddles. When greetings of peace are reserved for associates. When witnesses offer testimony without having been summoned. When people wear hides of sheep to conceal hearts of wolves. On that day, hearts will be more bitter than myrrh, more putrid than a carcass. So run and make haste! Run and make haste! Struggle, struggle! What a good place to reside Jerusalem will be when that day comes!

Then Aṣbagh ibn Nubātah rose, saying: commander of the faithful, what is the nature of the antichrist?

Aṣbagh, ʿAlī replied, the antichrist is Ṣayfī ibn ʿĀʾidh. Whoever trusts him will know misfortune. Whoever refuses him will know bliss. He will be killed at a plateau in the Levant known as the Plateau of Fīq at three in the afternoon at the hands of the Messiah, Jesus, son of Mary. After that the «great devastation»[43] will come! The sun will rise darkly from the west. On that day, «no soul will be helped by believing, if it has not previously attained belief and has not earned a reward in its belief by performing good deeds.»[44] On that day, no repentance shall be accepted, no deed shall rise up to the gates of heaven, and no sustenance shall be sent down.

Then ʿAlī said: My beloved, the messenger of God, made me swear that I would not recount what is to happen after that.

جاء إليه عليه السلام رجل فقال: يا أمير المؤمنين أخبرني عن القدَر . ٥٠٧

قال: بحر عميق فلا تَلِجْه .

فقال: يا أمير المؤمنين أخبرني عن القدر .

قال: سرّ الله عزّ وجلّ قد خفي عليك فلا تُفْشِه .

قال: يا أمير المؤمنين أخبرني عن القدر .

فقال عليه السلام: أيّها السائل إنّ الله عزّ وجلّ خلقك لما شاء أو لما شئت ؟

قال: بل لما شاء .

قال: فيستعملك لما شاء أو لما شئت ؟

قال: بل لما شاء .

قال: أيّها السائل ألست تسأل ربّك العافية ؟

قال: بلى .

قال: فمن أيّ شيء تسأله العافية ؟ أمن البلاء الذي ٱبتلاك به أو البلاءِ الذي ٱبتلى به غيرُه ؟[1]

قال: بل من البلاء الذي ٱبتلاني به هو .

قال: أيّها السائل ألست تقول لا حول ولا قوة إلّا ... بمَن ؟

قال: إلّا بالله العليّ العظيم .

قال: أيّها السائل أتعلم ما تفسيرها ؟

قال: علّمني ممّا علّمك الله يا أمير المؤمنين .

قال: فإنّ تفسيرها أنّ العبد لا يقدر على طاعة الله ولا تكون له قوّة في معصية في الأمرين جميعاً إلّا بالله عزّ وجلّ .

أيّها السائل ألك مع الله عزّ وجلّ مشيئة أو فوق الله مشيئة أو دون الله مشيئة ؟ فإن زعمت أنّ لك دون الله مشيئة فقد ٱكتفيت بها عن مشيئة

---

١ قرأتها (غيره) بخلاف رواية المخطوطات (غيرك) .

A man came to ʿAlī and said: Commander of the faithful, tell me about destiny. 5.7

It is a deep sea, ʿAlī replied, do not dive into it.

Commander of the faithful, tell me about destiny.

It is God's mystery that is concealed from you. Do not ask for it to be revealed.

Commander of the faithful, tell me about destiny.

O prober—has God created you for his purpose or for yours?

For his purpose, not mine.

Does he use you for his purpose or yours?

For his purpose, not mine.

O prober, do you not ask God for protection?

I do indeed.

From what do you ask his protection? A trial he has tested you with, or a trial that someone else has tested you with?

A trial that he has tested me with.

O prober, you say "There is no power and no strength save . . ." save from whom?

Save from God most high and most great.

O prober, do you know what that means?

Teach me from the knowledge that God gave you, commander of the faithful.

It means that no person has the power to obey God or to disobey him except through power that God grants him.

O prober, do you have any purpose that you can enact alongside God's purpose, or over and above God's purpose? Or any purpose that you can enact apart from God? If you believe that you have a purpose that you can enact apart from God, then you have sufficed yourself with

الله. وإن زعمت أنّ لك فوق الله مشيئة فقد زعمت أنّ قوّتك ومشيئتك غالبتان على قوّة الله ومشيئته. وإن زعمت أنّ لك مع الله عزّ وجلّ مشيئة فقد زعمت أنّ لك مع الله شركا في مشيئته. أيّها السائل إنّ الله عزّ وجلّ يُصِحّ ويُداوي منه الداء ومنه الدواء. أعقلت؟

قال: نعم.

فقال عليّ بن أبي طالب عليه السلام: الآن أسلم أخوكم فقوموا فصافحوه.

ثمّ قال عليه السلام: والله لو أنّ عندي رجلا من القَدَريّة لأخذت بصَليف رَقَبته ثمّ لا أزال أَحُزّها حتّى أقطعها. فإنّهم يهود هذه الأمّة ونصاراها ومجوسها.

٥.٨ جاء رجل من اليهود إلى عليّ بن أبي طالب عليه الصلاة والسلام فقال: يا أمير المؤمنين متى كان ربّنا عزّ وجلّ؟

فقال له عليه السلام: يا يهوديّ لم يكن ربّنا عزّ وجلّ فَكان وإنّما يقال متى كان لشيء لم يكن فكان. هو كائن بلا كَينونة كائن لم يزل ليس له قَبْل فهو قبل القبل وقبل الغاية. انقطعت الغايات عنده فهو غاية كلّ غاية.

٥.٩ سأله عليه السلام رجل عن تفسير لا حول ولا قوّة إلّا بالله.

فقال عليه السلام: تفسيرها أنّا لا نملك مع الله شيئا ولا نملك من دونه شيئا ولا نملك إلّا ما ملّكنا ممّا هو أملك به. فمتى ملّكنا ما هو أملك به كلّفنا ومتى أخذ منّا وضع عنّا ما كلّفنا. إنّ الله عزّ اسمه أمرنا تخييرا ونهانا تحذيرا وأعطانا على قليل كثيرا. لن يطاع ربّنا مُكرَها ولن يُعصى مغلوبا.

> that and dispensed with God's purpose. If you believe that you have a purpose that is over and above God's purpose, then you have believed that your strength and your purpose can overpower God's strength and God's purpose. If you believe that you have a purpose that you enact alongside God's purpose, then you have believed that you have partnership with God in the enactment of his purpose. O prober, truly, God makes you ill and cures you; the illness is from him, so too the cure. Do you understand?

Yes, the man replied.

Then ʿAlī ibn Abī Ṭālib said: Now your brother has truly accepted Islam. Stand up and shake his hand.

He added: If a man from the Qadarites fell into my hands, I would grab the side of his neck and hack it until I cut it off. They are the Jews of this community, its Christians, its Magians.

A Jew came to ʿAlī ibn Abī Ṭālib and asked: commander of the faithful, when did our lord come into existence? 5.8

ʿAlī said to him: God was never brought into existence such that he should become existent. "When did he come into existence?" is said of a thing that was not in existence then afterward came into existence. He is existent without coming into existence, existent unceasingly. He has no before, for he is before the before, before the first limit. All limits end with him, for he is the limit of every limit.

A man asked ʿAlī to explain the dictum "There is no power or strength save from God." 5.9

ʿAlī replied: It means that we are not masters of anything in partnership with God; that we are not masters of anything against his will; and that we are not masters of anything without him being its real master—when we are, we are given it as a burden to carry, and when it is taken from us, the burden is lifted. Truly, God has commanded us to do things while giving us a choice, and prohibited us from doing things while giving us a warning. He has given us much in return for little. Our obedience does not burden him, and our disobedience does not threaten him.

٥.١٠ جاء رجل إلى أمير المؤمنين عليه الصلاة والسلام فقال: يا أمير المؤمنين إنّي رجل فقير لا مال لي ولا ولد.

فقال له: أين أنت عن كتاب الله عزّ وجلّ في قوله تبارك وتعالى ﴿ فَقُلْتُ ٱسْتَغْفِرُوا۟ رَبَّكُمْ إِنَّهُۥ كَانَ غَفَّارًا ۞ يُرْسِلِ ٱلسَّمَآءَ عَلَيْكُم مِّدْرَارًا ۞ وَيُمْدِدْكُم بِأَمْوَٰلٍ وَبَنِينَ وَيَجْعَل لَّكُمْ جَنَّـٰتٍ وَيَجْعَل لَّكُمْ أَنْهَـٰرًا ﴾

فقال له: علّمني كيف أستغفر.

فقال: تقول: اللّٰهمّ إنّي أستغفرك من كلّ ذنب قوي عليه بدني بعافيتك أو نالته قدرتي بفضل نعمتك أو بسطت إليه يدي بسابغ رزقك أو اتّكلت فيه عند خوفي منه على أناتك أو عوّلت فيه على كريم عفوك أو وثقت منه[1] بحلمك.

اللّٰهمّ وأستغفرك من كلّ ذنب خُنت فيه أمانتي أو بخست بفعله نفسي أو خطئت به على بدني أو قدّمت فيه لذّتي أو آثرت فيه شهوتي أو قهرت فيه من منعني.

اللّٰهمّ وأستغفرك من كلّ ذنب سبق عليّ في علمك أنّي فاعله فدخلت فيه بإرادتي واجترحته بمحبّتي أو أتيته بشهوتي[2] ثمّ أحلت عليك ربّي[3] فلم أغالبك بفعلي إذ كنت كارها لمعصيتي. لكن سبق علمك فيّ فحلمت عنّي فلم تُدخلني فيه جبرا ولم تحملني عليه قسرا ولم تظلمني فيه شيئا. فاغفر لي يا إلٰهي إنّه لا يغفر الذنوب إلّا أنت.[4]

٥.١١ وسئل عليه الصلاة والسلام:

كم بين السماء والأرض؟

فقال: دعوة مستجابة.

قيل: فكم بين المشرق والمغرب؟

قال: مَسيرة يوم للشمس.

---

١ ي: (رتعت فيه).

٢ هـ: تضيف (وقد نهيتني عنه لمخالفتك).

٣ هـ: تضيف (في التقدير).

٤ هـ: تضيف (يا أرحم الراحمين).

5.10 A man came to the commander of the faithful and said: commander of the faithful, I am a poor man, with no money and no children.

ʿAlī replied: Have you not heard God's words in his book, «Ask your lord for forgiveness, for he is the most forgiving. He will send down the sky in torrents and provide you with wealth and progeny. He will give you gardens. He will give you rivers.»[45]

Teach me how to ask God for forgiveness, said the man.

ʿAlī answered: Say this:

I seek your forgiveness, God, for every sin that my body committed using the fortitude you gave it; for every sinful act my strength acquired using the favors you bestowed upon it; for every sinful thing my hand stretched out to grasp, fortified by your sustenance; for every sin I hesitated at but committed anyway, relying upon your patience, believing in your forgiveness, and trusting that you would not strike me in your wrath.

I seek your forgiveness, God, for every sin by which I betrayed my trust, or short-changed my soul, or transgressed upon my body, or gave precedence to my pleasures, or preference to my desires, and for the times when I answered roughly any who would try to stop me.

I seek your forgiveness, God, for every sin that you knew I would commit, but that I entered into of my own will, perpetrating it blithely, and coming to it through my own desires. I tried to deceive you, lord, but could not vanquish you. You disliked my disobedience, but had prior knowledge about me, and so were patient. You did not force me to sin, nor push me into it. No, you did me no injustice there. Forgive me, God. None can forgive sins but you.

5.11 ʿAlī was asked:

What is the distance between the sky and the earth?

An answered prayer, he replied.

What is the distance between east and west?

The sun's day-long trek.

٥.١٢ البَراء بن عازب قال: دخلت على عليّ عليه السلام فقلت:
يا أمير المؤمنين سألتك بالله ألّا خصصتني بأعظم ما خصّك به رسول الله صلّى الله عليه وآله وسلّم ممّا خصّه به جبريل عليه السلام ممّا أرسله به الرحمٰن عزّ وجلّ.

فقال: لولا ما سألتَ ما نشرتُ ذكر ما أريد أن أستره حتّى أُضمَّنَ لحدي.

إذا أردت أن تدعو بٱسم الله الأعظم فاقرأ من أوّل الحديد ستّ آيات وآخر الحشر ﴿هُوَ ٱللَّهُ ٱلَّذِي لَآ إِلَٰهَ إِلَّا هُوَ﴾ إلى آخرها. فإذا فرغت فتكلّمت فقل: يا من هو كذلك ٱفعل بي كذا وكذا فوالله لو دعوت به على شقيّ لسعد.

قال البراء: فوالله لا أدعو بها لدنيا أبدا.

قال عليّ عليه السلام: أصبت. كذا أوصاني رسول الله صلّى الله عليه وعلى آله وسلّم غير أنّه أمرني أن أدعو بها في الأمور الفادحة.

٥.١٣ وقال أبو عطاء: خرج علينا أمير المؤمنين عليّ بن أبي طالب عليه الصلاة والسلام محزونا يتنفّس فقال: كيف أنتم وزمان قد أظلّكم تُعطّل فيه الحدود ويُتّخذ المال فيه دُوَلا ويُعادى أولياء الله ويوالى فيه أعداء الله.

قلنا: فإن أدركنا ذلك الزمان فكيف نصنع؟

قال: كونوا كأصحاب عيسى عليه السلام: نُشروا بالمَناشير[1] وصُلبوا على الخشب. موت في طاعة الله عزّ وجلّ خير من حياة في معصية الله.

---

[1] م: في الحاشية (بالمآشير).

5.12 This report goes back to al-Barāʾ ibn ʿĀzib. He said: I went to ʿAlī ibn Abī Ṭālib and said to him:

Commander of the faithful, I ask you in the name of God. Bestow upon me the loftiest part of the special knowledge that God's messenger bestowed upon you, from that knowledge which Gabriel bestowed upon him, from that knowledge with which the Merciful sent him.

ʿAlī replied: If you had not asked in God's name, I would not have revealed to you what I had intended to conceal until I am laid in my grave.

If you wish to call upon God by his greatest name, then recite the first six verses from "Iron."[46] Then recite the last verse of "Resurrection," from «He is God, there is no god but him» till the end of the surah.[47] When you are done reciting and are beginning your supplication, say: "O God, you who are such and such, do with me such and such." By God, even were you to pray in this way for a wretch, he would be saved.

Al-Barāʾ said: By God, I will never use this prayer to pray for worldly things.

Good, ʿAlī replied. This is the special knowledge God's messenger bestowed upon me, and he instructed me to save this prayer for momentous affairs.

5.13 Abū ʿAṭāʾ said: The commander of the faithful, ʿAlī ibn Abī Ṭālib, came to us one day, troubled and sighing deeply, and said: How will you cope with a time that has almost come upon you, in which punishments for major crimes will be disregarded, and wealth will be the only thing for which people compete? A time in which God's elite will be hunted down, and God's enemies pledged allegiance to?

If that time comes upon us, we asked him, what should we do?

Be like the followers of Jesus, ʿAlī replied, who were hacked to pieces with saws and crucified on planks of wood for believing. Being killed for refusing to renounce God is better than being spared for capitulating.

قام إليه عليه السلام عبّاد بن قيس فقال: يا أمير المؤمنين أخبرنا ما الإيمان وما الإسلام. ٥.١٤

فقال: نعم يا ٱبن قيس. إنّ الله جلّ ثناؤه ٱبتدأ الأمور بعلمه فيها وٱصطفى لنفسه ما شاء وٱستخلص ما أحبّ. فكان ما أحبّ أنّه ٱختار الإسلام فجعله دينا لعباده. ٱشتقّه من ٱسمه لأنّه السلام ودينه الإسلام الذي ٱرتضاه لنفسه فنحَله من أحبّ من خلقه ثمّ شرّفه فسهّل شرائعه لمن ورده وعزّز أركانه على من حاربه. هيهات من أن يَصطلِمه مُصطلم. جعله عزّا لمن والاه وسلما لمن دخله وهدى لمن ٱئتمّ به ونورا لمن ٱستضاء به وبرهانا لمن تمسّك به وزينة لمن تجلّله وعونا لمن ٱنتحله وشرفا لمن عرفه وحجّة لمن نطق به وشاهدا لمن خاصم به وفَلْجا لمن حاجّ به وعلما لمن وعاه وفهما لمن رواه وحكما لمن قضى به وحلما لمن لَحَن به ولُبّا لمن تدبّره ويقينا لمن عقله وفهما لمن تفطّن به وعِبرة لمن ٱتّعظ به وحبلا وثيقا لمن تعلّق به ونجاة لمن صدّق به ومودّة لمن أصلح وزُلفى لمن ٱقترب وراحة لمن فوّض ولباسا لمن ٱتّقى وكفاية لمن آمن وأمنا لمن أسلم ورَوحا للصادقين.

فالإسلام أصل الحقّ والحقّ سبيل الهدى. صَفْقته الحسنى ومأثُرته المجد. فهو أبلج المنهاج نيّر السراج مُشرق المنار ذاكي المصباح رفيع الغاية يسير المسلك جامع الحِلية قديم العِدّة متنافَس السُّبقة أليم النقمة قصد الصادقين واضح البرهان عظيم الشأن كريم الفُرسان.

فالإيمان منهاجه والتقوى عُدّته والصالحات مناره والعفّة مصابيحه والمحسنون فرسانه والموت غايته والدنيا مِضماره والقيامة حَلَبته والجنّة سُبقته والنار نقمته.

5.14 ʿAbbād ibn Qays rose and asked ʿAlī: Commander of the faithful, tell us: What is faith? And what is Islam?

I shall tell you, Ibn Qays, ʿAlī replied. God created all things knowing about them. He then selected what he wanted, picking out what he loved; what he loved was Islam, which he favored and made into a path for his servants. He derived its name from his name, for he is *al-Salām*, Peace, and his religion is Islam. He was pleased with this religion, and gifted it to the creatures he loved. He exalted it, made the paths to its watering holes smooth, and protected its ramparts from those who would attack it. No saboteur can ever sabotage it. He made it a source of might for whomsoever pledges allegiance to it, a place of safety for whomsoever enters into it, right guidance for whomsoever takes it as his leader, light for whomsoever seeks illumination by it, proof for whomsoever holds fast to it, an ornament for whomsoever exalts it, an aid for whomsoever treads its path, an honor for whomsoever recognizes it, an attestation for whomsoever speaks by its strength, a witness for whomsoever litigates with it, victory for whomsoever debates with it, knowledge for whomsoever retains it, comprehension for whomsoever relates its merits, wisdom for whomsoever judges by it, maturity for whomsoever gains intelligence from it, rationality for whomsoever ponders it, conviction for whomsoever understands it, comprehension for whomsoever reflects upon it, a lesson for whomsoever takes heed from it, a stout rope for whomsoever links himself to it, salvation for whomsoever is true to it, an affectionate bond for whomsoever does good deeds, closeness to God for whomsoever comes nigh unto him, comfort for whomsoever gives himself to him, clothing for the pious, sustenance for the believer, security for the devoted, and well-being for the truthful.

Islam is the foundation of truth, and truth is the road of right guidance. Clasping its hand results in a beautiful reward, and its brilliance bestows nobility. Is path is lit, its sun bright, its road illuminated, its lamp burning, its goal high, its course true, its jewels countless. It is ancient in the counting of years, an arena where the prize can be won, or a painful chastisement received. It is the objective of the truthful. Its proof is clear, its eminence great, and its champions noble.

Its path is faith, its provision piety, its road good deeds, its lamp chastity, its champions the pious, its end death, its racecourse this world, its arena the day of resurrection, its prize paradise, and its punishment hellfire.

فمُعتصَم السعداء بالإيمان وخذلان الأشقياء بالعصيان من بعد إيجاب الحجّة عليهم بالبيان إذا وضح لهم منار الحقّ وسبيل الهدى. فتارك الحقّ مُشوَّهة يوم التغابن خلقته داحضة حجّته عند فوز السعداء بالجنّة.

فبالايمان يُستدلّ على الصالحات وبالصالحات يُستدلّ على التقوى وبالتقوى يُرهب الموت وبالموت تُختم الدنيا وفي الدنيا تُحرَز الآخرة وفي القيامة تُزلَف الجنّة وبالجنّة تكون حسرة أهل النار وفي ذكر أهل النار موعظة أهل التقوى.

والتقوى غاية لا يهلك من قصدها ولا يندم من عمل بها. لأنّ بالتقوى فاز الفائزون وبالمعصية خسر الخاسرون.[1] وليذّكّر أهل التقوى فإنّ الخلق لا مَقصَر لهم في القيامة دون الوقوف بين يدي الحكَم العدل مُرقلين في مضمارها نحو القَصَبة العليا إلى الغاية القصوى مُهطعين بأعناقهم نحو داعيها قد شُخِصوا من مستقَرّ الأجداث والمقابر إلى ضرورة الأبد لكلّ أهلها.[2] قد انقطعت بالأشقياء الأسباب وأَفضَوا إلى عذاب شديد العقاب فلا كرّة لهم إلى دار الدنيا. وافتقروا من الخيرات ولم يُغن عنهم الذين آثروا طاعتهم على طاعة المُتَعال وفاز السعداء بولاية الإيمان.

فالإيمان يا ابن قيس على أربعة أركان: الصبر واليقين والعدل والجهاد.

والصبر من ذلك على أربعة أركان: على الشّوق والشفقة والزهد والترقّب. فمن اشتاق إلى الجنّة سلا عن الشهوات. ومن أشفق من النار رجع عن الحرمات. ومن زهد في الدنيا هانت عليه المصيبات. ومن ترقّب الموت سارع في الخيرات.

واليقين من ذلك على أربعة أركان: على تبصِرة الفطنة وموعظة العبرة وتأويل الحكمة وسنّة الأوّلين.[3] فمن أبصر الفطنة تأوّل الحكمة. ومن تأوّل الحكمة تبيّن

---

١ ه: (المبطلون).

٢ ي: (لكلّ دار أهلها).

٣ م، ي: سقطت بعض الجمل والكلمات من هذه الفقرة. ورواية نهج البلاغة، الحكمة #٣٠، ص. ٦٣٢ مثل رواية ه التي أثبتُّها.

The blissful take refuge in faith. The wretched are debased by their continued disobedience to God even after Islam's proofs have been eloquently presented to them and the path of truth and the road of right guidance have become clearly visible. Whosoever rejects truth after all this—his shape will be made hideous on the day of loss and gain,[48] his arguments voided, that day when the blissful attain the garden.

Faith guides you to deeds, deeds guide you to piety, piety makes you heed death, and death will end this world. It is in this world that the hereafter can be attained, and it is on the day of resurrection that paradise will be brought close. People who are thrown into the fire will be in agony because they are barred from the garden. This reminder about people who are thrown into the fire is a warning that the pious will heed.

None who strive for piety perish, and none who live by it regret. It is by piety that victors are victorious, and by disobedience that losers lose. Let the pious take heed. There is no place for any creature on the day of resurrection other than before the just arbiter. Running swiftly in the racetrack toward the final pole, the finish line, pulled by the neck toward the caller, disturbed from the repose of graves, they will be handed over to the eternal distress that awaits each one of them. All means will be cut off for the wretched, who will be given over to severe punishment. There will be no return for them to the earth. Divested of good deeds, the people they preferred to obey rather than God will do nothing for them. And the blissful will win the kingdom of faith.

Faith, Ibn Qays, stands on four pillars: forbearance, conviction, justice, and struggle against evil.

Forbearance too stands on four pillars: Longing, fear, rejection of worldliness, and expectant waiting. Whosoever longs for the garden is diverted from indulging desires. Whosoever fears the fire retreats from the forbidden. Whosoever rejects worldliness makes light of calamities. And whosoever awaits death hastens to perform good deeds.

Conviction also stands on four pillars: Perceptive sagacity, counsel offered by this world's lessons, interpretation of God's wisdom, and following the practice of the earlier prophets. Whosoever perceives with sagacity interprets God's wisdom. Whosoever interprets God's wisdom recognizes these lessons. Whosoever recognizes these lessons recognizes the path trodden by earlier prophets. And whosoever recognizes the path trodden by

العبرة. ومن تبيّن العبرة عرف السنّة ومن عرف السنّة فكأنّما كان في الأوّلين. فاهتدى إلى التي هي أقوم.

والعدل من ذلك على أربعة أركان: على غامض الفهم وغَمرة العلم وزهرة الحكم وروضة الحلم. فمن فهم فسّر جمل العلم. ومن علم شرائع غرائب الحُكم دلّته على معادن الحلم[1] فلم يضلّ. ومن حلم لم يفرّط في أمره وعاش في الناس حميدا.

والجهاد من ذلك على أربعة أركان: على الأمر بالمعروف والنهي عن المنكر والصدق في المواطن وشَنَآن الفاسقين. فَمن أمر بالمعروف شدّ ظهر المؤمنين. ومن نهى عن المنكر أرغم أنف المنافقين. ومن صدق في المواطن قضى ما عليه. ومن شنئ الفاسقين فقد غضب لله عزّ وجلّ. ومن غضب لله جلّ وعزّ غضب الله جلّ ثناؤه له.

ذلك الأيمان يا ابن قيس ودعائمه وأركانه. أفهمت؟

قال: نعم يا أمير المؤمنين. أرشدك الله فقد أرشدت.

[1] م، ي: (ومن علم شرع غرائب الحكم. ومن شرع غرائب الحكم دلّته على معادن الحلم) ورواية نهج البلاغة، الحكمة #٣٠، ص. ٦٣٢، تختلف عن رواية م، ي، هـ.

earlier prophets is like someone who has lived with them and who has been guided to the steadfast faith.

Justice in its turn stands on four pillars: Deep comprehension, abundant knowledge, blossoms of wisdom, and flowerbeds of restraint. Whosoever comprehends, understands particulars from the generalities of knowledge. Whosoever knows the path of wondrous wisdoms is guided to the repositories of self-control and does not stray. And whosoever possesses restraint, eschews extremes in his affairs, and lives among people respected and loved.

And struggle against evil stands on four pillars: Enjoining good, forbidding evil, valor in battle, and abhorring the corrupt. Whosoever commands good strengthens the believers' resolve. Whosoever forbids evil cuts off the hypocrites' noses. Whosoever is valorous in battle has discharged his duty. And whosoever abhors the corrupt has been roused to anger for the sake of God—so God will be roused to anger on his behalf.

This is faith, Ibn Qays, and its columns and pillars. Do you understand?

Yes, I understand, commander of the faithful, Ibn Qays replied. May God guide you, for you have guided me.

الباب السادس

في المروي عنه عليه السلام من غريب كلامه

٦.١ كان عليه السلام يعلّم أصحابه الصلاة على النبيّ صلّى الله عليه وعلى آله وسلّم يقول: اللّهمّ داحي المَدحوّات وبارئ المسموكات وجبّار القلوب على فِطراتها شقيّها وسعيدها.

اجعل شرائف صلواتك ونوامي بركاتك ورأفة تحنّنك على محمّد عبدك ورسولك الفاتح لما ٱغتلق والخاتم لما سبق والمعلن الحقّ بالحقّ والدافع جَيشات الأباطيل والدامغ صولات الأضاليل[1] كما حُمّل.

فٱضطلع قائما بأمرك لطاعتك مستوفزا في مرضاتك لغير نَكَل في قُدم ولا وهن في عزم واعيا لوحيك حافظا لعهدك ماضيا على نفاذ أمرك حتّى أورى قبسا لقابس وأنار علَما لحابس. آلاء الله تصل بأهله أسبابه.

به هديت القلوب بعد خَوضات الفتن والأَثَم فأبان موضحات الأعلام ونائرات الأحكام ومنيرات الإسلام.

فهو أمينك المأمون وخازن علمك المخزون وشهيدك يوم الدين وبعيثك نعمة ورسولك بالحقّ رحمة.

اللّهمّ ٱفسح له مَفسحا في عدلك[2] وٱجزه مضاعفات الخير من فضلك وٱجعل له

---

١ م، ه: سقطت بعض الكلمات فأتت (والدامغ جيشات الأباطيل).

٢ م: (عدلك أو عدنك) وفي رواية نهج البلاغة، خطبة ٧١ ص. ١٤٨: (ظلّك).

Chapter 6

Sayings with Unusual Words

ʿAlī used to teach his companions how to invoke blessings on the prophet, saying: 6.1

O God, unfolder of lands unfolded, creator of heavens raised high, compeller of hearts, wretched or blissful—

Let your noblest blessings, your manifold graces, your merciful compassion, all be showered upon Muḥammad, your servant and messenger—who opened what was locked, came as a seal for what had come before, rightfully announced the truth, repelled the forces of evil, and crushed the assault of the errant, as he had been charged.

He undertook your command vigorously and obeyed you, rising to serve your pleasure, with no fetters on boldness, or weakness of resolve, comprehending your revelation, safeguarding your compact, and executing your command, until he had ignited the flame of truth for whomsoever sought a burning brand, and lit the torches signaling the road to paradise for people who had tied up their camels not knowing where to go. God's favors bestow his means on his people.

It was through Muḥammad that hearts were guided after being steeped in sedition and sin. He directed them with brilliant signposts, blazing rules, and the luminous ways of Islam.

He is the trustee whom you entrusted with your message, custodian of your treasure of knowledge, your witness on judgment day, your emissary sent as a blessing, your messenger sent with truth and as the embodiment of mercy.

O God, give him an expansive share of your justice. Reward him with a goodly recompense, multiplied manifold by your generosity. Grant him a pure and unmuddied recompense from the font of your flowing reward and abundant magnanimity.

مهنّآت غير مكدّرات من فوز ثوابك المحلول وجزيل عطائك المعلول.

اللّٰهمّ أعلِ على بناء البانين بناءه وأكرم لديك نُزُله ومثواه وأتمم له نوره وآجزه من آبتعاثك له مقبول الشهادة ومرضيّ المقالة ذا منطق عدل وخطّة فصل وحجّة وبرهان عظيم.

٦٠٢

وقال عليه السلام:

ذمّتي رهينة وأنا به زعيم لمن صرّحت له العبر ألّا يهيج على التقوى زرع قوم ولا يظمأ على التقوى سِنخ أصل.

ألَا وإنّ أبغض خلق الله إلى الله رجل قَمَش علما غارّا بأغباش الفتنة عِميا بما في غيب الهُدنة سمّاه أشباهه من الناس عالما ولم يَغنَ فيه يوما سالما. بكّر فآستكثر ممّا قلّ منه فهو خير ممّا كثُر حتّى إذا ما آرتوى من آجن وآكتنز من غير طائل قعد بين الناس قاضيا لتخليص ما آلتبس على غيره. إن نزلت به إحدى المبهمات هيّأ حشوا رأيا من رأيه. فهو من قطع الشبهات في مثل غزل العنكبوت لأنّه لا يعلم إذا أخطأ أأخطأ أم أصاب. خبّاط عَشَوات ركّاب جهالات لا يعتذر ممّا لا يعلم فيسلم ولا يعضّ في العلم بضِرس قاطع فيغنم يذروا الرواية ذَرْو الريح الهشيم. تبكي منه الدماء وتصرخ منه المواريث ويُستحَلّ بقضائه الفرج الحرام. لا مليءٌ والله بإصدار ما ورد عليه ولا أهل لما قُرّظ به.

تفسير غريبه:

قوله (لا يَهيج) يريد: لا يجفّ. و(السِنخ): الأصل، وأضاف أحدهما إلى الآخر لآختلاف لفظيهما. وأراد أنّه من عمل لله عملا لم يفسد ذلك العمل ولم يبطل كما يفسد النبتُ ولكنّه لا يزال ناضرا. و(أغباش الفتنة): ظُلَمها. و(الهُدنة): السكون. أراد أنّه لا يعرف ما في الفتنة من الشرّ ولا في السكون من الخير. و(لم يَغنَ) أي

O God, let his palace be lofty above all others. Give honor to his resting place and his station at your side. Perfect his light.[49] Reward him for being an exemplary messenger—one whose testimonial was accepted and whose words convinced, a man of just speech, decisive action, and magisterial evidence.

6.2

ʿAlī said: For those to whom life's lessons have spoken plainly, I give my pledge: The fields sown by the pious will not wither. The roots planted by them will not shrivel from thirst.

The most hateful of God's creation in his eyes is a man who collects bits of religious knowledge, heedless of the black beasts of sedition, blind to the mysteries of stillness. People of the same ilk call him a scholar, but he has not spent even a full day in learning. He is hasty and thinks he has in abundance what he actually possesses little of. Yet true knowledge is far superior to anything he has amassed. When he has drunk his fill of stagnant water and increased his hoard without profit, he sits down to judge among the people, to elucidate what others have found perplexing. When an impenetrable case comes to him, he assembles jumbled thoughts from his own opinions and gives judgment. In cutting through uncertainties, his words are as weak as the spider's gossamer thread.[50] For when he errs, he does not know whether he has erred or judged correctly. He stomps about in the gloom and rides the steed of ignorance. He does not excuse himself from a case which he does not understand, else he would be protected from erring. He has not bitten into knowledge with strong teeth, or else he would earn something good. He flings around hadith reports just as the wind scatters dry leaves.[51] The lifeblood of the unjustly executed weeps from his injustice and inheritances scream from his wrongdoings. Prohibited private parts are made lawful in his judgments. By God, he is not qualified to send forth with a legal pronouncement cases that come to water at his watering hole, nor is he deserving of the adulation lavished upon him.

Explanation of the unusual words in this passage:

By saying "does not wither [*lā yahīju*]" he means: "not dry up." "Origin [*al-sinkh*]" means root: he puts them in a construct, since the words are different although they mean the same thing; he meant by this expression that whosoever performs a good deed for God, that deed will not be lost or damaged like unwatered plants, but rather will

لم يلبث في العلم يوما تامّا. و (الآجِن): الماء المتغيّر. و (إحدى المبهمات): المسألة المعضلة. وقوله (خبّاط عشوات): هو الذي يخبط في الظلم. وقوله عليه السلام (ولا يعضّ في العلم بضرس قاطع): اي لم يُتقنه ولم يُحكمه. وقوله عليه السلام (لما قرّظ به): التقريظ المدح.

٦٠٣

و روى ٱبن عبّاس قال:

رأيتُ أمير المؤمنين عليّا عليه الصلاة والسلام يوم صفّين وعلى رأسه عِمامة بيضاء وكأنّ عينيه سراجا سَليط وهو يُحمِّش أصحابه إلى أن ٱنتهى إليّ وأنا في كَثْف فقال:

معشر المسلمين استشعِروا الخشية وعَنّوا الأصوات وتجلببوا السكينة وأكملوا اللؤم وأخفّوا الجُنَن وأقلقوا السيوف في الغِمد قبل السلّة وٱلحَظوا الشَّزْر وٱطعنوا الشزر (أو النَّتر أو اليَسر: كُلّا قد سمعت) ونافِحوا بالظُّبى وصِلوا السيوف بالخُطى والرماح بالنَّبل. وٱمشوا إلى الموت مِشية سُجُحًا (أو سَجحاء). وعليكم الرُّواق المطنّب فٱضربوا ثَبَجه. فإنّ الشيطان راكد في كِسره نافج حِضنيه مفترش ذراعيه. قد قدّم للوثبة يدا وأخّر للنكوص رجلا.

تفسير غريبه:

(السليط): الزيت. (يُحمّش أصحابه) أي يَذمُرهم ويغضّبهم. و(الكَثْف): الجماعة. وقوله (وعنّوا الأصوات) أي ٱحبسوها وٱخفوها. و (اللؤم): جمع لَأمة وهي الدرع. و (الجُنَن): التّرسة. يقول: اجعلوها خفافا. و (أقلقوا السيوف): أي سهّلوها قبل أن تحتاجوا إلى ذلك لئلّا تعسر. و (الظُّبى): جمع ظُبة السيف أي حدّه. وقوله (وصلوا السيوف بالخطى): أي إذا قصرت عن الضرائب تقدّمتم وأسرعتم. وقوله (والرماح بالنبل): أي إذا قصرت الرماح بعد من تريدون طعنه رميتموه بالنبل. وقوله (مِشية سُجُحا): أي سهلة. و (الرُّواق): رواق البيت المشدود بالأطناب. و (الحضنان): الجنبان. وقوله (وٱلحظوا الشّزر):

always remain fresh. “Black beasts of sedition [*aghbāsh al-fitnah*]”: the “darknesses of sedition.” “Stillness [*al-hudnah*]” is “tranquility”—he means that such a man does not know the evil inherent in sedition, nor the good inherent in tranquility. “He has not spent [*lam yaghna*],” i.e. a man who has not “devoted” a full day in learning. “Stagnant [*ājin*]”: water that has changed state. “An impenetrable case [*iḥdā l-mubhamāt*]” is a matter that confounds him. The phrase “stomps in the gloom [*khabbāṭu ʿashawāt*]” means that he “stomps about in the darkness.” The phrase “He has not bitten into knowledge with strong teeth [*wa-lā yaʿaḍḍu fī l-ʿilmi bi-ḍirsin qāṭiʿ*]” means “he has no expertise in it.” In “adulation lavished [*limā qurriẓa bihī*],” “adulation” is “praise.”

6.3 It has been narrated by Ibn ʿAbbās, who said: I saw the commander of the faithful, ʿAlī, at the Battle of Ṣiffīn—a white turban on his head, eyes shining like two oil lamps—rousing his followers to battle, until he reached me. I was with a contingent and he addressed us, saying:

Muslims! Clothe yourselves with fear of God, lower your voices, and envelop your bodies with calm. Put on full armor, carry light shields, and rattle your swords in their sheaths before you are called upon to draw them. Glower fiercely at the enemy, and throw your spears from the right and the left (or: aim at the upper part of the body, or: throw them forcefully—I have heard all these narrated). Fight with your blades, and leap forward so that they pierce your enemy. If spears fall short, use arrows. Approach death with gentle courage. Go for the pitched tent. Cut off its center pole, for Satan is hiding in its flap, heaving his flanks, spreading out his arms. He has a hand in front ready to attack, and a foot at the back ready to flee.

Explanation of the unusual words in this passage:

“Olive oil [*salīṭ*]”: i.e. oil. “Rousing his followers to battle [*yuḥammishu aṣḥābahū*]” means he was “inciting and stirring them.” “Contingent [*kathf*]”: “battle group.” The phrase “lower your voices [*wa-ʿannū l-aṣwāt*]” means “keep them controlled, keep them down.” “Full armor [*luʾam*]” is the plural of *laʾmah*, meaning “breastplate.” “Shield [*junan*]” is a protective plate—he is saying, make them light. “Rattle your swords [*aqliqū l-suyūf*]”: i.e. loosen them before you need to draw them so they do not stick. “Blades [*al-ẓubā*]” is the plural of *ẓubah*, i.e., the sword’s edge. The phrase “Leap forward so that your swords pierce your enemy [*wa-ṣilū l-suyūf bi- l-khuṭā*]” means if they fall short of striking distance, go forward with them swiftly. The phrase “If spears fall short, use arrows [*wa-l-rimāḥ bi-l-nabl*]” means if your spears fall short of the enemy whom you are attempt-

هو النظر بمؤخَّر العين نظر العدوّ. و (الطعن اليَسر): ما كان حذاء وجهك. و (الشزر): عن يمينك وشمالك. و (النَّتر): الطعن الخَلس.

٦.٤ وقال عليه الصلاة والسلام:

من أراد البقاء، ولا بقاء، فَلْيُباكِر الغداء وليُقلّ غِشيان النساء وليُخفّف الرداء.

قيل: يا أمير المؤمنين وما خفّة الرداء؟

قال عليه السلام: قلّة الدَّين.

كنى بالرداء عن الظهر لأنّه يقع عليه. يقول: (فليخفّف ظهره ولا يثقله بالدين.)

٦.٥ رأى عليه الصلاة والسلام رجلاً في الشمس فقال:

قم عنها فإنّها مُبخِرة مُجفِرة تُتفِل الريح وتُبلي الثوب وتُظهر الداء الدفين.

قوله عليه السلام (مُجفِرة): اي تقطع شهوة النساء. وقوله (تُتفِل الريح): اي تُنتنها والإسم (التَّفَل). يقال (امرأة تَفِلَة) أي أنتن ريحها. وقوله (الداء الدفين): هو المستتر الذي قد قهرته الطبيعة. يقول: فالشمس تعينه على الطبيعة وتظهره.

٦.٦ قال عليه الصلاة والسلام:

إنّ مِن ورائكم أمورا مُتماحلة رُدُحا وبلاء مُكلِحا مُبلِحا.

(المتماحلة): الطوال يعني فتنا يطول أمرها. و (الرُّدُح): جمع رَداح وهي العظيمة. يقال ذلك للكتيبة إذا عظمت وللمرأة إذا كبرت عجيزتها. وقوله (مُكلِحا): اي يُكلِح الناس لشدّته. يقال (كَلَح الرجل وأكلحه الهمّ). و (المُبلِح): من قولك (بلَح الرجل) إذا انقطع من الإعياء فلم يقدر أن يتحرك.

ing to strike, hit them with arrows. The phrase "Approach with gentle courage [*mishyah sujuḥ*]" means "with ease." "Tent [*al-ruwāq*]" is a pavilion fastened with ropes. "Flanks [*al-ḥiḍnān*]": sides. The phrase "Glower fiercely [*wa-l-ḥaẓū l-shazr*]" means glancing with the side of the eye toward the enemy. "Aiming at the upper part of the body [*al-ṭaʿn al-yasr*]" is that strike which is aimed at the face; "from the right and the left [*al-shazr*]" is from your wind and lee; and "forcefully [*al-natr*]" is a powerful strike.

6.4 ʿAlī said: While no one lives forever, let whosoever wishes to live long rise early in the morning, abstain from too much sex, and wear a light robe.

He was asked, what do you mean by a light robe, commander of the faithful? He replied: Freedom from excessive debt.

By "robe," he was alluding to the back, because it is worn over it. He is saying: "Let him lighten the burden on his back, and not weigh it down with debt."

6.5 ʿAlī saw a man in the sun, and said: Come out of it. It makes your breath foul and impacts your prowess. It makes you malodorous, fades your clothes, and brings buried diseases to the surface.

"Impacts your prowess [*mujfirah*]" means it suppresses desire for women. "Makes your breath foul [*tutfil al-rīḥ*]": i.e. makes it malodorous; the noun is *al-tafal*; a "foul-breathed woman [*tafilah*]" is one whose odor is bad. "Buried disease [*al-dāʾ al-dafīn*]" is that disease which is hidden, that your natural immunity has suppressed. He means the sun aids it in combating your natural immunity and brings it out.

6.6 ʿAlī said: Fast catching up with you are long-lasting, colossal seditions, and scowling, debilitating trials.

"Long-lasting [*al-mutamāḥilah*]" indicates seditions that will drag on for years. "Colossal [*al-ruduḥ*]" is the plural of *radāḥ*, meaning that which is large; it is applied to a battalion if it is large, and to a woman if her buttocks are big. The word "scowling [*mukliḥan*]" means people are oppressed by its force; it is said: "The man scowled [*kalaḥa*]," and "Anxiety wore him down [*aklaḥahū*]." "Debilitating [*al-muballiḥ*]" is used in phrases such as "The man was debilitated [*ballaḥa*]," when he stops working due to fatigue and is unable to move.

٦٠٧

وقال عليه الصلاة والسلام:

البيت المعمور نِتَاقُ الكعبة من فوقها.

قوله عليه السلام (نتاق الكعبة): أي مُطِلّ عليها من فوقها من قول الله تعالى ﴿ وَإِذْ نَتَقْنَا ٱلْجَبَلَ فَوْقَهُمْ كَأَنَّهُ ظُلَّةٌ ﴾.

٦٠٨

وقال عليه الصلاة والسلام:

خذ الحكمة أنّى أتتك فإنّ الكلمة من الحكمة تكون في صدر المنافق فتَلَجلج حتّى تسكن إلى صاحبتها.

يقال: (لجلج اللقمة في فيه) إذا أدارها ولم يُسغها. وأراد عليه السلام أنّ الكلمة قد يعلمها المنافق فلا تزال تتحرك في صدره ولا تسكن حتّى يسمعها المؤمن أو العالم فيَثْقَفها[1] فتسكن في صدره إلى أخواتها من كلم الحكمة.

[1] م: في المتن (فيثبتها)، مصحّحة في الحاشية (فيثقفها). ي: (فيتقنها). هـ: (فيثبها).

ʿAlī said: The Heavenly House is directly over the Kaʿbah, on high.[52] 6.7

ʿAlī's phrase "directly over the Kaʿbah [*nitāq al-Kaʿbah*]" means "overlooking it from on high," and comes from God's words: «When we placed the mountain directly over them, from on high, as though it were a canopy . . .».[53]

ʿAlī said: Seize wisdom no matter where you find it. A wise maxim may reside in the breast of the hypocrite, yet it quivers and trembles until it settles in the breast of its rightful owner. 6.8

People say: "He made the morsel in his mouth quiver and tremble [*lajlaja*]," when he turned it around and around and did not swallow it. ʿAlī meant that a hypocrite may know a wise maxim, but it is agitated in his breast and does not settle, until an ordinary believer or religious scholar hears it and picks it up, such that it settles in his breast, taking comfort next to its kin, namely, other wise maxims.

الباب السابع

في المروي عنه من نوادر كلامه وملح ألفاظه عليه السلام

قال زيد بن أسلم: وصف أمير المؤمنين عليّ بن أبي طالب عليه السلام المؤمن فقال: ٧.١

صفة المؤمن قوّة في دينه وجُرأة في لينه وإيمان في يقينه وخوض في فقه وعمل في علم ونشاط في هدى وبرّ في ٱستقامة وكَيس[1] في رفق. لا يغلبه فرجه ولا يفضحه بطنه. نفسه منه في عناء والناس منه في إعفاء لا يَغتاب ولا يتكبّر.

وقال عليه السلام: أعجب ما في هذا الإنسان قلبُه وله مَوادّ من الحكمة وأضداد من خلافها: فإن سنح له الرجاء أذلّه الطمع وإن هاج به الطمع أهلكه الحرص وإن ملكه اليأس قتله الأسف. إن عرض له الغضب ٱشتدّ به الغيظ وإن أسعد بالرضى نسي التحفّظ. وإن ناله الفزع شغله الحذر وإن ٱتّسع له الأمن ٱستلبته الغِرّة. وإن أفاد مالا أطغاه الغنى وإن أصابته فاقة مسّه الجزع. وإن نَهِكه الجوع قعد به الضعف وإن أفرط به الشّبَع كظّته البِطنة. فكلّ تقصير به مضرّ وكلّ إفراط به مفسد. ٧.٢

كان عليه الصلاة السلام إذا نظر إلى الهلال يقول: ٧.٣

أيّها الخلق المطيع لله الدائر السريع المتردِّد في منازل التقدير المتصرّف في فلك التدبير. آمنت بمن نوّر بك الظلَم وأوضح بك البُهَم وجعلك آية من آيات ملكه وعلامة

---

[1] ي: (كسب).

Chapter 7

Unique Sayings and Pithy Words

7.1 Zayd ibn Aslam said: The commander of the faithful, ʿAlī ibn Abī Ṭālib, described the believer thus:

The believer is strong in his religion, bold yet gentle. He believes with conviction, studies matters of religious practice, performs deeds with knowledge, and receives guidance with enthusiasm. He is kind yet firm, sensible yet gentle. His private parts do not rule him, and his belly does not shame him. He wearies himself by constant chiding, while never causing others unease. He does not indulge in malicious gossip, nor behave arrogantly.

7.2 ʿAlī said: The most wondrous part of the human being is the heart. It has elements of wisdom, and others that are quite the opposite. If the heart is lifted by hope, ambition debases it; if ambition boils over, greed destroys it; and if disappointment takes hold, regret kills it. If aggravated, its rage runs rampant; and if made happy, it forgets to be circumspect. If fear takes hold, caution preoccupies it; and if safety is secured, heedlessness strips it away. If it gains property, the wealth makes it a tyrant; and if poverty touches it, it panics. If hunger emaciates it, weakness ensconces it; and if satiety is excessive, the surfeit oppresses it. Every deficiency harms it, and every excess injures it.

7.3 Whenever ʿAlī looked at the new moon, he would say:[54]

Obedient creature of God, revolving quickly and regularly through the stations of destiny, moving in the sphere of his steering, I place my faith in the one who illumined darkness and clarified ambiguity through you, who made you a sign of his dominion and a symbol of his authority. He humbled

من علامات سلطانه. فٱمتهنك بالزيادة والنقصان والطلوع والأُفول والإنارة والكسوف. في كلّ ذلك أنت له مطيع وإلى إرادته سريع.

سبحانه فما أعجب ما دبّر في أمرك وألطف ما صنع في شأنك. جعلك مفتاح شهر حادث لأمر حادث.

جعلك الله هلال بركة لا تَمحَقه الأيّام وطهارة لا تُدنّسه الأعوام هلال أمنة من الآفات وسلامة من السيّئات. هلال سعد لا نحس فيه ويمن لا نَكَد فيه ويسر لا يمازجه عسر وخير لا يشوبه شرّ. هلال أمن وإيمان ونعمة وإحسان وسلامة وإسلام.

اللّهمّ ٱجعلنا مِن أرضى مَن طلع عليه وأزكى من نظر إليه وأسعد من تعبّد لك فيه.

اللّهمّ وفِّقنا للتوبة وٱعصمنا من الحَوبة وأوزعنا شكر النعمة وألبسنا خير[1] العافية وأتمم علينا بٱستكمال طاعتك فيه المنّة لك، إنّك المنّان الحميد.

٧٠٤ وقال عليّ عليه الصلاة السلام في حقّ العالم: من حقّ العالم أن لا تُكثر عليه السؤال ولا تُعنِته في الجواب ولا تُلِحّ عليه إذا كسل[2] ولا تأخذ بثوبه إذا نهض ولا تُفشي له سرّا ولا تغتاب عنده أحدا. وأن تجلس أمامه وإذا أتيته قصدته بالتحيّة وسلّمت على القوم عامّة. وأن تحفظ سرّه ومَغيبه ما حفظ أمر الله عزّ وجلّ.

فإنّما العالم بمنزلة النخلة. تنتظر متى يسقط عليك منها شيء. والعالم أفضل من الصائم القائم الغازي في سبيل الله تعالى. وإذا مات العالم ٱنثلم بموته في الإسلام ثُلمة لا تُسدّ إلى يوم القيامة. وإذا مات العالم شيّعه سبعة وسبعون ألفا من مُقرّبي السماء.

---

١ في رواية الصحيفة السجادية، ص. ١٤٢: (جنن).

٢ ي: (كَلّ).

you by making you wax and wane, rise and set, illumine and eclipse. In all of this, you obey him and are quick to his will.

God be praised! How marvelous is his planning regarding you! How sublime is his craftsmanship regarding you! He made you a key for a new month, for a new situation.

May God render you a crescent of grace uneffaced by the passing days, and of purity undefiled by the passing years; a crescent of security from calamities, and safety from evil deeds; a crescent of felicity free of misfortune, of blessings free of adversity, of ease unmixed with hardship, and of good unpolluted by evil; a crescent of security and faith, bounty and virtue, safety and commitment.

O God, of all the people over whom this moon rises, place us among those who please you the most. Of all who gaze at it, place us among the purest. Of all who worship you under it, place us among the happiest.

O God, motivate us to repent, preserve us from misdeeds, move us to give thanks for your blessings, envelop us with health, and complete your favors upon us by perfecting our obedience to you. You are the best benefactor and the most praiseworthy.

7.4 ʿAlī said about the rights of a learned man: You owe it to a learned man that you not bombard him with questions, dog him for answers, press him when he is tired, hold him back by his robe when he rises, expose his secrets, nor tell him tales about people. Moreover, you should sit facing him, and greet him individually when you come to his class before addressing others present collectively. You should preserve his secrets and defend him in his absence. Abide by this, as long as he preserves God's commandments.

A learned man is like a date palm; you can expect a date to drop on you at any moment. A learned man is worthier than one who fasts, prays, and fights in the path of God. When a learned man dies, Islam sustains a breach not plugged till the day of resurrection. When a learned man dies, his bier is escorted by seventy-seven thousand of God's cherished angels.

٧.٥ وقال عليه الصلاة السلام: أيُّها الناس إنّ أوّل وقوع الفتن أهواء تُتّبَع وأحكام تُبتدَع يُخالَف فيها حُكم الله ويُعظِّم عليها رجالٌ رجالا. ولو أنّ الحقّ أُخلص فعُمل به لم يَخْفَ على ذي حِجى ولكنّه يؤخذ ضِغْث من هذا وضغث من هذا فيُخلَط فيُعمل به. فعند ذلك يَستولي الشيطان على أوليائه وينجو ﴿ٱلَّذِينَ سَبَقَتْ لَهُم مِّنَّا ٱلْحُسْنَىٰ﴾.

خبر الناقوس

٧.٦ مرّ عليّ عليه الصلاة والسلام ومعه الحارث الأعوَر رحمه الله تعالى. فإذا دَيرانيّ يضرب بالناقوس. فقال عليّ: يا حارث أتعلم ما يقول هذا الناقوس؟ قال: الله ورسوله وٱبن عمّ رسوله أعلم. قال: إنّه يصف مَثَل خراب الدنيا. يقول:

طفًّا طفًّا حقًّا حقًّا[1]   يا ٱبن الدنيا مَهْلًا مهلا

إنّ الدنيا قد غرّتنا   وٱستهوتنا وٱستغوتنا

لسنا ندري ما فرّطنا   فيها إلّا أن قد مِتنا

ما من يوم يمضي عنّا   إلّا هَدّ منّا ركنا

زِنْ ما تأتي زن ما تأتي   زن ما تأتي زن ما تأتي

وَزْنًا وزنًا وزنًا وزنا   تَفنى الدنيا قَرْنًا قرنا

يا ٱبن الدنيا جمعًا جمعا   يا ٱبن الدنيا سَرْطًا سرطا

ما من يوم يمضي عنّا   إلّا أثقل منّا ظهرا

---

[1] م، ي: سقطت المصراع. وفي المصراع الثاني والأبيات التالية اختلافات صغيرة. وروايتهما قريبة من رواية الديوان، ص. ٤٨٨.

7.5 ʿAlī said: O people! The first manifestation of sedition is the following of whims and the prescribing of innovating rules—whims and rules by which God's decree is disobeyed and men are aggrandized by other men. If the truth were sincerely adhered to and practiced, it would not be concealed from the intelligent. But a bit is taken from this, and a bit from that, mixed together and acted upon. At that moment, Satan gains complete mastery over his followers, and only «those for whom our blessings have been decreed»[55] will be saved.

The report of the church gong

7.6 ʿAlī was passing by a Christian monastery accompanied by al-Ḥārith al-Aʿwar, when they heard a monk ringing the gong. Ḥārith, do you know what this church gong is saying, ʿAlī asked. God, his messenger, and his messenger's cousin know best, answered Ḥārith. The gong is describing the ruin of this world, ʿAlī explained. It is saying:[56]

Soon, yes, soon, and truly, truly
  This world's sons, go slowly, slowly
This world has indeed deceived us
  and seduced us and misled us
We don't see how much we've transgressed
  in it, but we all will soon die
There is not a day that goes by
  that does not assault our buttress
Weigh what comes then, weigh what comes
  Weigh what comes then, weigh what comes
Weight for weight, yes, weight for weight
  This world's dead, whole generations
Son of this world, gath'ring, gath'ring
  Son of this world, guzzling, guzzling
There is not a day that goes by
  That does not increase our burden

إنّ المولى قد خبّرنا أنّا نُحشر غُرلا بُهما
قد ضيّعنا دارا تبقى واستوطنّا دارا تفنى

فقال الحارث لعلي عليه الصلاة والسلام: أَوَتعلم النصارى ذلك؟ قال: لا يعلم ذلك إلا نبيّ أو صِدّيق أو وصيّ نبيّ. فإنّ علي من علم النبيّ وعلم النبيّ من علم جبريل وعلم جبريل من علم الله تبارك وتعالى.

شرط له عليه الصلاة والسلام في شِراء دار ٧.٧

اشترى شُريح دارا وكتب كتابا وأشهد شهودا.

فبلغ ذلك عليّ بن أبي طالب عليه السلام فقال له: يا شريح اشتريت دارا؟ قال: نعم. وأشهدت شهودا؟

قال: نعم.

قال: احذر أن تكون قد اشتريت من غير مالك ووزنت مالا من غير حِلّ. وسوف يأتيك من لا ينظر في بيّنتك ولا يسألك عن كتابك ويُزعجك عنها فتكون قد خسرت الدارين الدنيا والآخرة. ولو أنّك حين أردت شراء الدار أو إذا أراد أحد شراء دار جاءني لكنت أكتب له كتابا أُزهّد فيه البائع المغرور والمشتري.

قلت: وما كنت تكتب؟[1]

قال: كنت أكتب:

بسم الله الرحمٰن الرحيم

هذا ما اشترى عبد ذليل من ميّت قد أُزعج بالرحيل. اشترى منه دارا من دُور الآفات من الجانب الفاني من عسكر الهالكين ومجمع الغافلين.

---

[1] كذا في المخطوطات. قد يكون الراوي للخبر شريح نفسه وإن لم يأت ذكره فهو فاعل (قلت).

God in heaven has informed us
Intact bodies resurrected
We have foregone life unending
Settling in the house of death.

Do the Christians know their gong says this? Ḥārith asked. None can know it, ʿAlī replied, except a prophet, his staunchest supporter, or his legatee. Indeed, my knowledge comes from the prophet, the prophet's from Gabriel, and Gabriel's from God.

Stipulations set by ʿAlī when buying a house

7.7

Shurayḥ bought a house, wrote up a contract, and called witnesses to attest to the purchase. The news reached ʿAlī ibn Abī Ṭālib, who asked: Shurayḥ, did you buy a house? Shurayḥ replied that he had. Did you have witnesses attest to the contract? Shurayḥ replied that he had. ʿAlī responded: Beware of buying with money other than yours, of weighing out coins gained from unlawful sources. Soon there will come to you one who will not look at your testimonials nor ask for the written contract, but will rudely dislodge you from the house.[57] Then you will have lost both abodes: this world and the hereafter. If you—or anyone else who wants to buy a house—had come to me, I would have written up a different kind of contract, one in which I would have dissuaded the deluded seller as well as the buyer. What would you have written? Shurayḥ asked, and he replied: I would have written:

In the name of God, the compassionate, the merciful

This is what a humble servant has bought, from a soon-to-be-dead man who will be forced to depart the world. The humble servant bought from the soon-to-be-dead man one of the houses of calamity, located in a soon-to-perish district, in the camp of the dead, and the assembly of the heedless.

يجمع هذه الدارَ حدود أربعة: فالحدّ الأوّل ينتهي إلى الآفات. والحدّ الثاني ينتهي إلى عِظَم المصيبات. والحدّ الثالث ينتهي إلى الغفلات. والحدّ الرابع ينتهي إلى الشيطان المُغوي والهوى المُردي. وإليه يشرع باب هذه الدار التي اشتراها هذا المزعج بالأجل من هذا المغرور بالأمل. فما أدرك مشتري هذه الدار فعل[1] مبلبل الأجسام وقاصم الجبابرة مثل كسرى وقيصر وسابور الأكبر وتُبّع وحِمير.[2] ما أوضح الحقّ لذي عينين. إنّ الرحيل حقّ أحد اليومين.

٧.٨ وقال عليه والسلام في رسالته لرفاعة:

لا حِمى إلّا من ظَهر مؤمن وظهر فرس مجاهد وحريم بئر وحريم نهر وحريم حصن.

والحرمة بين الرجال والنساء وهي الحجب.

وحريمٌ بين الحلال والحرام لا مَرتَع فيه. وحريم لا يؤمَن في الأوّلين والآخرين.

وحريمٌ حرمته الرحِم.

وحريمٌ ما جاوز الأربع من الحرائر.

وحريمٌ القضاء.

٧.٩ وقال عليه الصلاة والسلام: إنّي لأستحيي من الله تعالى أن يكون ذنب أعظم من عفوي أو جهل أعظم من حلمي أو عورة لا يواريها ستري أو خَلّة لا يسدّها جودي.

---

١ م، ي، ه: (فعلى). صحّحها السويدان في تحقيقه للدستور (فعل) وكذا أثبتّها.

٢ ه: تضيف (ومن جمع مالا إلى مال فأكثر وبنى وشيّد وزخرف وأزجر ونظر بزعمه للولد ووعد وأوعد أشخصوا والله جميعا إلى موقف العرض والحساب والثواب والعقاب وسيقع الأمر بفصل القضاء ويقتصّ للجمّاء من القرناء ﴿وَخَسِرَ هُنَالِكَ ٱلْمُبْطِلُونَ﴾ [الغافر ٤٠:٧٨]، ﴿وَقُضِيَ بَيْنَهُم بِٱلْحَقِّ وَهُمْ لَا يُظْلَمُونَ﴾ [الزمر ٣٩:٦٩]. شهد على ذلك التواني بن الفاقة والغرور بن الأمل والحرص بن الرغبة واللهو بن اللعب ومن أخلد إلى محلّ الهوى ورغب عن الآخرة).

There are four limits to this house: The first limit extends to calamity. The second limit extends to great catastrophe. The third limit extends to heedless acts. The fourth limit extends to Satan the deceiver and destructive desire. Into this side opens the door of this house, which this person soon to be expelled by death has bought from that person deceived by false hopes. The buyer of this house has not grasped the reality of the actions of the putrefactor of bodies, the crusher of despots such as Chosroes, Caesar, Sābūr, Tubbaʿ, and Ḥimyar. O how clear is the truth for one who has two eyes! Departure from this world is assured, if not today then tomorrow.

7.8 ʿAlī wrote in a letter to Rifāʿah:

The back of a believer and the back of a warrior's horse are not to be violated; nor wells, rivers, or fortresses.

The inviolable space between men and women is upheld by veils and screens.

The lawful and unlawful are distinct; there can be no pasturing in an unlawful field. The unlawful was not safe for past generations, and it is not safe for those yet to come.

Marriage between close blood relatives is unlawful.

Marrying more than four free women is unlawful.

The law is inviolable.

7.9 ʿAlī said: I would be ashamed before God if there were a transgression greater than my forgiveness, a fit of anger greater than my forbearance, a shame that my robe could not conceal, or a need that my generosity could not fill.

٧.١٠ وقال عليه الصلاة والسلام: إنّ النعمة موصولة بالشكر والشكر متعلّق بالمزيد وهما مقرونان في قَرَن. فلن ينقطع المزيد من الله عزّ وجلّ حتّى ينقطع الشكر من العباد.

٧.١١ وقال عليه الصلاة والسلام: أربعٌ يُمِتنَ القلب: الذنب على الذنب ومُلاحاة الأحمق وكثرة مُشافنة النساء والجلوس مع الموتى.

قيل: ومن الموتى يا أمير المؤمنين؟

قال: كلّ عبد مُترَف.

٧.١٢ وقال عليه الصلاة والسلام: يا أيّها الناس من علم من أخيه مروءة جميلة فلا يسمعنّ فيه الأقاويل. ومن حسنت علانيته فنحن لسريرته أرجى. ألَا لا يزيدنّ أحدكم نفسه شكّاً. فإنّ من علم من أخيه مروءة جميلة فسمع فيه الأقاويل فقد شكّك نفسه. ألَا وإنّ الرامي قد يرمي وقد تخطئ السهام وباطل ذلك يبور.

ألَا وإنّ بين الحقّ والباطل أربع أصابع (وأشار بأصابعه الأربع فوضعها بين العين والأذن). فالحقّ أن تقول: رأيته بعيني. والباطل أن تقول: سمعته بأذني.

٧.١٣ وقال عليه الصلاة والسلام: من عزفت نفسه عن دنيّ المطامع كملت محاسنه ومن كملت محاسنه حُمد والمحمود محبوب ولن يحبّ العباد عبداً إلّا بعد حبّ الله عزّ وجلّ إيّاه. فتكون المحبّة درجة إلى نيل صلاح معاشه مع وفور معاده. ومن ٱجتمعت له الخصلتان كملت سعادته. والشقيّ الكامل الشقاء من كان بخلاف ذلك.

٧.١٤ وقال عليه الصلاة والسلام: ليس الخير أن يكثر مالك وولدك ولكنّ الخير أن يكثر علمك وأن يعظم حلمك وأن تباهي الناس بعبادة ربّك. فإن أحسنت حمدت الله عزّ وجلّ وإن أسأت ٱستغفرت الله.

ʿAlī said: Blessings are connected to gratitude and gratitude is linked to further blessings. The two are tied together in a single tether. God will not cut off his blessings unless his servants sever their gratitude. 7.10

ʿAlī said: Four things kill the soul: Sinning incessantly, arguing with a fool, too much dallying with women, and keeping company with the dead. 7.11

He was asked: Who are the dead, commander of the faithful?

All those mired in luxury, he replied.

ʿAlī said: O people, whoever knows his brother to be a decent man should not give ear to rumors about him. If a man's behavior is virtuous, I have good hope for his intentions. Do not sow doubts in your heart about him; whoever knows his brother to be a decent man and still gives ear to rumors about him unnecessarily casts his own heart into doubt. An archer may shoot, and his arrows may go astray—the injustice of this can destroy you. 7.12

The span of four fingers separates truth and falsehood (and he gestured with his four fingers, placing them between his eye and his ear). Truth is saying: "I saw with my eyes." Falsehood is saying: "I heard with my ears."

ʿAlī said: Whosoever turns his soul away from base ambitions perfects his character, whosoever perfects his character is praiseworthy, and the praiseworthy man is loved. God's servants do not love a man unless God loves him. This love becomes a means for him to gain a decent living in this world and abundant reward when he returns to God. The bliss of a person for whom the two come together is perfected. The perfect wretch, on the other hand, is one whose state is the antithesis of this. 7.13

ʿAlī said: Possessing great wealth and having many children are not the mark of excellence; excellence is obtained through great knowledge and abundant kindness, and by vying with people in worshiping the lord. If you do good, praise God. If you do ill, ask him for forgiveness. 7.14

ولا خير في الدنيا إلّا لرجلين: رجل أذنب ذنبا فهو يتدارك ذلك بتوبة ورجل يسارع في الخيرات.

ولا يقلّ عمل مع تقوى وكيف يقلّ ما يُتقبّل.

وقال عليه الصلاة والسلام: ٧.١٥

إنّ أبغض الخلق إلى الله رجلان: ٧.١٥.١

رجل وكّله الله عزّ وجلّ إلى نفسه فهو جائر عن قصد السبيل مشعوف بكلام بدعة قد لَهِج منها بالصوم والصلاة. فهو فتنة لمن ٱفتتن به ضالّ عن هدى من كان قبله مضلّ لمن ٱفتتن به حياته وموته حمّال لخطايا غيره رهين بخطيئته.

ورجل قَمَش جهلا في جُهّال الناس بالأباطيل والأضاليل. نصبها عُدّة من حبائل غرور وقول زور. قد حمل الكتاب على رأيه وٱستعطف الحقّ على هواه. يزيّن العظائم ويهوّن كبير الجرائم. لم يراقب من خلقه فيسكت حيث لا يعلم. قد ٱغترّ مع ذلك فسّاقا تصدّقه يَستجهل بهم أشباهَ الناس.

وجافٍ مُتجافٍ أعمى حيران. يدعو إلى العمى ويرى البصر في ترك النظر. يقول أقف عند الشبهات وفيها وقع. ويقول أعتزل البدع وفيها ٱضطجع. فهو في الناس رجل. الصورة صورة إنسان والقلب قلب حيوان. بهيمة بل البهيمة خير منه. فهو في الأحياء في التقلّب والموت أغلب عليه في الصفة. ٧.١٥.٢

عَشوةٌ غارٌّ بأغباش الفتنة غُمر بما في رَيث الهُدنة. قد سمّاه أشباه الناس عالما ولم يَغنَ فيه يوما سالما. بكر فٱستكثر وما قلّ منه خير ممّا كثُر. حتّى إذا ٱرتوى من عين آجن وٱكتنز من غير طائل جلس بين الناس قاضيا ضامنا لتخليص

There is no good in this world except for two kinds of men: one who commits a sin but atones for it by repenting, and one who hastens to perform good deeds.

No deed is too small if it is performed with piety. How can something that is accepted ever be too small?

ʿAlī said: 7.15

The most hateful creatures in God's eyes are two: 7.15.1

The first is a man whom God has given up on and left to his own devices, who strays from the straight path. Enamored of heretical innovations, he prescribes them in fasting and prayer, and incites people who are taken in by him. Having lost the path of right guidance his predecessors followed, he leads his own followers astray in his lifetime and after his death. Without a doubt, he will bear the burden of their sins, while remaining ransomed to the consequences of his own transgressions.

The second is a man who collects bits of ignorance—fabrications and fictions—from the most ignorant of people. He sets these deceptive snares and false reports as his stock. He interprets the book according to his whim and bends the truth to his desires. He makes grave sins look attractive and minimizes major transgressions. Blithely unconscious of his creator, he does not keep silent when he does not know. Despite all these faults, he manages to seduce other wicked people into believing him. With their support, he makes fools of those who are human only in form.

7.15.2 Many a harsh, coarse man, blind and confused, calls others to his blindness, and sees true vision in not thinking. He says "I pause when I have doubts," when in fact he has fallen headlong into the pit of doubt. He says "I stay away from heretical innovations," when in fact he has made innovations his bedfellows. In people's eyes he is a man—yes, his form is human, but his heart is bestial. He is a bovine animal, no, bovine animals are better than him.[58] He moves like the living, but death has taken control of his spirit.

This man oppresses others. He is heedless of the black beasts of sedition, ignorant of the mysteries of calm. People who are human only in form call him a scholar, but he has not spent even a full day in learning. He is hasty and thinks he possesses a lot. Yet true knowledge is far superior to anything he has amassed. When he has drunk his fill of stagnant water and increased his store without profit, he sits down to judge among the people, to elucidate

ما ٱلتبس على غيره. وإن خالف قاضيا فسّقه ولم يأتمّ في حكمه بمن خَلَفه. وإن نزلت به إحدى المبهمات المعضلات هيّأ لها حشوا رأيا من رأيه ثمّ قطع. فهو من لَبس الشبهات في مثل غزل العنكبوت لأنّه لا يدري أصاب أم أخطأ. لا يحسب العلم في شيء ممّا أنكر ولا يدري أنّ وراء ما بلغ مذهبا. إن قاس شيئا بشيء لم يكذّب نظره وإن أظلم عليه أمر اكتتم به لما يعلم من جهل نفسه لكي لا يقال له لا يعلم ثمّ جسر فحكم.

فهو مفتاح عشوات ركّاب شبهات خبّاط جهالات. لا يعتذر ممّا لا يعلم فيسلم ولا يَعَضّ في العلم بضِرس قاطع فيغنم. يذروا الرواية ذَرْوَ الريح الهشيم. تبكي منه المواريث وتصرخ منه الدماء ويُستحَلّ بقضائه الفرج الحرام. لا مليءٌ والله بإصدار ما أورد عليه ولا هو أهل لما قُرّظ من ٱدّعائه في علم الحقّ.

٧.١٥.٣ ألَا وإنّ أحبّ الناس إلى الله لعبد أعانه الله جلّ ثناؤه على نفسه فٱستشعر الخوف وتجلبب الحزن وأضمر اليقين وتجنّب الشكّ والشبهات وتوهّم الزوال فهو منه على بال. قد زهرت مصابيح الهدى في قلبه فقرّب به البعيد وهوّن به الشديد. فكّر فٱستكثر ونظر فأبصر. حتّى إذا ٱرتوى من عَذب فُرات سهلت موارده فشرب نَهَلا وسلك سبيلا سهلا. لم يدع مَظلِمة إلّا أبصر جَلاءها ولا مُبهَمة إلّا عرف مَداها.

قد خلع سرابيل الشهوات وتخلّى من الهموم إلّا همّا واحدا ٱنفرد به دون الهموم الشاغبة الشاغلة للعقول فخرج من صفة العمى ومشاركة الهوى فصار من مفاتيح الهدى ومغاليق أبواب الردى. وٱستفتح بما فتح به العلم[1] أبوابه فخاض بحاره وقطع غِماره ووضحت له سبله ومناره. قد ٱستمسك من العُرى بأوثقها ومن الحبال

[1] م، ي: (العالم).

what others have found perplexing. When his opinion goes against another judge's view, he tells people the other is immoral. He does not follow his predecessors in his judgments. When an impenetrable case comes to him, he assembles jumbled thoughts from his own opinions then gives judgment. His words are as weak as the spider's gossamer thread.[59] For when he errs he does not know whether he has erred or judged correctly. He does not know that beyond the place he has reached there is yet another path. If he comes up with an analogy, comparing one case to another, he never doubts his own opinion. If a case becomes too dark for him to grasp, he hides this fact, for he knows he is ignorant, and does not want it said that he does not know. Then he boldly passes judgment.

This man is the key to darkness, one who mounts the steed of sophistry and stomps about in ignorance. He does not recuse himself from a case which he does not understand, else he would be protected from erring. He has not bitten into knowledge with strong teeth, or else he would earn something good. He flings around hadith reports just as the wind scatters dry leaves.[60] Inheritances weep from his injustice, the lifeblood of the unjustly executed screams from his wrongdoing, and prohibited private parts are made lawful in his judgments. By God, he is not qualified to send forth with a legal pronouncement cases that come to water at his watering hole, nor is he deserving of praise for his extravagant claims of his perfect knowledge of truth.

7.15.3

The most beloved person in God's eyes is one who, with God's help, keeps his base soul under control. He wears the garment of fear and dons the robe of grief. A man of conviction, he divests himself of doubt and awaits the approaching end of his life on earth, always mindful of this approaching end. The lamp of guidance shines forth from his heart. With its light, he brings the distant close and makes tribulations easier to bear. He thinks deeply and gains much, he looks hard and acquires perception. When he finds sweet water, the path to it becomes smooth for him, and he drinks his fill. He now sees how to dispel every darkness, and knows the boundaries of every ambiguity.

He has removed the garment of desire and divested himself of aspirations. Putting aside the tumultuous aspirations that occupy most minds, he holds on to just one. Escaping the grip of blindness and the companionship of whim, he becomes himself a key to right guidance and a lock in the door of perdition. He seeks to open the door of knowledge, plunging into its sea and venturing into its depths. Its paths and beacons shine bright for him. Grasping the stoutest

بأمتنها. فهو من اليقين على مثل ضياء الشمس. قد نصب نفسه لله عزّ وجلّ في أرفع الأمور من إصدار كل وارد عليه وردّ كلّ فرع إلى أصله. فالأرض الذي هو فيها مشرقة بضياء نوره ساكنة إلى قضائه. فرّاج عشوات كشّاف مبهمات دفّاع معضلات مصباح ظلمات دليل فلَوات. لا يدع للخير مَطلبا إلّا قصده. فالعلم ثمرة قلبه ومنى نفسه التي إليها يقصد وإيّاها يحاول. بقية أبقاه الله عزّ وجلّ لدينه وحجّته. خليفة من خلائف أنبياء الله بلزوم طريقتهم والدعاء إلى ما كانت عليه دعوتهم والقيام بحجّتهم. قد أمكن الكتابَ من زمامه فهو قائده وإمامه يضع رحله حيث حلّ ثقَله. والناس عن الصراط ناكبون ﴿فِي غَمْرَةٍ سَاهُونَ﴾ وفي حيرة يعمهون.

وقال عليّ عليه الصلاة والسلام: ألا وإنّ الناس سبع طبقات: ٧.١٦

فالطبقة الأولى الفراعنة. يدعون الناس إلى عبادتهم. أما إنّهم لا يأمرونهم أن يصلّوا لهم ولا يصوموا ولكنّما يأمرونهم بطاعتهم فيطيعونهم فبطاعتهم لهم في معصية الله جلّ ثناؤه قد اتّخذوهم أربابا من دون الله جلّ ثناؤه. والطبقة الثانية جبابرة. أكلُهم الرِبا وبيعهم السُحت. والطبقة الثالثة فُسّاق. قد تشرّدوا من الدين كما يتشرّد الشارد من الإبل. والطبقة الرابعة أصحاب الرياء. ليس يعبدون إلّا الدينار والدرهم. والطبقة الخامسة قرّاء مخادعون. يطلبون الدنيا بزيّ الصالحين. والطبقة السادسة فقراء. إنّما همّ أحدهم أن يشبع شَبعة من الطعام لا يبالي أحلالا أخذها أم حراما. والطبقة السابعة الذين أثنى الله جلّ وعزّ عليهم فقال ﴿وَعِبَادُ ٱلرَّحْمَٰنِ ٱلَّذِينَ يَمْشُونَ عَلَى ٱلْأَرْضِ هَوْنًا وَإِذَا خَاطَبَهُمُ ٱلْجَاهِلُونَ قَالُوا سَلَامًا﴾. ثمّ قال عليه السلام: والذي فلق الحبّة وبرأ النسمة إنّهم ﴿ٱلَّذِينَ يَرِثُونَ ٱلْفِرْدَوْسَ هُمْ فِيهَا خَالِدُونَ﴾.

of handles and the strongest of ropes, he has the conviction of someone who sees all things as clearly as the light of the sun. Doing what he does for God, he follows the highest standards, sending back any who come to his watering hole with the right answers, and tracing every branch to its root. The land in which he lives is illumined by the radiance of his light, and is peaceful due to his justice. He removes misfortunes, elucidates ambiguities, and repulses calamities. He is a lamp in the darkness and a guide in the wilderness. He pursues every repository of good and seeks it wherever it may be found. Knowledge is his heart's yield and his soul's desire. This is what he aspires to and strives to attain. He is the one remaining sage, whom God has preserved for his religion and maintained as his proof. The true successor of God's prophets, he follows their path, calls to their religion, and conveys their proofs. Entrusting his reins to the holy book, he takes it as his leader, and lays down his saddle in the place where the book has deposited its precious belongings, abiding there. This is his life, while other people are turning away from the path,[61] «erring in droves»,[62] and milling about blindly in their confusion.

7.16

ʿAlī said: There are seven categories of men:

The first category is false monarchs;[63] they call people to worship them. They do not demand that their subjects bow to them in prayer or fast for them as a form of worship, but rather, they command their obedience. By obeying these pharaohs and disobeying God, people make them their lords and thereby reject God. The second category is tyrants; they practice usury, and trade unlawfully. The third category is the depraved; they have bolted from religion just as runaway camels bolt from the herd. The fourth category is the duplicitous; they worship nothing but silver and gold. The fifth category is fraudulent Qur'an reciters; they seek worldly things while wearing the garb of the pious. The sixth category is beggars; all they think about is filling their stomachs with food, not caring whether they acquire it lawfully or unlawfully. The seventh category is people whom God has praised, saying: «God's servants are those who tread lightly upon the earth; if the ignorant address them, they say "Peace!"»[64] By the one who made the seed sprout and created humans, these are the people «who will inherit paradise, living there forever.»[65]

ثمّ ٱلتفت عليه السلام إلى كميل بن زياد رحمه الله تعالى فقال: يا كميل ٱطلبهم. قال كميل: وأين أطلبهم يا أمير المؤمنين؟ قال: في أطراف الأرض تجدهم. قد ٱتّخذوا الأرض فراشا والماء طيبا والقرآن شعارا والدعاء دثارا. باكي العيون دَنِسي الثياب. يَقرضون العيش قرضا إن غابوا لم يُفقَدوا وإن شهدوا لم يُعرفوا وإن خطبوا لم يزوَّجوا وإن قالوا لم يُنصَت لقولهم. يدفع الله عزّ وجلّ بهم العاهات والآفات والبلايا عن الناس وبهم يسقِي الله عزّ وجلّ العباد الغيث من السماء وينزّل القطر من السحاب. اولئك عباد الله حقّا حقّا.

٧.١٧ وقال عليه الصلاة والسلام: الناس سبع طبقات لا يصلح بعضها إلّا ببعض ولا غنى لبعضها عن بعض. فمنها جنود الله تعالى ومنها كتّاب العامّة والخاصّة ومنها قضاة العدل ومنها كتّاب الدواوين ومنها أهل الجزية والخراج والذمّة ومُسلِمة الناس ومنها التجّار وأهل الصناعات ومنها الطبقة السفلى من ذوي الحاجة والمسكنة. فكلّ قد سمّى الله سهمه ووقف على حدّه في فريضته في كتابه أو سنّة نبيّه صلّى الله عليه وعلى آله وسلّم عهدا منه عندنا محفوظا.

فالجنود بإذن الله عزّ وجلّ حصون الرعيّة وزَين الولاة وعزّ الدين وسبيل الأمن والخفض وليس تقوم الرعيّة إلّا بهم. ثمّ لا قِوام للجند إلّا بما يُخرج الله جلّ وعزّ لهم من الخراج الذي يَقوَون به على جهاد عدوّهم ويعتمدون عليه فيما أصلحهم ويكون من وراء حاجاتهم. ثمّ لا نَماء لهذين الصنفين إلّا بالصنف الثالث من القضاة والعمّال والكتّاب بما يُحكمون من الأمور ويُظهرون من الإنصاف ويجمعون من المنافع ويؤتَمنون عليه من خواصّ الأمور وعوامّها. ولا قوام لهم جميعا إلّا بالتجّار وذوي الصناعات فيما يجمعون من مَرافقهم ويقيمون من أسواقهم ويَكفونهم من الرفق بأيديهم ممّا لا يبلغه رفق غيرهم. ثمّ الطبقة السفلى من أهل الحاجة والمسكنة الذين يَحِقّ رفدهم في الله عزّ وجلّ لكلّ طبقة.[١]

---

١ م، ي: (سعة).

ʿAlī then turned toward Kumayl ibn Ziyād, and said: Seek them, Kumayl! Where should I seek them, commander of the faithful? Kumayl asked. You will find them at the ends of the earth, replied ʿAlī, they have taken the earth as bedding, its water as perfume, God's book as garment, and prayer as robe. Their eyes weep, their clothing is dusty, and they have severed all ties with this world. If they leave they are not missed, and if present they remain unknown. If they ask for a hand in marriage they are refused, and if they speak they are not heeded. Yet it is because of them that God turns away scourges, calamities, and trials from the world. It is because of them that God gives people water to drink, by sending rain from the sky, droplets from the clouds. They are the servants of God. Truly. Yes, truly.

7.17

ʿAlī said: People can be divided into seven categories, each category sustained by the others and needing the others. These categories are: God's soldiers; scribes who write for the elite or for the public; judges who dispense justice; government clerks; people who pay poll taxes and land taxes: "protected peoples,"[66] conquered peoples who have converted to Islam; traders and artisans; and the lowest category, that of the poor and needy. God has prescribed a role for each, drawing the boundaries through the laws mandated in his book or in the practice of his prophet. This is a covenant from him, one that we preserve.

Soldiers serve with God's permission as protection for the general public as the ornament of governors, the might of religion, and the path to security and ease. The public is not sustained except through them. Soldiers in turn are not sustained except by the land tax that God has ordained to be used for their maintenance, through which they gain strength to fight their enemy, and upon which they depend to improve their living conditions and fulfill their basic needs. These two groups prosper only with the help of the third—judges, tax collectors, and clerks, who conduct the affairs of society, establish justice, collect taxes, and are honest stewards of the specific or general affairs assigned to them. All these groups are sustained by the traders and artisans who gather together the stuff of life, set up markets, and suffice the other groups in their daily needs with services that no one else can perform. Then comes the lowest category, that of the poor and needy. People in all other categories must help them.

ولكلّ على الوالي حقّ بقدر ما يصلحه ولا يَخرج الوالي من حقيقة ما ألزمه الله تبارك وتعالى وتوطين نفسه على لزوم الحقّ والصبر عليه فيما خفّ أو ثقل.

٧.١٨ وقال عليه السلام: إنما أنت أحد رجلين: إمّا ٱمرؤ سخت نفسك بالبذل في الحقّ ففيمَ ٱحتجابك من واجب حقّ تعطيه وخُلُق كريم تُسديه؟ وإمّا مبتلى بالمنع فما أسرع كفّ الناس عن مسئلتك إذا يئسوا من بذلك.

٧.١٩ وقال عليه الصلاة والسلام: حقّ المسلم على المسلم سبع خصال: يسلّم عليه إذا لقيه ويجيبه إذا دعاه ويعوده إذا مرض ويتبع جنازته إذا مات ويحبّ له ما يحبّ لنفسه ويكره له ما يكره لها والمواساة في ماله.

٧.٢٠ وقال عليه الصلاة والسلام: الناس ثلاثة أصناف: زاهد معتزم وصابر على مجاهدة هواه وراغب مُنقاد لشهوته. فالزاهد لا يعظّم ما آتاه الله فرحا به ولا يكثر على ما فاته أسفا. والصابر نازعته إلى الدنيا نفسه فقدعها وتطلّعت إلى لذّاتها فمنعها. والراغب دعته إلى الدنيا نفسه فأجابها وأمرته بإيثارها فأطاعها فدنّس بها عِرضه ووضع لها شرفه وضيّع لها آخرته.

٧.٢١ وقال عليه الصلاة والسلام: الجهاد ثلاثة: أوّل ما يُغلَب عليه من الجهاد اليدُ ثمّ اللسان ثمّ القلب. فإذا كان القلب لا يعرف معروفا ولا ينكر منكرا نُكس فجُعل أعلاه أسفله.

Each group has rights that the governor should uphold to the best of his ability. The governor should not transgress the sphere of God's mandate for him. He should train his soul to cleave to truth and forbearance in all things light or burdensome.

ʿAlī said: You can be one or the other: Either you have a generous soul and spend freely on what is right—and if so, why hold back from giving where you should? Why relinquish your noble qualities? Or you are a man who is afflicted with refusal. O how quickly people will stop soliciting you when they realize it is of no use! 7.18

ʿAlī said: The believer owes the believer seven things: He should greet him when he sees him, answer him when he calls, visit him when he is sick, follow his bier when he dies, wish for him what he wishes for himself, dislike for him what he dislikes for himself, and help him with money if he is in need. 7.19

ʿAlī said: People are of three types: A person who is resolute in rejecting worldliness, a person who is patient in fighting his passions, or a covetous person who is led by his desires. The person who rejects worldliness does not revel in what God has given him, nor wastes time regretting what he has not obtained. The patient man reins in the base soul that pulls him toward the world, and stops it from directing its gaze at worldly pleasures. But the covetous person answers his base soul when it calls him to the world and obeys it when it commands him to give the world preference. He sullies his honor by it, abases his character for it, and forfeits his afterlife for it. 7.20

ʿAlī said: Righteous struggle is of three types: The first to be overcome in this struggle is the hand, next the tongue, and next the heart. If the heart cannot recognize good or decry evil, it is upended and turned topsy-turvy. 7.21

٧.٢٢ وقال عليه الصلاة والسلام: ثلاثة وآثنان ليس لهم سادس: ملك يطير بجناحين ونبيّ أخذ الله عزّ وجلّ بضَبعيه وساع مجتهد وطالب يرجو ومقصّر في النار. اليمين والشمال مَضِلّة والطريق المنهج عليه باقي الكتاب وآثار النبوّة. هلك بعدُ مَن آدّعى وخاب من آفترى. إنّ الله عزّ وجلّ أدّب هذه الأمّة بالسيف والسوط ليس لأحد عند الإمام فيهما هَوادة. فآستتروا ببيوتكم وأصلحوا ذات بينكم.

٧.٢٣ وقال عليه الصلاة والسلام في توحيد الله عزّ وجلّ:

إنّ أوّل الديانة معرفة الله تعالى وكمال معرفته توحيده وكمال توحيده الإخلاص له والإخلاص له نفي الصفات عنه بشهادة كلّ صفة أنّها غير الموصوف وشهادة الموصوف أنّه غير الصفة وشهادتهما جميعا بالتنبيه على أنفسهما بالحَدَث الممتنِع من الأزل. فمَن وصف الله عزّ وجلّ فقد حدّه ومن حدّه فقد عدّه ومن عدّه فقد أبطل أزله ومن قال (كيف؟) فقد آستوصفه ومن قال (فيمَ؟) فقد ضمّنه ومن قال (علامَ؟) فقد أخلى منه ومن قال (أين؟) فقد نعته ومن قال (إلى؟) فقد عدّاه. عالم إذ لا معلوم وقادر إذ لا مقدور وربّ إذ لا مربوب ومصوِّر إذ لا مصوَّر. فكذلك ربّنا تبارك وتعالى وفوق ما يصفه الواصفون.

٧.٢٤ وقال عليه الصلاة والسلام في مثله من توحيد الله عزّ وجلّ: إنّ الله عزّ وجلّ واحد بغير تشبيه ودائم بغير تكوين خالق بغير كُلفة قائم بغير مَنصَبة موصوف بغير غاية معروف بغير محدوديّة باق بغير تسوية عزيز لم يزل قديم في القِدَم. زاغت القلوب لمَهابته وذَهِلت الألباب لعزّته وخضعت الرقاب لقدرته. لا يخطر على القلوب له مبلغ كُنهه ولا يَعتقد ضميرُ التسكين من التوهّم في إمضاء مشيئته.

ʿAlī said: There are three and two more, no sixth: An angel who flies on two wings; a prophet whom God has grasped by his two arms; and a man who strives to perform good deeds. A seeker who hopes for God's forgiveness; and a sinner who will go to hell. The tracks to the right and the left lead into the wilderness. The true path is found by following the remnants of the book and the traces of prophecy. Whosoever makes false claims will perish and whosoever slanders will flounder. God has disciplined this community by the sword and the whip. The leader must not shrink from applying these punishments. So keep to your homes, and make peace among yourselves. 7.22

Regarding the oneness of God, ʿAlī said: 7.23

The first part of religion is knowledge of God. Knowledge of him is perfected by the declaration of his oneness. The declaration of his oneness is perfected by sincere allegiance to him. Sincere allegiance to him is achieved by negating all attributes from him, by the testimony of every attribute that it is other than the thing described, the testimony of every described thing that it is other than the attribute, and the testimony of both of these that they have newly come into being and thus cannot be eternal. Whosoever describes God has circumscribed him. Whosoever circumscribes him has quantified him. And whosoever quantifies him has invalidated his eternity. Whosoever asks "How?" has sought a description of him. Whosoever asks "In what?" has confined him. Whosoever asks "On what?" has made another space empty of him. Whosoever asks "Where?" has defined him. Whosoever asks "Where to?" has made him cross over a path. God was knowledgeable when there was nothing to be known, powerful when there was nothing to wield power over, lord when there was no one to be lord over, creator when there was nothing created. This is our lord, blessed and elevated, beyond any description.

Another exposition by ʿAlī on God's oneness: God is one without likeness, everlasting without having come into being, creating without effort, existent without locatability, describable only as ceaseless, known only as unbounded, remaining forever without having been assembled, unceasingly mighty, ancient in primeval existence. Hearts quiver from awe of him. Minds are struck with wonder when contemplating his majesty. Heads bow to his power. Hearts cannot plumb the depth of his essence. The imagination 7.24

لا تبلغه العلماء بألبابها ولا أهل التفكّر بتدبير أمورها بأكثر ممّا وصف جلّ وعزّ به نفسه.

٧.٢٥ وقال عليه الصلاة والسلام: إنّ للمكروه غايات لا بدّ أن ينتهي إليها فينبغي للعاقل أن ينام لها إلى حين ٱنقضائها فإنّ إعمال الحيلة فيها قبل تصرّمها زيادة في مكروهها.

٧.٢٦ وقال عليه الصلاة والسلام: دارئ عن المؤمن ما ٱستطعت فإنّ ظهره حِمى الله عزّ وجلّ ونفسه كريمة على الله وله يكون ثواب الله سبحانه فظالمه خصم الله فلا يكن خصمك.

٧.٢٧ وقال عليه الصلاة والسلام: والله ليسبقنّ إلى جنّات عدن يوم القيامة أقوام ما كانوا بأكثر الناس صلاة ولا صياما ولا حجّا ولا عمرة ولكن على قدر عقولهم.

٧.٢٨ أخبرنا أبو القاسم عبد الملك بن الحسن بن إبراهيم قراءة عليه قال: أخبرنا أبو بكر محمّد بن القاسم بن فَهْد بن أحمد ابن عيسى بن صالح البزّاز قال: أخبرنا أبو الحسن أحمد بن مطرّف بن سوّار البُستيّ قال: حدّثنا العبّاس بن الفضل ابن شاذان قال: حدّثنا محمّد بن حميد وحجّاج بن حمزة بن سويد العِجليّ قالا: حدّثنا زيد بن الحُباب قال: حدّثنا عيسى بن الأشعث عن جُويبر عن الضحّاك عن النزّال بن سَبرة[١] عن عليّ بن أبي طالب عليه الصلاة والسلام قال:

مَن ٱبتدأ غذائه بالملح أذهب الله عنه سبعين بابا من الشرّ.
ومن أكل سبع تمرات عَجْوَة قتلت كلّ دابّة في بطنه.
ومن أكل إحدى وعشرين زبيبة حمراء لم ير في جسده شيئا يكرهه.
واللحم يُنبت اللّحم.
والثريد طعام العرب.
والشُّفارِجات تُعظّم البطن وتُرخي الأليتين.

١ هـ: تضيف (الهلالي ثم العامري).

cannot adequately grasp the execution of his will. Learned scholars with their intellects and thinkers with their powers of prediction know nothing of the Almighty beyond what he has described of himself.

7.25 ʿAlī said: All adversities move toward an inexorable culmination. Until then, the intelligent man should sleep. Attempts to stop hardships before they have run their course will only increase their harm.

7.26 ʿAlī said: Defend the believer as much as you are able, for God protects his back, holds his soul dear, and has prepared a reward for him. Whosoever oppresses the believer will have God as adversary. Do not make God your adversary.

7.27 ʿAlī said: By God, a group of people will enter the Garden of Eden first on the day of resurrection. These people did not pray or fast more than others, nor perform the hajj or ʿumrah pilgrimage to Mecca more often than others. The honor is due to the worth of their minds.

7.28 Abū l-Qāsim ʿAbd al-Malik ibn al-Ḥasan ibn Ibrāhīm reported to us, saying: Abū Bakr Muḥammad ibn al-Qāsim ibn Fahd ibn Aḥmad ibn ʿĪsā ibn Ṣāliḥ al-Bazzāz reported to us, saying: Abū l-Ḥasan Aḥmad ibn Muṭarrif ibn Sawwār al-Bustī reported to us, saying: Al-ʿAbbās ibn al-Faḍl ibn Shādhān recounted to us, saying: Muḥammad ibn Ḥamīd and Ḥajjāj ibn Ḥamza ibn Suwayd al-ʿIjlī recounted to us, saying: Zayd ibn al-Ḥubāb recounted to us, saying: ʿĪsā ibn al-Ashʿath recounted to us, from Juwaybir, from al-Ḍaḥḥāk, from al-Nazzāl ibn Sabrah, from ʿAlī ibn Abī Ṭālib, who said:

Begin your meal with a taste of salt and God will remove from you seventy varieties of harm.

Eat seven Medinese *ʿajwah* dates daily. They will kill any worms in your stomach.

Eat twenty-one red raisins daily and you will not see any illness in your body.

Meat produces meat.

Tharīd porridge is the staple of the Arabs.

Laden trays distend the stomach and swell the buttocks.

ولحم البقر داء وشحمها[1] دواء ولبنها شفاء.

والشحم يُخرج من الداء مثله.

والسمك يذيب الجسد.

ولن تستشفي النُّفَساء بشيءٍ أفضل من الرُّطَب.

والمرء يسعى بجَدّه والسيف يقطع بحدّه.

من أراد البقاء، ولا بقاء، فليباكر الغداء وليُقِلّ غِشيان النساء وليخفّف الرداء.

قيل: يا أمير المؤمنين وما خفّة الرداء؟ قال: قلّة الدَّين.

١ هـ: (وسمنها).

The flesh of the cow brings disease, its fat cures, and its milk heals.

Animal fat removes its measure in disease from your body.

Fish emaciates.

There is nothing better for healing after childbirth than fresh dates.

Man strives with his luck, until the sword cuts with its edge.

While no one lives forever, whosoever wishes to live long should rise early in the morning, abstain from too much sex, and wear a light robe.

ʿAlī was asked, What do you mean by a light robe, commander of the faithful? Freedom from excessive debt, he replied.

الباب الثامن

في أدعيته ومناجاته

أخبرني أبو عبد الله محمّد بن منصور بن شِيكان التستريّ مجيزا قال: أخبرنا محمّد بن الحسن بن غراب قال: حدّثنا القاضي أحمد بن محمّد قال: حدّثنا القاضي موسى بن إسحٰق قال: حدّثنا عبد الله بن أبي شيبة قال: حدّثنا محمّد بن فضيل عن عبد الله الأسديّ قال: ٨.١

كان أمير المؤمنين يقول في مناجاته:

إلٰهي لولا ما جهلت من أمري ما شكوت عثراتي ولولا ما ذكرت من الإفراط ما سفحت عبراتي. إلٰهي فآمحُ مُثبِتات العثرات بمرسَلات العبرات وهَبْ كثير السيئات لقليل الحسنات. ٨.١.١

إلٰهي إن كنت لا ترحم إلّا المُجِدّين في طاعتك فإلى من يفزع المقصّرون؟ وإن كنت لا تقبل إلّا من المجتهدين فإلى من يلتجئ المخطئون؟ وإن كنت لا تكرم إلّا أهل الإحسان فكيف يصنع المسيئون؟ وإن كان لا يفوز يوم الحشر إلّا المتّقون فبمن يستغيث المذنبون؟ ٨.١.٢

إلٰهي إن كان لا يجوز على الصراط إلّا من أجازته براءة عمله فأنّى بالجواز لمن لم يتب إليك قبل دنوّ[1] أجله؟ ٨.١.٣

إلٰهي إن حُجب عن موحِّديك نظر تغمّد لجناياتهم أوقعهم غضبك بين المشركين في كرباتهم. إلٰهي فأوجب لنا بالإسلام مذخور هباتك وآستصف لنا ما كدّرته الجرائم بصفو صِلاتك. ٨.١.٤

إلٰهي ارحم غربتنا إذا تضمّنتنا بطون لحودنا وعُمّيت علينا باللبِن سقوف بيوتنا وأُضجعنا على الأيمان في قبورنا وخُلفنا فُرادى في أضيق المضاجع وصرعتنا المنايا ٨.١.٥

١ ي: سقطت (دنوّ). م: سقطت في المتن وأضيفت في الحاشية (حلول). ع: (آنقضاء).

Chapter 8

Prayers and Supplications

Abū ʿAbd Allāh Muḥammad ibn Manṣūr ibn Shīkān al-Tustarī reported to me, authorizing me to transmit the report, saying: Muḥammad ibn al-Ḥasan ibn Ghurāb reported to us, saying: Judge Aḥmad ibn Muḥammad recounted to us, saying: Judge Mūsā ibn Isḥāq recounted to us, saying: ʿAbd Allāh ibn Abī Shaybah recounted to us, saying: Muḥammad ibn Fuḍayl recounted to us, from ʿAbd Allāh al-Asadī, saying: 8.1

The commander of the faithful ʿAlī would say in his supplications:

God, if I were not ignorant of my affairs I would not complain about my misfortunes. If I did not recollect my transgressions, I would not shed copious tears. God, wash away the traces of my misfortunes with my flowing tears, and grant me forgiveness for my many offences in lieu of my paltry good deeds. 8.1.1

God, if you are merciful only to those who are assiduous in obeying you, where will reprobates turn for sanctuary? If you accept only those who strive, where will transgressors take refuge? If you are generous only to those who perform beautiful deeds, what will wrongdoers do? If none but the pious win on the day of resurrection, where will sinners seek safe haven? 8.1.2

God, if only the innocent are allowed to cross the celestial bridge, what will happen to those who did not repent before their time ran out? 8.1.3

God, if those who profess your oneness transgress and you veil from them your protective gaze, your wrath will fling them into the pit of catastrophes alongside those who assign partners to you. God, by Islam's grace, bestow on us your treasured gifts. Purify with your forgiveness what our crimes have sullied. 8.1.4

God, have mercy on our exile when the bellies of our tombs embrace us, when the solid roofs of our new homes hem us in with crushing darkness, when we are laid to rest on our sides in the grave, when we are made to sleep alone in the narrowest of beds, when the fates prostrate us in the vilest of 8.1.5

في أنكر المصارع وصرنا في ديار قوم كأنّها مأهولة وهي منهم بَلاقِع.

٨.١.٦ إلٰهي فإذا جئناك عُراة مغبرّة من ثرى الأجداث رؤوسنا وشاحبة من تراب الملاحد وجوهنا وخاشعة من أهوال القيامة أبصارنا وجائعة من طول القيام بطوننا وبادية هناك للعيون سوآتنا ومُثقلة من أعباء الأوزار ظهورنا ومشغولين بما قد دهانا عن أهلينا وأولادنا فلا تضاعف علينا المصائب بإعراض وجهك الكريم عنّا وسلب عائدة ما مَثّله الرجاء منّا.

٨.١.٧ إلٰهي ما حَنّت هذه العيون إلى بكائها ولا جادت متسرِّبة بمائها ولا شهرت بنحيب المثكِلات فَقْد عزائها إلّا لما سلف من نفورها وإبائها وما دعاها إليه عواقب بلائها. وأنت القادر يا كريم على كشف غمّائها.

٨.١.٨ إلٰهي ثَبِّت حلاوة ما يستعذبه لساني من النطق في بلاغته بزهادة ما يرفعه قلبي من النصح في دلالته.

٨.١.٩ إلٰهي أمرت بالمعروف وأنت أولى به من المأمورين وأمرت بصلة السُّؤال وأنت خير المسؤولين.

٨.١.١٠ إلٰهي كيف يُقبل بنا اليأس عن الإمساك كما لَهجنا بطِلابه وقد ٱدّرعنا من تأميلنا إيّاك أسبغ أثوابه؟

٨.١.١١ إلٰهي إذا تلونا من صفاتك ﴿شَدِيدُ ٱلعِقَابِ﴾ أشفقنا وإذا تلونا منها ﴿ٱلغَفُورُ ٱلرَّحِيمُ﴾ فرحنا. فنحن بين أمرين لا يؤمننا سخطك ولا تؤيسنا رحمتك.

٨.١.١٢ إلٰهي إن قصرت بنا مساعينا عن ٱستحقاق نظرك فما قصرت رحمتك بنا عن دفاع نقمتك.

٨.١.١٣ إلٰهي كيف تفرح بصحبة الدنيا صدورنا وكيف تلتئم في عمرانها أمورنا وكيف يخلص فيها سرورنا وكيف يملكنا باللّهو واللعب غرورنا وقد دعتنا بٱقتراب آجالنا قبورنا؟ إلٰهي كيف نبتهج بدار حُفرت لنا فيها حفائر صَرعتها وقلّبتنا بأيدي المنايا حبائل غَدرتها وجرّعتنا مكرَهين جُرَع مَرارتها ودلّتنا العبر على ٱنقطاع عيشتها؟ إلٰهي فإليك نلتجئ من مكايد خُدعتها وبك نستعين على عبور قَنطرتها وبك تستعصم الجوارح على

prostrations, when we take up residence in an abode which appears inhabited, but which is a true deadland.

8.1.6 God, when we come to you naked, our heads covered with the earth of the grave, faces pale from the dirt of the tomb, eyes lowered from the terrors of the resurrection, bellies hungry from prolonged standing, private parts uncovered and visible to all eyes, backs burdened with the heavy weight of sins, when we are too preoccupied with our own travails to think of our spouses and children—do not multiply our suffering by turning away your noble face from us, or by seizing from us the gift of our hope in you.

8.1.7 God, my eyes have not been moved to weeping, they have not been liberal with streaming tears, and have not exhibited the grief of a wailing, bereaved mother, except because of their prior avoidance of you and scorn for your religion, and because of the consequences of their trials. Power to alleviate their suffering, generous one, rests with you alone.

8.1.8 God, harmonize my honeyed tongue's eloquent speech with the lack of worldliness taught to my heart by its guiding counselor.

8.1.9 God, you commanded us to perform good deeds but are worthier of performing good deeds than we. You commanded us to give to petitioners, but you are the best of those petitioned.

8.1.10 God, how could despair make us hold back from asking you for what we have always asked, when our hope in you has clothed us with an all-protective armor?

8.1.11 God, when we read in the Qurʾan that «severe of punishment»[67] is one of your attributes we are afraid, and when we read that «forgiving, merciful»[68] is among them we rejoice. We are constantly between two states: Your wrath does not allow us to be reassured, and your mercy does not allow us to lose hope.

8.1.12 God, even if our efforts are too little for us to deserve your kindly gaze, yet your mercy does not fall short of defending us from your punishment.

8.1.13 God, how can our hearts take pleasure in this world, how can our affairs in it prosper, our joy in it be pure, or our delusions lead us to play and frolic, when our graves beckon to us with the approaching end of our lives? God, how can we take joy in an abode where the pit into which it will pitch us is already dug, and its deceptions' snares toss us into fate's hands? In a world that makes us swallow gulp after gulp of its bitter draught, and whose lessons prove to us that our lives too will be cut off? God, it is to you we turn from the trickeries of its deception. It is you we ask for help in crossing its bridge.

خلاف شهوتها وبك نستكشف جلابيب حيرتها وبك يقوّم من القلوب ٱستصعاب جهالتها.

٨.١.١٤ إلٰهي كيف للدُّور أن تمنع من فيها من طوارق الرزايا وقد أُصيب في كلّ دار سهم من أسهم المنايا.

٨.١.١٥ إلٰهي ما نُفجَع بأنفسنا عن الديار إن لم توحشنا هنالك من مُرافَقة الأبرار. إلٰهي ما تضرّنا فُرقة الإخوان والقرابات إذا قرّبتنا منك ياذا العطيّات.

٨.١.١٦ إلٰهي ٱرحمني إذا ٱنقطع من الدنيا أثري وٱمّحى من المخلوقين ذكري وصرت في المَنسيّين كمن قد نُسي. إلٰهي كبرت سِنّي ودَقّ عظمي ورقّ جلدي ونال الدهر منّي وٱقترب أجلي ونفِدت أيّامي وذهبت شهوتي وبقيت تَبِعتي وٱمتحَت محاسني وبلي جسمي وتقطّعت أوصالي وتفرّقت أعضائي. إلٰهي فٱرحمني.

٨.١.١٧ إلٰهي أفحمتني ذنوبي وٱنقطعت مقالتي فلا حجّة لي ولا عذر فأنا المُقرّ بجرمي والمعترف بإساءتي والأسير بذنبي والمرتهَن بعملي المتهوِّر في خطيئتي المتحيّر عن قصدي المنقطَع بي. إلٰهي فصلّ على محمّد وعلى آل محمّد وٱرحمني برحمتك وتجاوز عنّي.

٨.١.١٨ إلٰهي إن كان صغر في جنب طاعتك عملي فقد كبر في جنب رجائك أملي. إلٰهي كيف أنقلب بالخيبة من عندك محروما وكان ظنّي بجودك أن تقلبني مرحوما. كلّا إنّي لم أسلّط على حسن ظنّي بك قُنوط ظنّ الآيسين فلا تُبطل صدق رجائي لك بين الآملين.

٨.١.١٩ إلٰهي إن كنّا مرحومين فإنّا نبكي على ما ضيّعناه في طاعتك ما تستوجبه وإن كنّا محرومين فإنّا نبكي إذا فاتنا من جوارك ما نطلبه.

٨.١.٢٠ إلٰهي عظم جرمي إذ كنت المبارِز به وكبر ذنبي إذ كنت المطالِب به إلّا أنّي إذا ذكرت كثرة ذنوبي وعظيم غفرانك وجدت الحاصل لي بينهما عفو رضوانك.

It is from you that our bodies seek aid in battling its temptations. It is you whose support we entreat in stripping off the robes of its perplexities. It is you who will remove the hard shell of ignorance with which it has covered our hearts.

8.1.14 God, how can our homes protect us from calamities, when each home conceals within its walls an arrow from death's quiver.

8.1.15 God, we shall not panic at being removed from the familiarity of our homes if you grant us the companionship of the pious in our next dwelling. God, separation from brothers and relatives will not hurt us if you bring us close to you, O giver of bounties!

8.1.16 God, have mercy on me when all traces of me have become erased from this world, when any recollection of me has been wiped from the memories of its people, when I am entirely forgotten. God, I am advanced in age, my bones have become brittle, my skin fragile, time has taken its toll on me, the end of my life has drawn near, and my days have run out. My desires are gone, but my sins remain. My beauties are obliterated, my body has decayed, my joints have disintegrated, and my limbs have fallen apart. God, have mercy on me!

8.1.17 God, sins have silenced me. My words have come to an end. I have no argument and no excuse. I acknowledge my crime and confess my wickedness. I am a prisoner of my sins, pledged to my heinous deeds, someone who has rushed headlong into iniquity. I am bewildered about my purpose, cut off from all. God, shower your blessings on Muḥammad and his progeny, and cover me in your mercy.[69] Forgive me.

8.1.18 God, even if my deeds are tiny next to what is due to you, my hope has grown large in the shelter of my confidence in you. God, how could I return from your presence disappointed and deprived? Never! I fully expect that your generosity will send me back laden with the favor of your mercy. I do not let hopeless despair crush my expectations of your goodness, so do not quash my confidence in you. I place all my hopes in you.

8.1.19 God, if you have mercy on us, we shall weep at our shortcomings in rendering you the obedience you deserve. If you deprive us of your mercy, we shall weep at the loss of the shelter we sought in you.

8.1.20 God, my offence is great for I have challenged you. My sin is grave and you will hold me accountable. But when I weigh the multitude of my sins against the immensity of your forgiveness, I find the balance in favor of your pardon.

إلٰهي إن أوحشتني الخطايا من محاسن لطفك فقد آنسني اليقين بمكارم عطفك. ٨.١.٢١

إلٰهي إن أنامتني الغفلة عن الإستعداد للقائك فقد أنبهتني المعرفة بكريم آلائك. ٨.١.٢٢

إلٰهي إن عزب لبّي عن تقويم ما يُصلحني فما عزب إيقاني بنظرك فيما ينفعني. ٨.١.٢٣

إلٰهي جئتك ملهوفا قد أُلبست عَدَمي وفاقتي وأقامني مقام الأذلّين بين يديك ذلّ حاجتي. ٨.١.٢٤

إلٰهي كَرُمتَ فأكرمني إذ كنت من سُؤَّالك وجد بمعروفك فاخلطني بأهل نوالك. ٨.١.٢٥

إلٰهي أصبحت على باب من أبواب مِنَحك سائلا وعن التعرّض لغيرك بالمسألة عادلا. وليس من جميل امتنانك أن تردّ سائلا ملهوفا ومضطرّا لانتظار أمرك مألوفا.[1] ٨.١.٢٦

إلٰهي أقمتُ على قَنطَرَة الأخطار مبلُوًّا بالأعمال وبالإعتبار فأنا الهالكُ إن لم تُعِنْ عليها بتخفيفِ الآصار. ٨.١.٢٧

إلٰهي أمِنْ أهل الشقاء خلقتني فأُطيل بكائي؟ أم من أهل السعادة فأبشّر رجائي؟ ٨.١.٢٨

إلٰهي لولم تَهدني إلى الإسلام ما اهتديت ولو لم تُطلق لساني بدعائك ما دعوت ولو لم ترزقني الأيمان بك ما آمنت ولو لم تعرّفني حلاوة نعمتك ما عرفت ولو لم تبيّن شديد عقابك ما استجرت. ٨.١.٢٩

إلٰهي إن أقعدني التخلّف عن السبق مع الأبرار فقد أقامتني الثقة بك على مَدارج الأخيار. ٨.١.٣٠

إلٰهي نفسا أعززتَها بتأييد إيمانك كيف تُذلّها بين أطباق نيرانك؟ إلٰهي لسانا كسوته من وحدانيّتك أنقى أثوابها كيف تُهوي إليه من النار شُعلات التهابها؟ ٨.١.٣١

إلٰهي كلّ مكروب فإليك يلتجي وكلّ محزون فإيّاك[2] يرتجي. ٨.١.٣٢

إلٰهي سمع العابدون بجزيل ثوابك فخشعوا وسمع المذنبون بسعة رحمتك فقنعوا وسمع المُولّون عن القصد بجودك فرجعوا وسمع المجرمون بسعة غفرانك فطمعوا حتّى ازدحمت عصائب العصاة من عبادك ببابك وعَجّ منهم إليك عجيج الضّجيج بالدعاء في بلادك. ولكلّ أمل ساق صاحبه إليك مُحتاجا ولكلّ قلب تركه يا ربِّ ٨.١.٣٣

١ ع: (لانتظار خيرك المألوف).

٢ هـ: تضيف (يسأل و).

God, when my errors distance me from your gracious kindness, conviction in your generous affection brings me comfort. 8.1.21

God, when heedlessness lulls me to sleep instead of preparing for my meeting with you, awareness of your generous favors rouses me. 8.1.22

God, even if my mind has deserted me in setting right my affairs, my conviction that you are concerned for my well-being has not. 8.1.23

God, I have come to you in deep sorrow, robed in destitution and poverty. The degradation that my need has prompted has placed me before you as the humblest of the humble. 8.1.24

God, you are generous, so be generous to me, one of your mendicants. Be munificent with your gifts, and place me among the people who receive them. 8.1.25

God, I stand this morning as a mendicant at your favor's door, having turned away from all but you. Your beautiful kindness cannot dismiss a mournful beggar, one who must wait upon your command. 8.1.26

God, I stand at the bridge of dangers, on trial for immoral deeds and unheeded lessons. If you do not lighten my burden and help me cross I will perish. 8.1.27

God, have you created me as one of the wretched, who weeps long and hard? Or as one of the blissful, awaiting fulfillment of hopes? 8.1.28

God, if you had not guided me to Islam I would never have been guided. If you had not loosened my tongue in prayer to you I would never have prayed. If you had not blessed me with belief in you I would never have believed. If you had not acquainted me with the sweetness of your favors I would never have known them. If you had not elucidated for me the terrors of your punishment I would never have sought protection. 8.1.29

God, my lack of deeds has kept me from being at the forefront with the pious, yet my trust in you has placed me upon the path of the upright. 8.1.30

God, how can you debase between the layers of your fire a soul you have honored with belief? God, how can you scorch with its blazing flames a tongue you have clothed with your oneness's spotless robes? 8.1.31

God, every distressed person turns to you for succor. Every sorrowful soul puts his hopes in you. 8.1.32

God, worshipers hear of your bountiful reward and bow down. Sinners hear of your vast mercy and are comforted. Strayers hear of your generosity and turn back. Offenders hear of your vast forgiveness and have hope. Throngs of wrongdoers from among your servants crowd your door, and a 8.1.33

وجيف الخوف منك مُهتاجا فأنت المسئول الذي لا تَسودّ لديه وجوه المَطالب ولا يردّ نائله[1] قاطعات المَعاطب.

٨.١.٣٤ إلٰهي إذا أخطات طريق النظر لنفسي بما فيه كرامتها فقد أصبت طريق الفزع إليك بما فيه سلامتها.

٨.١.٣٥ إلٰهي إن كانت نفسي ٱستسعدتني متمرِّدة على ما يُرديها فقد ٱستسعدتها الآن بدعائك على ما يُنجيها.

٨.١.٣٦ إلٰهي إن قسطت في الحكم على نفسي بما فيه حسرتها فقد أقسطت في تعريفي إيّاها من رحمتك أسباب رأفتها.

٨.١.٣٧ إلٰهي إن قطعني قلّة الزاد في المسير إليك فقد وصلته بذخائر ما أعددته من فضل تعويلي عليك.

٨.١.٣٨ إلٰهي إذا ذكرت رحمتك ضحكت لها عيون وسائلي وإذا ذكرت سخطك بكت له عيون مسائلي. إلٰهي أدعوك دعاء من لم يرجُ غيرك في دعائه وأرجوك رجاء من لم يقصد غيرك في رجائه. إلٰهي كيف أُسكت بالإفحام لسان ضراعتي وقد أقلقني ما أبهم عليّ من مصير عاقبتي.

٨.١.٣٩ إلٰهي قد علمتَ حاجة جسمي إلى ما تكفّلت له من الرزق في حياتي وعرفت قلّة ٱستغنائي عنه في الجنّة بعد وفاتي فيا من سمح لي به متفضّلا في العاجل لا تمنَعْنيه يوم فاقتي إليه في الآجل.

٨.١.٤٠ إلٰهي إن عذّبتني فعبد خلقته لما أردت فعذّبته وإن رحمتني فعبد ألفيته مسيئا فأنجيته.

٨.١.٤١ إلٰهي لا ٱحتراس من الذنب إلّا بعصمتك ولا وصول إلى عمل الخيرات إلّا بمشيئتك فكيف لي بإفادة ما سلبتني فيه مشيئتك؟ وكيف لي بٱحتراس من الذنب ما لم تدركني فيه عصمتك؟

٨.١.٤٢ إلٰهي أنت دللتني على سؤال الجنّة قبل معرفتها فأقبلت النفس بعد العرفان على

١ ع: (ولم تزر بنزيله).

clamorous uproar of prayer arises in your lands. Each person comes with a wish that has driven him to you in his need. Each comes with a heart, lord, that fear's palpitations have left bewildered. You are the one petitioned, at whose door entreaty's face is never blackened, whose seeker destruction's sword never turns away.

8.1.34 God, if I have missed the honorable path of looking out for my soul, I have found the safe path of seeking refuge in you.

8.1.35 God, if my soul has found me blithely bent on doing things that will destroy it, I have delighted it now by praying to you to save it.

8.1.36 God, if I have oppressed my soul by consigning it to sorrowful regret in the hereafter, I have also shown it justice by describing to it your mercy and the reasons why you will be kind.

8.1.37 God, the paucity of my provisions cuts me off from journeying to you, but I augment them now with stores of copious tears.

8.1.38 God, when I think of your mercy, my entreaty's eyes smile. When I think of your wrath, my supplication's eyes weep. God, I pray to you, never having prayed to any but you. I place my hopes in you, never having placed my hopes in any but you. God, how do I silence my solicitation's tongue, when I am frightened, not knowing what my end will be?

8.1.39 God, you know my body's dependence on your sustenance in this life. You know that I cannot do without your care in paradise after my death. God, you who have graciously granted me sustenance now, do not forbid it to me tomorrow, on the day I am most in need of it.

8.1.40 God, if you punish me, it is because I am your servant whom you have created for your purpose and punished. If you have mercy on me, it is because I am your servant whom you have found sinful yet saved.

8.1.41 God, there is no way to avoid sinning except by your grace. There is no way to do good except through your will. How can I bring forth something your will has stripped away? How can I stop sinning if your grace does not extend to me?

8.1.42 God, you taught me to ask for heaven before I knew of it; thus my soul learned of it and asked for it. Will you teach your supplicants to ask for your grace yet forbid it to them? You are generous, praiseworthy in all that you do, mighty and generous one. God, if I am unworthy of being granted the

مسئلتها. أفتدلّ على خيرك السُّؤّال ثمّ تمنعه وأنت الكريم المحمود في كلّ ما تصنعه يا ذا الجلال والإكرام. إلٰهي إن كنت غير مستأهل لما أرجو من رحمتك فأنت أهل أن تجود على المذنبين بفضل سعتك.

إلٰهي نفسي قائمة بين يديك وقد أظلّها حسن توكّلها عليك فٱصنع بي ما أنت أهله وتغمّدني برحمتك. ٨.١.٤٣

إلٰهي إن كان دنا أجلي ولم يقرّبني منك عملي فقد جعلت الإعتراف بالذنب وسائل عللي. فإن عفوت فمن أولى منك بذلك؟ وإن عذّبت فمن أعدل منك في الحكم هنالك؟ ٨.١.٤٤

إلٰهي إنّك لم تزل بارًّا بي أيّام حياتي فلا تقطع برّك بي بعد وفاتي. ٨.١.٤٥

إلٰهي كيف آيَسُ من حسن نظرك بعد مماتي وأنت لم تولِني إلّا الجميل في حياتي؟ ٨.١.٤٦

إلٰهي إنّ ذنوبي قد أخافتني ومحبّتي لك قد أجارتني فتوَلَّ في أمري ما أنت أهله وعُد بفضلك على من غَمَره جهله يا من لا تخفى عليه خافية صلّ على محمّد وعلى آل محمّد وٱغفر لي ما خفي عن الناس من أمري. ٨.١.٤٧

إلٰهي ليس ٱعتذاري إليك ٱعتذار من يَستغني عن قبول عذره فٱقبل عذري يا خير من ٱعتذر إليه المسيئون. ٨.١.٤٨

إلٰهي إنّك لو أردت إهانتي لم تهدني ولو أردت فضيحتي لم تعافِني فمتّعني بما له هديتني وأدم لي ما به سترتني. ٨.١.٤٩

إلٰهي لولا ما ٱقترفت من الذنوب ما خِفت عقابك ولولا ما عرفت من كرمك ما رجوت ثوابك وأنت أكرم الأكرمين بتحقيق آمال الآملين وأرحم من ٱسترُحِم في تجاوزه عن المذنبين. ٨.١.٥٠

إلٰهي نفسي تمنّيني بأنّك تغفر لي فأكرم بها أمنيّتي فقد بشّرت بعفوك وصدق كرمك مبشِّرات تَمنّيها وهب لي بجودك مقصِّرات تَجَنّيها. ٨.١.٥١

إلٰهي ألقتني الحسنات بين جودك وكرمك وألقتني السيئات بين عفوك ومغفرتك وقد رجوت أن لا يَضيع بين ذَيْنِ وذِين مسيء ومحسن. ٨.١.٥٢

mercy I ask you for, it is still worthy of your generosity that you bestow your grace upon sinners.

God, my soul stands before you, securely shaded by its beautiful trust in you. Do with me, then, what is worthy of you and cover me with your mercy! 8.1.43

God, I have neared the end of my life without having performed deeds that would bring me close to you. But I have proffered a confession of my sins as intercessor for forgiveness. If you forgive, there is none worthier of it than you. If you punish, there is none fairer in judgment than you. 8.1.44

God, you have been kind to me all the days of my life. Do not cut off your kindness to me after I die. 8.1.45

God, why should I despair of your kindly gaze after my death, when you have shown me nothing but good during my life? 8.1.46

God, my sins frighten me, but I know that my love for you gives me protection. Discharge my affairs in the manner of which you are worthy. Assist with your grace one whose ignorance is total. God from whom nothing is hidden: Bless Muḥammad and the progeny of Muḥammad, and forgive me the sins I have concealed from people. 8.1.47

God, I proffer you my excuses, having no recourse if you do not accept them. Accept my apology, O kindest of all forgivers. 8.1.48

God, if you had wanted to debase me, you would not have guided me. If you had wanted to dishonor me, you would not have preserved me. So keep me in the faith to which you have guided me, and continue to conceal my faults. 8.1.49

God, if not for the many sins I have committed, I would not fear your punishment. If not for your generosity, I would not hope for your reward. You are the most generous of all in fulfilling the desires of the hopeful. You are the most merciful of all whose mercy is petitioned by sinners seeking pardon. 8.1.50

God, my soul encourages me to hope for forgiveness from you. Honor my hope, for its heralds have given glad tidings of your pardon and bounty. You are generous, so forgive my soul's wicked iniquities. 8.1.51

God, my good deeds have placed me between your bounty and generosity, and my bad deeds between your pardon and forgiveness. My hope is strong that between these two and those two, a man who has done both good and bad will not perish. 8.1.52

إلٰهي إذا شهد لي الإيمان بتوحيدك وٱنطلق لساني بتمجيدك ودلّني القرآن على فضائل جودك فكيف لا يبتهج رجائي بحسن موعودك؟ ٨.١.٥٣

إلٰهي تَتابُع إحسانك يدلّني على حسن نظرك فكيف يشقى ٱمرؤ أوليته منك حسن النظر؟ إلٰهي إن نظرت إليّ بالهلكة عيون سخطك فما نامت عن ٱستنقاذي منها عيون رحمتك. ٨.١.٥٤

إلٰهي إن عرّضني ذنبي لعقابك فقد أدناني رجائي من ثوابك. ٨.١.٥٥

إلٰهي إن غفرت فبفضلك وإن عذّبت فبعدلك فيا من لا يُرجى إلا فضله ولا يُخاف إلا عدله صلّ على محمّد وعلى آل محمّد وٱمنن عليّ بفضلك ولا تَستقصِ عليّ عدلك. ٨.١.٥٦

إلٰهي خلقت لي جسما وجعلت لي فيه آلات أطيعك بها وأعصيك وأغضبك بها وأرضيك وجعلت لي من نفسي داعيا إلى الشهوات وأسكنتني دارا مُلئت من الآفات وقلت لي ٱزدجر فبك أعتصم وبك أحترز وأستوفقك لما يرضيك وأسألك فإنّ سؤالي لا يُحفيك. ٨.١.٥٧

إلٰهي لو عرفت ٱعتذارا وتنصّلا هو أبلغ من الإعتراف به لأتيته فهب لي ذنبي بالإعتراف ولا تردّني في طلبي بالخيبة عند الإنصراف. ٨.١.٥٨

إلٰهي كأنّي بنفسي قد ٱضطجعت في حُفرتها وٱنصرف عنها المشيّعون من عشيرتها وناداها من شفير القبر ذو مودّتها و رحِمها المُعادي لها في الحياة عند صَرعتها ولم يَخْفَ على الناظرين إليها ذلّ فاقتها ولا على من قد رآها توسّدت الثرى عَجزحيلتها فقلت: ملائكتي قريب نأى عنه الأقربون وبعيد جفاه الأهلون وخذله المؤمّلون نزل بي قريبا وأصبح في اللحد غريبا وقد كان لي في دار الدنيا راعيا ولنظري إليه في هذا اليوم راجيا. فتُحسن عند ذلك ضيافتي وتكون أشفق عليّ من أهلي وقرابتي. ٨.١.٥٩

God, my faith testifies to your oneness, my tongue speaks of your glory, and the Qur'an tells me to believe in your munificent bounties. How could my hope not take joy in your beautiful promise? 8.1.53

God, your bounties come to me one after another, demonstrating your kindly regard. How could I be wretched? God, even if your wrath looks at me with a view to destroy, your mercy neither slumbers nor is neglectful of saving me from it. 8.1.54

God, my sin exposes me to your punishment, yet my hope draws me in to your reward. 8.1.55

God, if you forgive, it is because of your grace. If you punish, it is because of your justice. O gracious one, no grace is besought but yours, no justice is feared but yours. Bless Muḥammad and the progeny of Muḥammad, and bestow upon me your grace. Do not push me to the full limits of your justice. 8.1.56

God, you have created a body for me, placing in it instruments with which I obey or disobey you, through which I anger or please you. You placed in my body a base soul that calls me toward animal desires, housed me in a place filled with calamities, and said to me: "Stay back!" It is from you, then, that I seek protection against sinning. It is in you that I seek refuge. I ask your guidance in doing what will please you. I supplicate to you. My supplication does not tire you. 8.1.57

God, if I knew of an apology or defense more effective than confession I would have come to you with it. I confess my sins, so pardon them. Do not send me back empty-handed. 8.1.58

God, I see myself lying in the tomb: My family who came to bury me have left; friends call to me from the rim of the grave; relatives who had enmity for me in life look down on me, now prostrate. Now that the earth is my pillow, my degradation is not concealed to any who look, nor my helplessness in finding a way out. You say: "Angels, look! Here is a man whose relatives have distanced themselves from him. His kinfolk have rejected him and sent him far away. All those in whom he had placed his hopes have cast him off. He has come close to me, a stranger in the grave. In the worldly abode he was conscious of me, and today he is hopeful of my kindly regard." At that time, you, God, will proffer me your beautiful hospitality. You will be more compassionate to me than my family and my relatives. 8.1.59

إلٰهي سترت عليّ في الدنيا ذنوبا ولم تظهرها فلا تفضحني يوم ألقاك على رؤوس العالمين وآسترها عليّ هنالك يا أرحم الراحمين. ٨.١.٦٠

إلٰهي لو طبّقت ذنوبي بين السماء والأرض وخرقت النجوم وبلغت أسفل الثرى ما ردّني اليأس عن توقّع غفرانك ولا صرفني القنوط عن آنتظار رضوانك. ٨.١.٦١

إلٰهي سعت نفسي إليك لنفسي تستوهبها وفتحت أفواهَ آمال[١] لا تستوجبها فهب لها ما سألت وجد لها بما طلبت فإنّك أكرم الأكرمين بتحقيق أمل الآملين. ٨.١.٦٢

إلٰهي قد أصبت من الذنوب ما عرفت وأسرفت على نفسي بما قد علمت فآجعلني عبدا لك إمّا طائعا أكرمتني وإمّا عاصيا فرحمتني. ٨.١.٦٣

إلٰهي دعوتك بالدعاء الذي علّمتني فلا تحرمني من جِبائك الذي عرّفتني فمن النعمة أن هديتني لحسن دعائك ومن تمامها أن توجب لي محمود جزائك. ٨.١.٦٤

إلٰهي آنتظرت عفوك كما ينتظر المسيؤون ولست أيْئَس من رحمتك التي يتوقّعها المحسنون. إلٰهي جودك بسط أملي وشكرك قَبِل عملي فصلّ على محمّد وعلى آل محمّد وبشّرني بلقائك وأعظم رجائي لجزائك. إلٰهي أنت الكريم الذي لا يَخيب لديك أمل الآملين ولا يبطل عندك سَبْق السابقين. ٨.١.٦٥

إلٰهي إن كنت لم أستحقّ معروفك ولم أستوجبه فكن أنت أهل التفضّل به عليّ فالكريم لم يضع معروفه عند كلّ من يستوجبه. ٨.١.٦٦

إلٰهي مسكنتي لا يجبُرها إلّا عطاؤك وأمنيّتي لا يغنيها إلّا نعماؤك. ٨.١.٦٧

إلٰهي أستوفقك لما يُدنيني منك وأعوذ بك ممّا يَصرفني عنك. ٨.١.٦٨

إلٰهي أحبّ الأمور إلى نفسي وأعوَدها عليّ منفعة ما أرشدتها بهدايتك إليه ودللتها برحمتك عليه فآستعملها بذلك عنّي إذ أنت أرحم بها منّي. ٨.١.٦٩

---

١ م: (أملها). ي: (ملها). وسقطت فيهما (لا) التالية.

God, you have concealed my sins in this world and not revealed them. Do not shame me on the day I meet you before all the people of the world. Conceal my sins there too, merciful one. 8.1.60

God, even if my sins filled up the space between the sky and the earth, pierced the stars and reached the very ends of the earth, despair would not stop me from anticipating your forgiveness, and hopelessness would not prevent me from awaiting your acceptance. 8.1.61

God, my soul has come to you craving forgiveness, asking with the tongue of hope for favors it does not deserve. So grant it the pardon it beseeches. Bestow upon it what it seeks. You are the most generous of the generous. You fulfill the hopes of those who place their hopes in you. 8.1.62

God, I have committed many sins and you know them. I have oppressed my soul and you know it. Take me as your servant, whether obedient and honored, or disobedient but forgiven. 8.1.63

God, I pray to you with the prayer you taught me, so do not deny me the favors you have made known to me. It is your bounty that has guided me to beautiful prayer, and it will only be complete if you reserve for me your cherished reward. 8.1.64

God, I await your pardon like other wrongdoers, not despairing of the mercy anticipated by the pious. God, your generosity has given life to my hopes, and your acceptance has received my deeds. Bless Muḥammad and his progeny, and tell me I will meet you soon. Raise my hopes in your reward. God, you are the generous one at whose door no hope is disappointed, no petition invalidated. 8.1.65

God, even if I were lowly and did not deserve your grace—and indeed I have not earned it—you are worthy of bestowing it upon me. The generous do not bestow their bounty only on the deserving. 8.1.66

God, my destitution will not be mended except with your largesse. My hope will not prosper except through your grace. 8.1.67

God, I beseech your aid in doing what will bring me closer to you. I ask you to preserve me from doing what would turn me away from you. 8.1.68

God, the undertaking dearest to my soul, the one that will bring it the most benefit, is the task to which you have guided it, to which you, by your mercy, have directed it. Task my soul to it then, for you are more merciful toward it than I. 8.1.69

٨.١.٧٠ إلٰهي أرجوك رجاء من يخافك وأخافك خوف من يرجو ثوابك فقِني بالخوف شرّ ما أحذر وأعطني بالرجاء خير ما أحاذر.

٨.١.٧١ إلٰهي ٱنتظرت عفوك كما ينتظر المذنبون ولست آيسا من رحمتك التي يتوقّعها المحسنون.

٨.١.٧٢ إلٰهي مددت إليك يدا بالذنوب مأسورة وعينا بالرجاء مذرورة وحقيق لمن دعاك بالندم تذلّلا أن تجيب له بالكرم تفضّلا.

٨.١.٧٣ إلٰهي إن عرّضتني ذنوبي لعقابك فقد أدناني رجائي من ثوابك. إلٰهي لم أسلّط على حسن ظنّي بك قنوط الآيسين فلا تُبطل صدق رجائي لك بين الآملين.

٨.١.٧٤ إلٰهي إن ٱنقرضت بغير ما أحببت من السعي أيّامي فبالإيمان أمضتها الماضيات من أعوامي.

٨.١.٧٥ إلٰهي إن أخطأت طريق النظر لنفسي بما فيه كرامتها فقد أصبت طريق الفزع إليك بما فيه سلامتها.

٨.١.٧٦ إلٰهي ما أضيق الطريق على من لم تكن أنت دليله وما أوحش المسلك على من لم تكن أنت أنيسه.

٨.١.٧٧ إلٰهي ٱنهملت عبراتي حين ذكرت خطيئاتي وما لها لا تنهمل ولا أدري ما يكون إليه مصيري أو ماذا يَهجُم عليه عند البلاغ مسيري؟ وأرى نفسي تخاتلني وأيّامي تخادعني وقد خفقت فوق رأسي أجنحة الموت ورمتني من قريب أعين الفوت فما عذري وقد أوجس في مسامعي رافع الصوت؟ لقد رجوت ممّن ألبسني بين الأحياء ثوب عافيته ألّا يعرّيني منه بين الأموات بجود رأفته ولقد رجوت ممّن تولّاني باقي حياتي بإحسانه أن يُسعفني عند وفاتي بغفرانه.

يا أنيس كلّ غريب آنس في القبر وحشتي ويا ثاني كل وحيد ٱرحم في القبر وحدتي يا عالم السرّ وأخفى ويا كاشف الضرّ والبلوى كيف نظرك لي من بين ساكني الثرى وكيف صُنعك بي في دار الوحشة والبِلى؟ قد كنت بي لطيفا أيّام حياة الدنيا يا أفضل المنعمين في آلائه وأنعم المفضلين في نعمائه. كثرت عندي أياديك

God, I place my hope in you, yet fear you. I fear you, yet hope for your reward. Because I fear, save me from the evil I dread. Because I hope, give me the good I crave. 8.1.70

God, I await your pardon like other wrongdoers, without despairing of the mercy anticipated by the pious. 8.1.71

God, I stretch out to you a hand chained by its sins. Yet I look at you with an eye daubed with the collyrium of hope. It is only fitting that when someone calls out to you in humble repentance, you answer with kindly generosity. 8.1.72

God, even if my sins expose me to your punishment, my hope draws me close to your reward. God, I do not let hopeless despair crush my expectations of your goodness, so do not quash my confidence in you. I place my hope in you. 8.1.73

God, even if my days have run out with me neglecting to do as much good as you would have wished, I have still spent my years in faith. 8.1.74

God, if I have missed the honorable path of looking out for my soul, I have found the safe path of seeking refuge in you. 8.1.75

God, how narrow is the path for one who does not have you as a guide! And how rough the journey for one who does not have you as companion! 8.1.76

God, my tears pour down when I recollect my transgressions. How could it be otherwise when I do not know what my end will be? Or to what destination my journey will take me? I see that my soul has deceived me, my days have betrayed me, and now death's wings are fluttering over my head, its eyes closely observing me. What is my excuse, then, when I have heard the warning loud and clear with my own ears? I have hope that the one who clothed me in the garments of well-being when I was among the living will not strip me of them when I am dead, for he is generous and kind. I have hope that the one who took care of me with his bounties during the days of my life will envelop me with his forgiveness at my death. 8.1.77

O consoler of the stranger! Comfort me in my grave when I am lonely and terrified. O companion to every person who has no other, have mercy on me when I am left in my grave alone. O knower of secrets and concealed things, O remover of harm and troubles, how will you regard me when I am among those who live inside the earth? What will you do with me in the abode of lonely terror and decay? You have been kind to me during the days of my life. O most bestowing giver, O most giving bestower, your favors to me are abundant; I cannot count them. My hands are too straitened to offer you

فعجزت عن إحصائها وضِقت ذرعاً في شكري لك بجزائها. فلك الحمد على ما أوليت ولك الشكر على ما أبليت.

يا خير من دعاه داع وأفضل من رجاه راج بذمّة الإسلام أتوسّل إليك وبحرمة القرآن أعتمد عليك وبمحمّد صلّى الله عليه وعلى آله أتقرّب اليك فصلّ على محمّد وعلى وآل محمّد وٱعرف لي ذمّتي التي بها رجوت قضاء حاجتي وٱستعملني بطاعتك وٱختم لي بخير وأعتقني من النار وأسكنّي الجنّة ولا تفضحني بسريرتي حيّاً ولا ميتاً وهب لي الذنوب التي فيما بيني وبينك وأرضِ عبادك عنّي في مظالمهم قِبَلي وٱجعلني ممّن رضيت عنه فحرّمته على النار والعذاب وأصلح لي كلّ أموري التي دعوتك فيها في الآخرة والدنيا يا حنّان يا منّان يا ذا الجلال والإكرام يا حيّ يا قيّوم يا من له الخلق والأمر تباركت يا أحسن الخالقين يا رحيم يا كريم يا قدير فصلّ على محمّد وعلى آله الطيّبين.

وعليه وعليهم السلام ورحمة الله وبركاته إنّه حميد مجيد.

٨.٢ أخبرنا حمزة بن عبد الله قال: أخبرنا الحسين بن خالويه قال: حدّثنا ٱبن دريد قال: حدّثنا السكن بن سعيد عن محمّد بن عبّاد الكلبيّ عن أبيه قال: حدّثنا حَوثرة بن الهِرماس وكان شيخاً هِمّاً وذكر وفود بني دارم إلى أمير المؤمنين عليّ صلوات الله عليه وذكر حديث الإستسقاء بطوله وقال فيه:

فقام إليه منّا رجل من حِسل[1] فقال:

يا أمير المؤمنين جادَتك الأنواء وضَفا لديك البلاء وتمّت بك الآلاء وكُشفت بيمنك اللأواء. أتتك عَماعم من أفناء دارم تطوي إليك سُهوب الأملاء بالحراجيج الأَبلاء تَبُثّك أَزَبات[2] اللأواء ولَزَبات الشهباء. تزدلف بك وتستمطر بغرّتك وتستدفع البلوى بسنّتك.

---

١ م: في الحاشية (جُعَل بن حِسْل) مشكّلة.

٢ ي: (إرهاب). هـ: (أزمات).

adequate recompense, but I offer you praise for your bounties and gratitude for your trials.

O best of those to whom a caller calls, O worthiest of those in whom an aspirer places his hopes, I seek intercession with you through the covenant of Islam. I rely on you through the sanctity of the Qur'an. I seek closeness to you through Muḥammad. So bless Muḥammad and the progeny of Muḥammad, and acknowledge my covenant, through which I hope for the fulfillment of my petition. Make me act in obedience to you. End my days in goodness, free me from the fire, and give me a home in heaven. Do not shame me by revealing my secrets in life or in death. Pardon the sins I have committed against you. Convince those among your servants whom I have wronged to accept my regrets. Place me among those with whom you are pleased, saving me from the fire. Look into all the things I have prayed to you for in this world and the next. O compassionate one, O liberal one, O mighty and munificent one, O living one, O sustaining one, O master of creation and command, may you be blessed. O most beautiful creator. O merciful one, O generous one, O powerful one, bless Muḥammad and his pure progeny.

Peace, God's mercy and his grace upon him and upon them. Verily God is praiseworthy, noble.

8.2 Ḥamzah ibn ʿAbd Allāh reported to us, saying: al-Ḥusayn ibn Khālawayh reported to us, saying: Ibn Durayd recounted to us, saying: al-Sakan ibn Saʿīd recounted to us, from Muḥammad ibn ʿAbbād al-Kalbī, from his father, saying: Ḥawtharah ibn al-Hirmās recounted a report to us when he was a very old man. He remembered the delegation of the Dārim tribe that came to the commander of the faithful ʿAlī ibn Abī Ṭālib, and described in full the report of ʿAlī's prayer for rain, saying:

A man among us from the Ḥisl clan stood up and said:

May the rain-stars be generous to you, commander of the faithful! May reverence be abundant for you! May God's favors be granted us through you! May calamities be lifted by your grace! Scattered groups of people from Dārim have come to you, journeying through vast wildernesses on tall, strong camels, to complain to you of the hardships of their privation, and the sufferings brought on by this year of drought. They come to attain closeness to God through you, to beseech him for rain by the grace of your luminous presence, and to fend off this calamity by following your practice.

وقام إليه أبو سرادق فتكلّم بكلام قال في آخره: أنت ربيع الأيّام وملجأ[1] الأنام ومصباح الظلام وغاية المِعدام والسيّد الهمام والإمام[2] القمقام لا مُعتصَر عنك ولا معتصم دونك.

فقال أمير المؤمنين صلوات الله عليه: الحمد لله والصلاة على خير خلق الله وسلام على المُصطفَين من عباد الله. يا قنبر ناد: الصلاة جامعة. ثمّ نهض مُعتجِرا بنَصيف مُزبَرَق كأنّما غرّته البدر لِتمّه يكاد يُعشي الناظرين يؤمّ المسجد فصلّى ثمّ دنا من القبر فهَينَم بكلمات لم أُوجسهنّ ثمّ قام قانتا فقال:

اللّهمّ ربّ السبع الطباق والرُّقَع الوِثاق خالق الخلق وباسط الرزق عالم الخفيّات وكاشف الكربات ومجيب الدعوات وقابل الحسنات وغافر السيّئات ومُقيل العثرات ومُنزل البركات من فوق سبع سموات بعلمك من خزائن رحمتك وأكناف كرامتك على شاكري آلائك وكافري نعمائك من عبادك وقُطّان بلادك رأفة منك لهم ونعمة عليهم أنت غاية الطالبين وملاذ الهاربين.

أتاك مَلأٌ من عبادك بإزاء قبر نبيّك تزدلف إليك بعبدك وتشكو إليك ما أنت أعلم به.

اللّهمّ فإنّا نسألك بك فلا شيء أعظم منك وبما استقلّ به عرشك من عظمتك التي وسعت كلّ شيء السماء والأرض وملأت البرّ والبحر أن تصلّي على محمّد خاتم النبيين وسيّد الأوّلين والآخرين.

اللّهمّ كاشف الضرّ ومزيل الأَزْل أزِل عن عبادك ما قد غشيهم من آياتك وبرّح بهم من عقابك إنّه لا يكشف السوء إلا أنت إنك رؤوف رحيم.

---

[1] م: (عصرة).

[2] ي: (البطل).

Then Abū Surādiq went forward and spoke to him, ending with the following words: You are the spring of days, the succor of the world, a lamp in the darkness, the last resort of the indigent, a noble chieftain, and a magnanimous leader. There is no haven other than you, no refuge apart from you.

The commander of the faithful responded: God be praised! Blessings and peace upon the best of God's creation. Peace upon the chosen ones among God's servants. Qanbar, call out: "Gather for the prayer!"[70] Wearing a yellow head covering,[71] he rose like the moon in its fullness, blinding any who looked upon him, and headed for the mosque. He offered the ritual-prayer, then drew close to the prophet's grave, and whispered some words that I did not quite hear. After that, he stood up to beseech God for rain, entreating him thus:

O God, lord of the seven spheres and the interlinked heavens, creator of all creation, giver of sustenance, knower of secrets, remover of misfortunes, answerer of prayers, accepter of good deeds, forgiver of sins, steadier of stumblers. You send down your grace from on high in the seven skies, a grace that descends with your knowledge from your mercy's treasures and the shelters of your kindness upon those among your servants, the inhabitants of your lands, those who are thankful for your favors as well as those who are ungrateful for your gifts. You send it to them because of your own compassion and benevolence. You are the ultimate support for those who seek aid, the best refuge for those who would escape from calamity.

Your servants have come to you at the grave of your prophet, seeking to come close to you through your servant, complaining to you about a crisis that you know more about than anyone else.

O God, we beseech you in your own name, for there is nothing greater than you. We beseech you by the greatness borne upon your throne, a greatness that permeates the heavens and earth, a greatness that fills the land and the sea. We ask you to bless Muḥammad, seal of the prophets, the best of generations past and generations yet to come.

O God, remover of hardships, repealer of constraints. Remove from your servants this sign of yours which has enveloped them, this retribution of yours which has tested them sorely. None can remove hardship but you. You are most kind, most merciful.

الباب التاسع

في المحفوظ من شعره

٩.١ روى أبو عبد الله إبراهيم بن محمّد بن عرفة الأزديّ النحويّ نِفطَوَيه من شعر أمير المؤمنين عليّ صلوات الله عليه [بسيط]:

اَلْحَمْدُ لِلّٰهِ رَبِّي الْخَالِقُ الصَّمَدُ   فَلَيْسَ يَشْرَكُهُ فِي مُلْكِهِ أَحَدُ

هُوَ الَّذِي عَرَّفَ الْكُفَّارَ كُفْرَهُمُ   وَالْمُؤْمِنُونَ سَيَجْزِيهِمْ بِمَا وُعِدُوا

فَإِنْ تَكُنْ دَوْلَةٌ كَانَتْ لَنَا عِظَةً   وَهَلْ عَسَى أَنْ يُرَى فِي غَيِّهَا رَشَدُ

وَيَنْصُرُ اللّٰهُ مَنْ وَالَاهُ إِنَّ لَهُ   نَصْرًا وَيُمَثِّلُ بِالْكُفَّارِ إِذْ عَنَدُوا

فَإِنْ نَطَقْتُمْ بِفَخْرٍ لَا أَبَا لَكُمُ   فِيمَنْ تَضَمَّنَ مِنْ إِخْوَانِنَا أُحُدُ[1]

فَإِنَّ طَلْحَةَ[2] غَادَرْنَاهُ مُنْجَدِلًا   وَلِلصَّفَائِحِ نَارٌ بَيْنَنَا تَقِدُ

وَالْمَرْءَ عُثْمَانَ[3] أَرْدَتْهُ أَسِنَّتُنَا   فَجَيْبُ زَوْجَتِهِ إِذْ خُبِّرَتْ قِدَدُ

فِي تِسْعَةٍ وَلِوَاءٌ بَيْنَ أَظْهُرِهِمْ   لَمْ يَنْكُلُوا عَنْ حِيَاضِ الْمَوْتِ إِذْ وَرَدُوا

كَانُوا الذُّؤَابَةَ مِنْ فِهْرٍ وَأَكْرَمَهَا   حَيْثُ الْأُنُوفُ وَحَيْثُ الْفَرْعُ وَالْعَدَدُ

وَأَحْمَدُ الْخَيْرِ قَدْ أَرْدَى عَلَى عَجَلٍ   تَحْتَ الْعَجَاجِ أُبَيًّا[4] وَهْوَ مُجْتَهِدُ

فَظَلَّتِ الطَّيْرُ وَالضِّبْعَانُ تَرْكَبُهُ   فَحَامِلٌ قِطْعَةً مِنْهُ وَمُقْتَعِدُ

---

١ ي: (اللحد). ومثلها رواية الديوان، ص. ١٨٧.

٢ م: تضيف في المتن بعد البيت (يعني طلحة بن أبي طلحة العبدريّ وكان معه لواءُ المشركين يوم أحد). ي: تضيف نفس التعليق في الحاشية.

٣ م: تضيف في المتن بعد البيت (هو عثمان بن أبي طلحة قتله حمزة بن عبد المطّلب يوم أُحُد).

٤ م: تضيف في المتن بعد البيت (يعني أُبيّ بن خَلَف قتله النبيّ صلى الله عليه وعلى آله وسلّم بيده وطعنه طعنةً يوم أُحُد). ي: تضيف نفس التعليق في الحاشية.

Chapter 9

Verse

9.1 Nifṭawayh, Abū ʿAbd Allāh Ibrāhīm ibn Muḥammad ibn ʿArafah al-Azdī al-Naḥwī, transmitted the following poetry by the commander of the faithful, ʿAlī ibn Abī Ṭālib:[72]

Praise God! My lord is the eternal creator,
no partner shares his kingdom.
He apprised the disbelievers of their outcome
and will reward the believers as promised.
Our defeat is a lesson for us,
perhaps right will yet take the place of error.
God will give victory to his servants, victory comes from him;
he will make an example of the disbelievers for denying the truth.
Woe to you! If you speak boastingly of our brothers
whom Mount Uḥud took unto herself,
then remember Ṭalḥah whom we left dead on the ground,
swords glinting fire between us.
Remember ʿUthmān killed by our spears,
whose wife tore her shift to shreds.
With nine others, the banner between them,
who went to drink at the pools of death;
The best of Fihr and the noblest too,
proud-nosed, high-born, numerous.
With a swift spearthrust, Muḥammad the Good killed Ubayy
and left him writhing under a canopy of dust.
Vultures and hyenas fight over him,
one carries away a choice piece, another bides his time.

وَمَنْ قَتَلْتُم عَلَى مَا كَانَ مِنْ عَجَبٍ مِنَّا فَقَدْ صَادَفُوا خَيْرًا وَقَدْ سَعِدُوا
لَهُمْ جِنَانٌ مِنَ الفِرْدَوْسِ طَيِّبَةٌ لَا يَعْتَرِيهِمْ بِهَا حَرٌّ وَلَا صَرَدُ
صَلَّى الإِلَٰهُ عَلَيْهِمْ كُلَّمَا ذُكِرُوا فَرُبَّ مَشْهَدِ صِدْقٍ قَبْلَهُ شَهِدُوا
قَوْمٌ وَفَوْا لِرَسُولِ اللهِ وَٱحْتَسَمُوا شُمُّ العَرَانِينِ مِنْهُمْ حَمْزَةُ الأَسَدُ[1]
وَمُصْعَبٌ[2] كَانَ لَيْثًا دُونَهُ حَرِدًا حَتَّى تَرَمَّلَ مِنْهُ ثَعْلَبٌ جَسِدُ
لَيْسُوا كَقَتْلَى مِنَ الكُفَّارِ أَدْخَلَهُمْ نَارَ الجَحِيمِ عَلَى أَبْوَابِهَا الرُّصُدُ[3]

٩.٢.١ وقال عليه الصلاة والسلام في قتله عمرو بن عبد[4] وَدّ وكان عليه السلام حين قتله سقط عمرو فٱنكشف فتنحّى عنه وقال [كامل]:

أَعَلَيَّ يَقْتَحِمُ الفَوَارِسُ هٰكَذَا عَنِّي وَعَنْهُمْ خَبِّرُوا[5] أَصْحَابِي
اَلْيَوْمَ يَمْنَعُنِي الفِرَارَ حَفِيظَتِي وَمُصَمِّمٌ فِي الرَّأْسِ[6] لَيْسَ بِنَابِ
وَغَدَوْتُ أَلْتَمِسُ القِرَاعَ وَصَارِمٌ عَضْبٌ كَلَوْنِ المِلْحِ فِي أَقْرَابِ
آلَى ٱبْنُ عَبْدٍ حِينَ شَدَّ أَلِيَّةً وَحَلَفْتُ فَٱسْتَمِعُوا مِنَ الكَذَّابُ[7]
أَلَّا يَفِرَّ وَلَا يُهَلِّلَ فَٱلْتَقَى رَجُلَانِ يَضْطَرِبَانِ كُلَّ ضِرَابِ
وَصَدَدْتُ حِينَ رَأَيْتُهُ مُتَقَطِّرًا كَالجِذْعِ[8] بَيْنَ دَكَادِكٍ وَرَوَابِي

---

١ م، ي: سقط البيت. وأُثبت في الديوان، ص. ١٨٨ كما في رواية ه التي أثبتُّها.

٢ م: تضيف في المتن بعد البيت (مُصْعَب بن عُمَيْر صاحب لواء رسول الله عليه السلام قُتل يوم أحد). ي: تضيف نفس التعليق في الحاشية.

٣ م، ي: (الأصد). ورواية الديوان، ص. ١٨٨، مثل رواية ه التي أثبتُّها. م: تضيف في المتن بعد البيت (الأُصُد من الوَصِيد. يقال "أَوْصَدْتُ البابَ وآصَدْتُه" أيْ "أغلقتُه". والوصيد أيضا الفِناء، من قوله جلّ وعزّ ﴿وَكَلْبُهُمْ بَاسِطٌ ذِرَاعَيْهِ بِالْوَصِيدِ﴾ [سورة الكهف ١٨:١٨]). ي: تضيف نفس التعليق في الحاشية.

٤ م، ه: سقطت (عبد). أُثبتت في رواية الديوان، ص. ١٣٠، كما في رواية ي التي أثبتُّها.

٥ م: (أَخَرُوا) مشكّلة. ه: (أخبروا). ورواية الديوان، ص. ١٣٠، مثل رواية ي التي أثبتُّها.

٦ ه: (الهام).

٧ م: شُكّلت العبارة (مَن الكذّابُ) بالإقواء من حيث القافية ولكنّها الأصوب من حيث المعنى، لأنّ الإقواء كان غلطا عامًّا في الشعر القديم خصوصا بين الضمّة والكسرة كما أتى هنا (انظر الأخفش الأوسط، كتاب القوافي، ص. ٤١).

٨ م: (بالدرع). ه: (في الدرع). ورواية الديوان، ص. ١٣١ مثل رواية ي التي أثبتُّها.

Those whom you killed when you came upon us without warning
went on to earn reward and bliss.
For them, the delight of paradise,
a place neither too hot nor too cold.
May God bless them whenever their names are mentioned,
fighters in so many true battles.
They were loyal to God's messenger, men of restraint,
their noses proudly high-bridged, among them Ḥamzah the Lion.
Muṣʿab was also a lion protecting the prophet,
until a bloodsmeared jackal washed himself in his gore.[73]
Our dead are not like your dead—
God delivered yours into the fires of hell, its gates well-guarded.

The following are ʿAlī's verses upon his slaying of ʿAmr ibn ʿAbd Wadd.[74] ʿAmr fell when ʿAlī slew him and his private parts were exposed. ʿAlī moved away, saying: 9.2.1

Can horsemen attack me like this?
Tell my friends about me and them.
Today my fury prevents me from fleeing.
I am resolved, my aim unswerving.
I awoke this morning anticipating battle,
in my scabbard a sharp sword the color of salt.
Ibn ʿAbd swore an oath, bracing for battle, and I made a vow
—who is the liar among us?—
that we would neither flee nor hold back.
We met. We exchanged blows.
I turned away when I saw him fall,
a great palm tree tumbling to the ground between the knolls.
I held back and did not plunder his garments.
Had I been slain he would have stripped me of mine.

وَعَففتُ عَنْ أَثْوابِهِ وَلَوَ آنّنِي كُنْتُ المقَطَّرَ بَزَّنِي أَثْوَابِي
نَصَرَ الحِجَارَةَ مِنْ سَفَاهَةِ رَأْيِهِ وَنَصَرْتُ رَبَّ مُحَمَّدٍ بِصَوَابِ
لَا تَحْسَبَنَّ اللهَ خَاذِلَ دِينِهِ وَنَبِيِّهِ يَا مَعْشَرَ الأَحْزَابِ

٩.٢.٢ وجاءت أخت عمرو فوجدته قتيلا فقالت: من قتله؟ قالوا: علي بن أبي طالب. قالت: كفو كريم ثمّ قالت [بسيط]:

لَوْ كَانَ قَاتِلُ عَمْرٍو غَيْرَ قَاتِلِهِ بَكَيْتُهُ مَا أَقَامَ الرُّوحُ فِي جَسَدِي[١]
لَكِنَّ قَاتِلَهُ مَنْ لَا يُعَابُ بِهِ مَنْ كَانَ يُدْعَى قَدِيماً بَيْضَةَ البَلَدِ

٩.٢.٣ وقال عليه السلام في قتله عمرو بن عبد وَدّ [طويل]:

وَكَانُوا عَلَى الإِسْلَامِ إِلْباً ثَلَاثَةً فَقَدْ بَزَّ مِنْ تِلْكَ الثَّلَاثَةِ وَاحِدُ[٢]
وَفَرَّ أَبُو عَمْرٍو هُبَيْرَةُ لَمْ يَعُدْ لَنَا وَأَخُو الحَرْبِ المُجَرِّبُ عَائِدُ
نَهَتْهُمْ سُيُوفُ الهِنْدِ أَنْ يَقِفُوا لَنَا غَدَاةَ ٱلْتَقَيْنَا وَالرِّمَاحُ المَصَائِدُ[٣]

٩.٢.٤ وقال عليه السلام [طويل]:

ضَرَبْنَا غُوَاةَ النَّاسِ عَنْهُ تَكَرُّماً وَلَمَّا يَرَوْا قَصْدَ السَّبِيلِ وَلَا الهُدَى
فَلَمَّا تَبَيَّنَّا الهُدَى كَانَ كُلُّنَا عَلَى طَاعَةِ الرَّحْمٰنِ وَالحَقِّ وَالتُّقَى
نَصَرْنَا رَسُولَ اللهِ لَمَّا تَدَابَرُوا وَثَابَ إِلَيْهِ المُسْلِمُونَ ذَوُو الحِجَا

---

١ م: (لقد بكيت عليه آخر الأبد).
٢ م، ي: تضيف في المتن بعد البيت (ألبًا أي مجتمعين يقال: تألّبوا على الشيء أي ٱجتمعوا عليه).
٣ ي: (الصوابد).

He fought for the stone idol, a foolish choice,
while I fought in righteousness for Muḥammad's lord.
Do not think that God will disgrace his religion or his prophet,
O gathering of confederates.

ʿAmr's sister came on the scene to find her brother slain. Who killed him? she asked. ʿAlī ibn Abī Ṭālib, she was told. A noble equal! she exclaimed, and recited: 9.2.2

If ʿAmr's slayer had been any other man,
I would have wept till my soul left my body.
But his slayer is ʿAlī,
and the one long known as the city's champion is not to be faulted for being felled by him.

With regard to his slaying of ʿAmr ibn ʿAbd Wadd, ʿAlī also recited: 9.2.3

Three lined up against Islam,
one has been taken out.[75]
Abū ʿAmr Hubayrah fled and did not return,
only an experienced warrior would have come back.
Sharp Indian swords and keen hunting spears prevented them
from facing us on the morning we met in battle.

ʿAlī also recited: 9.2.4

Honoring him, our swords struck those who strayed from him,
they perceived neither the straight path nor his guidance.
When we recognized his guidance, we took the road of obedience to the Merciful,
the road of truth and piety.
We fought for God's messenger when they attacked.
The Muslims, people of perspicacity, turned to him.

٩.٣ وقال عليه السلام في يوم أُحُد [وافر]:

رَأَيْتُ الْمُشْرِكِينَ بَغَوْا عَلَيْنَا ... وَلَجُّوا فِي الْغَوَايَةِ وَالضَّلَالِ[1]

وَقَالُوا نَحْنُ أَكْثَرُ إِذْ نَفَرْنَا ... غَدَاةَ الرَّوْعِ بِالْأَسَلِ النِّهَالِ

فَإِنْ تَبْغُوا وَتَفْتَخِرُوا عَلَيْنَا ... بِحَمْزَةَ وَهْوَ فِي الْغُرَفِ الْعَوَالِي

فَقَدْ أَوْدَى بِعُتْبَةَ يَوْمَ بَدْرٍ ... وَقَدْ أَبْلَى وَجَاهَدَ غَيْرَ آلِ

وَقَدْ غَادَرْتُ كَبْشَهُمُ جِهَارًا ... بِحَمْدِ اللهِ طَلْحَةَ فِي الْمَجَالِ

٩.٤ وقال عليه الصلاة والسلام [متقارب]:

عَرَفْتُ وَمَنْ يَعْتَدِلْ يَعْرِفِ ... وَأَيْقَنْتُ حَقًّا فَلَمْ أَصْدِفِ

عَنِ الْحِكَمِ الْحُكْمُ آيَاتُهَا ... مِنَ اللهِ ذِي الرَّأْفَةِ الْأَرْأَفِ

رَسَائِلُ تُدْرَسُ فِي الْمُؤْمِنِينَ ... بِهِنَّ اصْطَفَى أَحْمَدَ الْمُصْطَفِي

فَأَصْبَحَ أَحْمَدُ فِينَا عَزِيزًا ... عَزِيزَ الْمُقَامَةِ وَالْمَوْقِفِ

فَيَا أَيُّهَا الْمُوعِدُوهُ سَفَاهًا ... وَلَمْ يَأْتِ جَوْرًا وَلَمْ يَعْنُفِ

أَلَسْتُمْ تَخَافُونَ أَمْرَ الْعَذَابِ ... وَمَا آمِنُ اللهِ كَالْأَخْوَفِ

وَلَمْ يُصْرَعُوا تَحْتَ أَسْيَافِهِ ... كَمَصْرَعِ كَعْبِ أَبِي الْأَشْرَفِ[2]

غَدَاةَ تَرَاءَى لِطُغْيَانِهِ ... وَأَعْرَضَ كَالْجَمَلِ الْأَخْنَفِ

فَأَنْزَلَ جِبْرِيلَ فِي قَتْلِهِ ... بِوَحْيٍ إِلَى عَبْدِهِ مُلْطَفِ

فَبَاتَتْ عُيُونٌ لَهُ مُعْوِلَاتٌ ... مَتَى يُنْعَ كَعْبٌ لَهَا تَذْرِفِ

---

١ م، ي: (الضلال).

٢ م، ي: تضيف في المتن بعد البيت (كعب بن الأشرف رئيسُ اليهود دَسَّ إليه النبيُّ صلى الله عليه وعلى آله وسلّم مَن قَتَلَه). ملاحظة: رواية مخطوطات الدستور لهذا البيت وكذلك رواية ابن هشام في السيرة النبوية ٢:١٤٣: "كعب أبي الأشرف" في حين أنّ كعب هذا مذكور في المصادر التاريخيّة باسم "كعب بن الأشرف".

'Alī recited the following verses about the Battle of Uḥud: 9.3

I see the polytheists, treacherous,
persistent in their errant and sinful ways.
They say: "We went home on the morning of that frightful battle
with spears that had drunk blood."
Treacherous in their fighting, they boast of slaying Ḥamzah;
he resides now in the highest station.
Let them remember that Ḥamzah killed 'Utbah in the Battle of Badr,
he slew many, and fought without weakness;
And let them remember that I prostrated Ṭalḥah, their ram,
in plain sight on the field. God be praised!

'Alī recited:[76] 9.4

I know, and one who is just knows.
I have true conviction.
I do not stray from the clear verses of wisdom
coming from a God who is kind, most kind.
A message that believers pore over,
a message that Muḥammad was chosen to deliver.
Muḥammad became mighty among us,
mighty at home and in battle.
You hotheads who threaten him
when he has not oppressed or done violence to anyone:
Do you not fear the great punishment?
You should know that one protected by God is not like the one who is fearful,
Not prostrated—yet—under his sword
like Ka'b.
The morning he came bringing mischief,
then stomped away like an injured camel.
God sent down Gabriel with instructions to kill him,
in a heavenly revelation to his servant.
Many an eye spent the night weeping over him,
bursting forth whenever Ka'b's death was mentioned.

فَقَالُوا لِأَحْمَدَ ذَرْنَا قَلِيلًا ... فَإِنَّا مِنَ النَّوْحِ لَمْ نَشْتَفِ
فَأَجْلَاهُمُ ثُمَّ قَالَ اظْعَنُوا ... فُتُوحًا عَلَى رَغْمِ الْآنُفِ
وَأَجْلَى النَّضِيرَ إِلَى غُرْبَةٍ[1] ... وَكَانُوا بِدَارٍ ذَوِي زُخْرُفِ
إِلَى أَذْرِعَاتٍ رَذَايَاهُمُ ... عَلَى كُلِّ ذِي دَبَرٍ أَعْجَفِ

٩٠٥ وقال عليه الصلاة والسلام [طويل]:

أَلَمْ تَرَ أَنَّ اللهَ أَبْلَى رَسُولَهُ ... بَلَاءَ عَزِيزٍ ذِي اقْتِدَارٍ وَذِي فَضْلِ
بِمَا أَنْزَلَ الْكُفَّارَ دَارَ مَذَلَّةٍ ... فَذَاقُوا هَوَانًا مِنْ إِسَارٍ وَمِنْ قَتْلِ
وَأَمْسَى رَسُولُ اللهِ قَدْ عَزَّ نَصْرُهُ ... وَكَانَ رَسُولُ اللهِ أُرْسِلَ بِالْعَدْلِ
فَجَاءَ بِفُرْقَانٍ مِنَ اللهِ مُنْزَلٍ ... مُبَيِّنَةٍ آيَاتُهُ لِذَوِي الْعَقْلِ
فَآمَنَ أَقْوَامٌ بِذَاكَ وَأَيْقَنُوا ... وَأَمْسَوْا بِحَمْدِ اللهِ مُجْتَمِعِي الشَّمْلِ
وَأَنْكَرَ أَقْوَامٌ فَزَاغَتْ قُلُوبُهُمْ ... فَزَادَهُمُ ذُو الْعَرْشِ خَبْلًا عَلَى خَبْلِ
وَأَمْكَنَ مِنْهُمْ يَوْمَ بَدْرٍ رَسُولَهُ ... وَقَوْمًا غِضَابًا فِعْلُهُمْ أَحْسَنُ الْفِعْلِ
بِأَيْدِيهِمُ بِيضٌ خِفَافٌ عَصَوْا بِهَا ... وَقَدْ حَادَثُوهَا بِالْجِلَاءِ وَبِالصَّقْلِ
فَكَمْ تَرَكُوا مِنْ نَاشِئٍ ذِي حَمِيَّةٍ ... صَرِيعًا وَمِنْ ذِي نَجْدَةٍ مِنْهُمُ كَهْلِ
تَبِيتُ عُيُونُ النَّائِحَاتِ عَلَيْهِمُ ... تَجُودُ بِإِسْبَالِ الرَّشَاشِ وَبِالْوَبْلِ
نَوَائِحُ تَنْعَى عُتْبَةَ الْغَيِّ وَابْنَهُ ... وَشَيْبَةَ تَنْعَاهُ وَتَنْعَى أَبَا جَهْلِ
وَذَا الرِّجْلِ تَنْعَى وَابْنَ جِدْعَانَ[2] مِنْهُمُ ... مُسَلَّبَةٌ حَرَّى مُبَيِّنَةُ الثُّكْلِ
ثَوَى مِنْهُمُ فِي بِئْرِ بَدْرٍ عِصَابَةٌ ... ذَوُو نَجَدَاتٍ فِي الْحُرُوبِ وَفِي الْمَحْلِ

---

١ م: (عَزَبَة) مشكّلة، وهي اسم قرية بالقرب من المدينة المنوّرة. ورواية ابن هشام في السيرة النبوية ٢:١٤٧ مثل رواية هـ، ي، التي أثبتُّها.

٢ هـ: (جذعان). ورواية الديوان، ص. ٣٤٢ مثله ولكن في الحاشية (جدعان). ي: ورد المصراع بغير تنقيط.

The al-Naḍīr tribe said to Muḥammad, "Leave us be for a while
for we are not done mourning."
But he expelled them all, saying "Be gone!
Scatter in groups and bands, willing or not."
He sent al-Naḍīr into exile
—they had been living in a beautifully decorated place—
To Adhriʿāt
on their weak, mangy, emaciated camels.

ʿAlī said:[77]

9.5

Don't you see that God has shown his messenger great generosity,
the generosity of a powerful, munificent God?
Consigning disbelievers to a place of humiliation,
where they taste the ignominy of captivity and death.
The evening found God's messenger mighty in victory—
God's messenger was sent in justice.
He brought the Furqān[78] revealed by God,
its verses clear for people of intelligence.
Some believed in it with conviction,
and, God be praised, by evening they were united.
Others denied it, their hearts strayed,
so the lord of the throne increased their corruption.
The messenger needed only God to oppose their evil in the Battle of Badr,
and he sufficed a people roused to righteous anger, whose acts were most beauteous.
In their hands, light and gleaming swords,
used in battle after long polishing and sharpening.
They left there hotheaded youths prostrate,
and generous men in their prime.
Mourning women spent the night spilling tears,
in drops and in torrents.
Mourners wail for ʿUtbah the Errant and his son.
They wail for Shaybah. They wail for Abu Jahl.

دَعَا الْغَيُّ مِنْهُمْ مَنْ دَعَا فَأَجَابَهُ — وَلِلْغَيِّ أَسْبَابٌ مُرَمَّةُ الْوَصْلِ
فَأَضْحَوْا لَدَى دَارِ الْجَحِيمِ بِمَعْزِلٍ — عَنِ الشَّغْبِ وَالْعُدْوَانِ فِي أَشْغَلِ الشُّغْلِ

٩٠٦

وقال عليه الصلاة والسلام يرثي النبيّ صلّى الله عليه وعلى آله وسلّم [طويل]:

أَلَا طَرَقَ النَّاعِي بِلَيْلٍ فَرَاعَنِي — وَأَرَّقَنِي لَمَّا اسْتَهَلَّ مُنَادِيَا
فَقُلْتُ لَهُ لَمَّا رَأَيْتُ الَّذِي أَتَى — أَغَيْرَ رَسُولِ اللهِ إِنْ كُنْتَ نَاعِيَا
فَحَقَّقَ مَا أَشْفَقْتُ مِنْهُ وَلَمْ يُبَلْ — وَكَانَ خَلِيلِي غُرَّتِي[1] وَجَمَالِيَا
فَوَاللهِ لَا أَنْسَاكَ أَحْمَدُ مَا مَشَتْ — بِيَ الْعِيسُ فِي أَرْضٍ وَجَاوَزْتُ وَادِيَا
وَكُنْتُ مَتَى أَهْبِطْ مِنَ الْأَرْضِ تَلْعَةً — أَجِدْ أَثَرًا مِنْهُ جَدِيدًا وَعَافِيَا[2]
جَوَادٌ تَشَظَّى الْخَيْلُ عَنْهُ كَأَنَّمَا — يَرَيْنَ بِهِ لَيْثًا عَلَيْهِنَّ ضَارِيَا[3]
مِنَ الْأُسْدِ قَدْ أَحْمَى الْعَرِينَ مَهَابَةً — تَفَادَى سِبَاعُ الْأُسْدِ مِنْهُ تَفَادِيَا
شَدِيدٌ جَرِيءُ النَّفْسِ نَهْدٌ مُصَدَّرٌ — هُوَ الْمَوْتُ مَغْدُوًّا عَلَيْهِ وَغَادِيَا
لِتَبْكِ رَسُولَ اللهِ خَيْلٌ مُغِيرَةٌ — تُثِيرُ غُبَارًا كَالضَّبَابَةِ كَابِيَا
وَيَبْكِ رَسُولَ اللهِ صَفٌّ مُقَدَّمٌ — إِذَا كَانَ ضَرْبُ الْهَامِ نَقْفًا تَفَانِيَا

١ ي: (عُدَّتي). ومثلها رواية الديوان ص. ٤٤٠.
٢ ي: (باليا).
٣ هـ: (ماضيا).

They wail for the one-legged man, for the son of the nose-cut one.[79]
Mothers stripped of sons, their hearts burning, their bereavement plain.
Many Meccans took up residence in the wells of Badr,
noble men, generous in war and drought.
Error called to them and they answered,
—but error's ropes are frayed and falling apart.
By afternoon they were residents of hell,
too preoccupied with their own troubles to make mischief or to hate.

ʿAlī said in an elegy for the prophet: 9.6

The crier brought the news at night,
alarming and disconcerting me when he started shouting it out.
When I saw what news he brought, I said to him:
"If your news is of a death, then anyone's but the messenger of God!"
But what I feared was true, and he did not care
that my friend had been for me brightness and beauty.
By God, I shall not forget you, Muḥammad,
as long as caravans carry me, as long as I cross dry rivers.
Whenever I reach a twisting ravine in the earth
I find traces of Muḥammad, new and old.
He was a swift courser: bold horsemen scattered from his charge,
as though a ferocious beast were bearing down upon them.
A lion among lions, he protected his lair by the awe he inspired,
and rapacious lions fled from him.
Strong, bold, and robust. He was Death itself—
whether the enemy came to him on the morning of battle or he to them.
Let horsemen weep for God's messenger as they sally on a raid,
steeds raising dust like enveloping mist.
Let the front lines weep for God's messenger when blows fall,
when skulls are fractured, and armies destroyed.

وقال عليه الصلاة والسلام في قوم من الزنادقة قتلهم وأحرقهم [رجز]: ٩.٧

لَمَّا رَأَيْتُ الأَمْرَ أَمْرًا مُنْكَرًا   أَجَّجْتُ نَارِي وَدَعَوْتُ قَنْبَرَا

وقال عليه السلام [طويل]: ٩.٨

لِمَنْ رَايَةٌ سَوْدَاءُ يَخْفِقُ ظِلُّهَا   إِذَا قِيلَ قَدِّمْهَا حُضَيْنُ تَقَدَّمَا
فَيُورِدُهَا فِي الصَّفِّ حَتَّى يَرُدَّهَا   حِيَاضَ المَنَايَا تَقْطُرُ المَوْتَ وَالدَّمَا
جَزَى اللهُ قَوْمًا قَاتَلُوا فِي لِقَائِهِمْ   لَدَى المَوْتِ يَوْمًا مَا أَعَزَّ وَأَكْرَمَا
وَأَطْيَبَ أَخْبَارًا وَأَكْرَمَ شِيمَةً   إِذَا كَانَ أَصْوَاتُ الرِّجَالِ تَغَمْغُمَا
رَبِيعَةَ أَعْنِي إِنَّهُمْ أَهْلُ نَجْدَةٍ   وَبَأْسٍ إِذَا لَاقُوا خَمِيسًا عَرَمْرَمَا[١]

وقال عليه الصلاة والسلام [طويل]: ٩.٩

أَرَى عِلَلَ الدُّنْيَا عَلَيَّ كَثِيرَةً   وَصَاحِبُهَا حَتَّى المَمَاتِ عَلِيلُ
لِكُلِّ اجْتِمَاعٍ مِنْ خَلِيلَيْنِ فُرْقَةٌ   وَكُلُّ الَّذِي دُونَ المَمَاتِ قَلِيلُ
وَإِنَّ افْتِقَادِي وَاحِدًا بَعْدَ وَاحِدٍ   دَلِيلٌ عَلَى أَنْ لَا يَدُومَ خَلِيلُ

---

١ م، ي: تضيف في المتن بعد البيت (حضين معجمةُ الضّاد وهوحضين بن المنذر أبو ساسان وكان معه رايةُ قومِه يومَ صفّين وعاش بعد ذلك دهرًا طويلاً).

ʿAlī said about a group of heretics whom he had killed and burned:[80]

9.7

When I saw it was evil
I kindled the fire and called to Qanbar.

ʿAlī said:[81]

9.8

Whose is the black banner, dappled with shadows?
When the call "Take it forward, Ḥuḍayn" is given, he sallies forth.
He takes it to water at the front line,
and fate's pools return it dripping death and blood.
May God reward the fighters who encountered death on that day,
a noble day, a gallant day,
A day of sweet report and noble character,
the voices of men raised in battlecries—
I speak of the tribe of Rabīʿah,
brave and mighty when it meets battalions.

ʿAlī recited:

9.9

I see this world has many ills,
its dweller sickens, then he dies.
Good friends meet then separate—
but short of death, all this is small.
I lose a friend and then one more,
sure proof that none remain forever.

٩.١٠ أخبرني أبو عبد الله محمّد بن منصور التستريّ مجيزا قال: أخبرنا أحمد بن محمّد بن خليل[1] قال: حدّثنا الحسين بن إبراهيم قال: حدّثنا محمّد بن أحمد بن رجاء قال: حدّثنا هارون بن محمّد قال: حدّثنا قَعنَب بن المُحرِز قال: حدّثنا الأصمعيّ قال: حدّثنا أبو عمرو بن العلاء المقرئ قال: حدّثني الذيّال بن حَرمَلة قال:

كان عليّ بن أبي طالب عليه الصلاة والسلام يغدو ويروح إلى قبر رسول الله صلّى الله عليه وعلى آله وسلّم بعد وفاته ويبكي تفجّعا ثمّ يقول: يا رسول الله ما أحسن الصبر إلّا عنك وأقبح البكاء إلّا عليك.

ثمّ يقول [منسرح]:

مَا غَاضَ دَمْعِي عِنْدَ نَازِلَةٍ ... إِلَّا جَعَلْتُكَ لِلْبُكَا سَبَبَا
إِذَا[2] ذَكَرْتُكَ مَيِّتاً سَفَحَتْ ... مِنِّي الجُفُونُ فَفَاضَ وَٱنْسَكَبَا

ثمّ يمرّغ وجهه في التراب ويبكي ويندب ويذكر ما حلّ به بعده ويقول في ذلك [كامل]:

مَاذَا عَلَى مَنْ شَمَّ تُرْبَةَ أَحْمَدٍ ... أَلَّا يَشُمَّ مَدَى الزَّمَانِ غَوَالِيَا
صُبَّتْ عَلَيَّ مَصَائِبٌ لَوْ أَنَّهَا ... صُبَّتْ عَلَى الأَيَّامِ عُدْنَ لَيَالِيَا

٩.١١ وأخبرني أبو عبد الله أيضا قال: أخبرنا الحسن بن عبد الله بن سعيد قال: حدّثنا أحمد بن عبد العزيز الجوهريّ قال: أخبرنا زكريّا بن يحيى عن الأصمعيّ عن سلمة بن بلال عن مجالد عن الشعبيّ قال:

قال عليّ بن أبي طالب عليه الصلاة والسلام لرجل كره صحبة رجل [هزج]:

---

١ ه: (جميل).

٢ م، ه: (وإذا) وهي زحاف من حيث الوزن، ربما يكون (وإذ). ي: سقط البيت.

9.10 Abū ʿAbd Allāh Muḥammad ibn Manṣūr al-Tustarī reported to me, with a license to transmit the report, saying: Aḥmad ibn Muḥammad ibn Khalīl reported to us, saying: Al-Ḥusayn ibn Ibrāhīm recounted to us, saying: Muḥammad ibn Aḥmad ibn Rajāʾ recounted to us, saying: Hārūn ibn Muḥammad recounted to us, saying: Qaʿnab ibn al-Muḥriz recounted to us, saying: Al-Aṣmaʿī recounted to us, saying: Abū ʿAmr ibn al-ʿAlāʾ al-Muqriʾ, recounted to us, saying: Al-Dhayyāl ibn Ḥarmalah recounted to me, saying:

ʿAlī ibn Abī Ṭālib would go morning and evening to the messenger's grave, weep, heartbroken, and exclaim, "O messenger of God! How beautiful is forbearance, except in your loss! How ugly is weeping, except over you!" Then he would recite:

My eyes brim over when misfortunes descend,
but the real reason for my tears is you.
Whenever I remember that you are gone,
my eyes overflow and tears come pouring again.

Then he would place his face on the grave, and rub it until it was covered in earth. He would weep and lament and recount the difficulties that had assailed him after Muḥammad's death, and recite:

One who inhales the fragrance of Muḥammad's grave
inhales musk and ambergris forever.
I have been burdened with hardships;
if the day was likewise burdened, it would turn into night.

9.11 Abū ʿAbd Allāh also reported to me, saying: Al-Ḥasan ibn ʿAbd Allāh ibn Saʿīd reported to us, saying: Aḥmad ibn ʿAbd al-ʿAzīz al-Jawharī recounted to us, saying: Zakariyyā ibn Yaḥyā reported to us, from al-Aṣmaʿī, from Salamah ibn Bilāl, from Mujālid, from al-Shaʿbī, saying:

ʿAlī ibn Abī Ṭālib said to a man whom he wanted to warn against another's company:

فَلَا[1] تَصْحَبْ أَخَا الْجَهْلِ وَإِيَّاكَ وَإِيَّاهُ
فَكَمْ مِنْ جَاهِلٍ أَرْدَى حَلِيمًا حِينَ آخَاهُ
يُقَاسُ الْمَرْءُ بِالْمَرْءِ إِذَا مَا هُوَ مَاشَاهُ
فَلِلشَّيْءِ مِنَ الشَّيْءِ مَقَايِيسٌ وَأَشْبَاهُ
وَلِلْقَلْبِ عَلَى الْقَلْبِ دَلِيلٌ حِينَ يَلْقَاهُ
وَفِي الْعَيْنِ غِنًى لِلْعَيْنِ إِنْ تَنْطِقَ أَفْوَاهُ

٩.١٢ وأخبرني أيضا مجيزا قال: أخبرنا أبو الفضل يحيى بن إبراهيم بن زياد القرقوبيّ قال: أخبرنا أحمد بن عبد الرحمٰن بن الجارود الرقّيّ قال: أخبرنا سليمان بن سيف قال: أخبرنا الأصمعيّ عن العلاء بن جرير عن أبيه عن الأحنف بن قيس[2] قال:

دخلت على أمير المؤمنين عليّ بن أبي طالب صلوات الله عليه وهو يصلّي الضحى فقلت له: يا أمير المؤمنين إلى متى هذا الدُّؤوب دؤوب بالليل ودؤوب بالنهار؟ فأشار إليّ أن أجلس فلمّا سلّم قال: ٱسمع وَٱفهم. وأنشد [بسيط]:

اِصْبِرْ عَلَى مَضَضِ الْإِدْلَاجِ بِالسَّحَرِ وَفِي الرَّوَاحِ عَلَى الْحَاجَاتِ وَالْبُكَرِ
لَا تَيْأَسَنَّ وَلَا تَحْزُنْكَ مَطْلَبَةٌ فَالنُّجْحُ يَتْلَفُ[3] بَيْنَ الْعَجْزِ وَالضَّجَرِ
إِنِّي رَأَيْتُ وَفِي الْأَيَّامِ تَجْرِبَةٌ لِلصَّبْرِ عَاقِبَةً مَحْمُودَةَ الْأَثَرِ
وَقَلَّ مَنْ جَدَّ فِي أَمْرٍ يُطَالِبُهُ وَٱسْتَصْحَبَ الصَّبْرَ إِلَّا فَازَ بِالظَّفَرِ

١ سقطت (ف) في رواية م، ي، هـ، ويجب ورودها لتصويب الوزن. ورواية الديوان، ص. ١٠٢ كما أثبتُّها.
٢ رواية الديوان، ص. ٢٠٤: (الأشعث بن قيس) وفيها أنّ هذه الأبيات قيلت في الصفّين.
٣ هـ: (فإنّما الهدي).

Do not befriend the fool.
  Beware of him, beware!
Many a fool has led into death
  the wise man who took him as brother.
The measure of a man
  is the man he walks with.
Each entity finds in another such,
  its true measure and like.
When the two meet, one heart finds in the other
  the proof he seeks.
The eye need not look into the eye
  when lips have spoken.

9.12 Al-Tustarī also recounted the following report to me, with a license to transmit, saying: Abū l-Faḍl Yaḥyā ibn Ibrāhīm ibn Ziyād al-Qarqūbī reported to us, saying: Aḥmad ibn ʿAbd al-Raḥmān ibn al-Jārūd al-Raqqī reported to us, saying: Sulaymān ibn Sayf reported to us, saying: Al-Aṣmaʿī reported to us, from al-ʿAlāʾ ibn Jarīr, from his father, from al-Aḥnaf ibn Qays, saying:

I entered the presence of the commander of the faithful, ʿAlī ibn Abī Ṭālib, while he was praying the noon prayer, and said: O commander of the faithful, how long will you strive like this, striving at night and in the daytime! He gestured that I should sit. When he had finished the prayer, he said: Listen and understand. Then he recited:

Bear the hardships of morning journeys patiently,
  and set out at daybreak in search of your desire.
Do not give up. Do not let setbacks grieve you.
  Weakness and vexation destroy any chance of victory.
My experience comes from the passage of days,
  I've seen that forbearance brings the best outcome.
One who strives to achieve a goal,
  with forbearance, achieves success.

٩.١٣ وأخبرني أيضا قال: وأُنشدنا لأمير المؤمنين عليّ بن أبي طالب صلوات الله عليه السلام [متقارب]:

أَصَمُّ عَنِ الكَلِمِ المُحفِظَاتِ	وأَحْلُمُ والحِلْمُ بِي أَشْبَهُ
وَإِنِّي لَأَتْرُكُ حُلْوَ الكَلَامِ	لِئَلَّا أُجَابَ بِمَا أَكْرَهُ
إِذَا مَا اجْتَرَرْتُ سَفَاهَ السَّفِيهِ	عَلَيَّ فَإِنِّي أَنَا الأَسْفَهُ
فَلَا تَغْتَرِرْ بِرُوَاءِ الرِّجَالِ	وَإِنْ زَخْرَفُوا لَكَ أَوْ مَوَّهُوا
فَكَمْ مِنْ فَتًى يُعْجِبُ النَّاظِرِينَ	لَهُ أَلْسُنٌ وَلَهُ أَوْجُهُ
تَرَاهُ يَنَامُ عَنِ المَكْرُمَاتِ	وَعِنْدَ الدَّنَاءَةِ يَسْتَنْبِهُ

٩.١٤ أخبرنا الحسين بن محمّد بن عيسى القمّاح قال: أخبرنا الحسن بن إسماعيل الضرّاب قال: حدّثنا عليّ بن عمر قال: حدّثني أحمد بن محمّد الأنباريّ قال: حدّثنا محمّد بن سهل قال: حدّثنا عبد الله بن محمّد البَلَويّ قال: حدّثنا عمارة بن يزيد قال: حدّثني مالك عن الزهريّ عن عبد الرحمٰن بن سعد عن جابر بن عبد الله قال:

سمعت عليًّا عليه الصلاة والسلام ينشد و رسول الله صلّى الله عليه وعلى آله وسلّم يسمع [بسيط]:

أَنَا أَخُو المُصْطَفَى لَا شَكَّ فِي نَسَبِي	مَعَهُ رُبِيتُ وَسِبْطَاهُ هُمَا وَلَدِي
جَدِّي وَجَدُّ رَسُولِ اللهِ مُنْفَرِدٌ	وَفَاطِمُ زَوْجَتِي لَا قَوْلَ ذِي فَنَدِ
صَدَّقْتُهُ وَجَمِيعُ النَّاسِ فِي بُهَمٍ	مِنَ الضَّلَالَةِ وَالإِشْرَاكِ وَالنَّكَدِ
اَلْحَمْدُ لِلهِ شُكْرًا لَا شَرِيكَ لَهُ	اَلْبَرُّ بِالعَبْدِ وَالبَاقِي بِلَا أَمَدِ

فقال له النبيّ صلّى الله عليه وعلى آله وسلّم: صدقت يا عليّ.

9.13 He also reported to me, saying: the following verses by the commander of the faithful, ʿAlī ibn Abī Ṭālib, were recited to us:

I turn a deaf ear to words that would rouse me to anger;
I am restrained, for restraint is worthier of me.
I leave off speaking even sweet words,
to guard against being answered by offensive ones.
If I bring upon myself the quarrel of an impetuous fool,
then I am a fool.
Do not be deceived by men's appearance,
though ornamented or duplicitiously charming.
Many a youth stuns with his looks,
but has several tongues and numerous faces.
You see him sleeping when it is time for virtuous deeds,
and fully awake for sordid doings.

9.14 Al-Ḥasan ibn Muḥammad ibn ʿĪsā al-Qammāḥ reported to us, saying: Al-Ḥasan ibn Ismāʿīl al-Ḍarrāb reported to us, saying: ʿAlī ibn ʿUmar recounted to us, saying: Aḥmad ibn Muḥammad al-Anbārī recounted to me, saying: Muḥammad ibn Sahl recounted to us, saying: ʿAbd Allāh ibn Muḥammad al-Balawī recounted to us, saying: ʿUmārah ibn Yazīd recounted to us, saying: Mālik recounted to us, from al-Zuhrī, from ʿAbd al-Raḥmān ibn Saʿd, from Jābir ibn ʿAbd Allāh, who said:

I heard ʿAlī recite the following verses, as the messenger of God listened:

I am Muḥammad's brother. My lineage is incontestable:
I was brought up with him; his two grandsons are my sons;
My grandfather and his grandfather are one;
and Fāṭimah is my wife. All true.
I believed in him when the world
was in the throes of error, polytheism, and adversity.
All praise and gratitude are due to God. He has no partner.
He is kind to his servants, and eternal, without end.

You have spoken true, ʿAlī, the prophet responded.

تمّ الدستور بحمد الله وحسن عونه.
فله الحمد دائما على نعمه التي لا تحصى
وصلّى الله على سيّدنا محمّد نبيّه وآله الطاهرين
وسلّم تسليما وحسبنا الله ونعم الوكيل.[1]

[1] ي: (تمّ الكتاب بعون الله تعالى وتوفيقه). هـ: (تمّ ذلك).

God be praised!
With his help, we have reached the end of the *Treasury*.
All praise is due to him for his immeasurable favors.
May God shower his blessings upon our leader,
his prophet Muḥammad, and upon Muḥammad's
pure progeny. Peace upon them all.
God is our sufficiency. He is the best guardian.

مائة كلمة

من كلام أمير المؤمنين عليّ بن أبي طالب
عليه السلام

المنسوب إلى

الجاحظ

One Hundred Proverbs

from

The Words of the Commander of the Faithful ʿAlī ibn Abī Ṭālib

compilation attributed to

Al-Jāḥiẓ

بسم الله الرحمن الرحيم

حدّثنا الشيخ الأديب أبو نصر محمّد بن سليمان بن محمّد: حدّثني الشيخ عبد الواحد بن أحمد الكرمانيّ قال: حدّثني أبو بكر هبة الله بن الحسن العلّاف القاضي بشيراز قال[1]:

حدّثني أبو بكر محمّد بن الحسن بن دريد قال: حدّثني أبو الفضل أحمد بن أبي طاهر صاحب أبي عثمان الجاحظ قال:

كان الجاحظ يقول لنا زمانا أنّ لأمير المؤمنين عليّ بن أبي طالب كرّم الله وجهه مائة كلمة تفي كلّ كلمة منها بألف كلمة من محاسن كلمات العرب. قال: وكنت أسائله دهرا طويلا أن يجمعها ويمليها عليّ وهو يعدني بها ويتغافل عنها ضنّا بها فلمّا كان في آخر عمره أخرج يوما جملة من مسوّدات[2] مصنّفاته فجمع منها تلك الكلمات فأخرجها ودفعها إليّ بخطّه. وكانت الكلمات المائة هذه:[3]

١ لو كُشف الغطاء ما ٱزددتُ يقينا

٢ الناس نِيام فإذا ماتوا ٱنتبهوا

٣ الناس بزمانهم أشبه منهم بآبائهم

٤ ما هلك ٱمرؤ عرف قدره

٥ قيمة كلّ ٱمرئ ما يُحسنه

٦ من عرف نفسه فقد عرف ربّه

٧ المرء مخبوء تحت لسانه

---

١ وردت هذه المقدّمة في ط. ووردت أيضا في خ بإسناد آخر: (وأخبرنا الفقيه أبو سعيد الفضل بن محمد الأستراباديّ حدّثنا أبو غالب الحسن بن علي بن القاسم حدثنا أبو عليّ الحسن بن أحمد الجهرميّ بعسكر مكرم حدّثني أبو أحمد الحسن ابن عبد الله بن سعيد حدّثني أبو بكر محمد بن الحسين بن دريد قال: قال أبو الفضل أحمد بن أبي طاهر صاحب أبي عثمان الجاحظ). اتّحدت رواية ط وخ في الراويَين الأخيرين.

٢ ا: سقطت (مسوّدات).

٣ خ: أوردت أربع كلمات أخرى: (الحذر الحذر فوالله لقد ستر كأنّه غفر / من أطال الأمل أساء العمل / الكاسب فوق قوته خازن لغيره / مسكين ابن آدم مكنون العلل مكتوم الأجل محفوظ العمل تؤلمه المقة وتقتله الشرقة). ط: أوردت واحدة من هذه: (الكاسب فوق قوته خازن لغيره). ث: أوردت كلمة أخرى: (لا ظهير كالمشاورة). ب: أوردت أربع كلمات أخرى: (الناس أبناء ما يحسنون / منع الموجود سوء الظن بالمعبود / رحم الله امرأ قال خيرا فغنم أو سكت فسلم / ليس العجب فيمن هلك كيف هلك إنّما العجب ممّن نجا كيف نجا).

In the name of God, the compassionate, the merciful

The religious scholar and litterateur, Abū Naṣr Muḥammad ibn Sulaymān ibn Muḥammad, recounted to us, saying: The religious scholar, ʿAbd al-Wāḥid ibn Aḥmad al-Kirmānī, recounted to me, saying: Abū Bakr Hibat Allāh al-ʿAllāf, who was judge in Shiraz, recounted to me, saying:[82]

Abū Bakr Muḥammad ibn al-Ḥasan ibn Durayd recounted to me, saying: Abū l-Faḍl Aḥmad ibn Abī Ṭāhir,[83] the friend of Abū ʿUthmān al-Jāḥiẓ, recounted to me, saying:

For years al-Jāḥiẓ had been telling us that the commander of the faithful, ʿAlī ibn Abī Ṭālib, had produced a hundred proverbs, each proverb worth a thousand of the best proverbs produced by the Arabs. I asked him many times to collect them and dictate them to me. He would promise to do so, but deliberately, stingily, forget. One day toward the end of his life, he brought out several earlier drafts of his own works, culled from them ʿAlī's proverbs, wrote them down with his own hand, and gave them to me.

The hundred proverbs are these:

1 Removing the veil will not increase my conviction.[84]

2 People are asleep; they awaken when they die.

3 People reflect their times more than they resemble their fathers.

4 The man who knows his worth will not perish.

5 The true worth of a man is measured by the good he does.

6 Whoever knows himself knows his lord.

7 A man is concealed behind his tongue.

٨ من عذب لسانه كثر إخوانه

٩ بالبرّ يُستعبد الحرّ

١٠ بشّر مال البخيل بحادث أو وارث

١١ لا تنظر إلى من قال ولكن ٱنظر إلى ما قال

١٢ الجزع عند البلاء تمام المحنة

١٣ لا ظفر مع البغي

١٤ لا ثناء مع الكبر

١٥ لا برّ مع شحّ

١٦ لا صحّة مع النَّهَم

١٧ لا شرف مع سوء الأدب

١٨ لا ٱجتناب من محرّم مع الحرص

١٩ لا راحة مع حسد

٢٠ لا محبّة مع مِراء[١]

٢١ لا سودد مع ٱنتقام

٢٢ لا زيارة مع زَعارَّة

٢٣ لا صواب مع ترك المشورة

٢٤ لا مروّة لكَذوب

٢٥ لا وفاء لمَلول[٢]

٢٦ لا كرم أعزّ من التقوى

٢٧ لا شرف أعلى من الإسلام

٢٨ لا معقل أحصن[٣] من الورع

٢٩ لا شفيع أنجح من التوبة

---

١ و: (مرء لجوج).

٢ ط، خ: (لملوك).

٣ ا، ط: (أحرز). و، خ، ث: (أحسن).

8 One whose tongue is sweet has many friends.

9 It is through kindness that the free man is enslaved.

10 Inform the miser's property of the imminent arrival of an accident or an heir.

11 Do not look at who said a thing, but at what was said.

12 Panic makes a calamity complete.

13 There can be no victory where there is treachery.

14 There can be no praise where there is arrogance.

15 There can be no kindness where there is miserliness.

16 There can be no health where there is gluttony.

17 There can be no honor where there is coarseness.

18 There can be no restraint from sinning where there is greed.

19 There can be no peace where there is envy.

20 There can be no love where there is hypocrisy.

21 There can be no right rule where there is vengeance.

22 There is no point in visiting someone who harbors hatred.

23 There can be no good judgment without consultation.

24 A liar has no shame.

25 A man who is quick to anger cannot be loyal.

26 There is no nobility mightier than piety.

27 There is no honor more exalted than Islam.

28 There is no refuge more protective than chastity.

29 There is no intercessor more effective than repentance.

٣٠ لا لباس أجمل من السلامة

٣١ لا داء أعيى من الجهل

٣٢ لا مرض أضنى من قلّة العقل

٣٣ لسانك يقتضيك ما عوّدته

٣٤ المرء عدوّ ما جهله

٣٥ رحم الله ٱمرأ عرف قدره ولم يتعدّ طوره

٣٦ النصح بين الملأ تقريع

٣٧ إعادة الإعتذار تذكير للذنب

٣٨ إذا تمّ العقل نقص الكلام

٣٩ الشفيع جناح الطالب

٤٠ نفاق المرء ذلّة

٤١ نعمة الجاهل كروضة في مَزبَلة

٤٢ الجزع أتعب من الصبر

٤٣ المسؤول حرّ حتّى يعد

٤٤ أكبر الأعداء أخفاهم مَكيدة

٤٥ من طلب ما لا يعنيه فاته ما يعنيه

٤٦ السامع للغِيبة أحد المغتابَين

٤٧ الذّل مع الطمع

٤٨ الراحة مع اليأس

٤٩ الحرمان مع الحرص

٥٠ من كثر مزاحه لم يخل من حقد عليه أو ٱستخفاف به

٥١ عبد الشهوة أذلّ من عبد الرقّ

٥٢ الحاسد مُغتاظ[1] على من لا ذنب له

---

١ ث: (ضاغن).

30 There is no garment more beautiful than good health.

31 There is no illness more chronic than ignorance.

32 There is no disease more debilitating than a lack of intelligence.

33 Your tongue brings forth what you have accustomed it to.

34 Man is the enemy of what he does not know.

35 May God have mercy on the man who, despite knowing his own worth, waits for his turn.

36 Advice in public is censure.

37 Repeated excuses recall the fault.

38 Where intelligence abounds, words are few.

39 The intercessor is the seeker's wing.

40 Two-facedness brings ignominy.

41 Blessings enjoyed by an ignoramus are like a garden in a garbage dump.

42 Panic tires more than forbearance.

43 A man who is petitioned is free until he makes a promise.

44 Your biggest enemy is the one who plots most secretly.

45 Whoever seeks what does not concern him will lose what does.

46 Whoever listens to gossip participates in it.

47 Avarice brings shame.

48 Resignation brings comfort.

49 Greed brings deprivation.

50 One who jokes too much will either be hated or ridiculed.

51 A slave to lust is baser than a slave in bondage.

52 An envious man resents even those who have done him no harm.

٥٣ كفى بالظفر شفيعاً للمذنب

٥٤ رُبَّ ساعٍ فيما يضرّه

٥٥ لا تتّكل على المنى فإنها بضائع النَّوكى

٥٦ اليأس حرّ والرجاء عبد

٥٧ من لانت أسافله صلبت أعاليه

٥٨ في كل جرعة شَرقة ومع كلّ أَكلة غصّة

٥٩ من أتي في عِجانه قلّ حياؤه وبَذُؤَ[١] لسانه

٦٠ السعيد من وُعظ بغيره

٦١ الحكمة ضالّة المؤمن

٦٢ الشَّرَه[٢] جامع لمساوئ العيوب

٦٣ ظنّ العاقل كهانة

٦٤ من نظر اعتبر

٦٥ العداوة شغل شاغل[٣]

٦٦ القلب إذا أُكره عمي[٤]

٦٧ الأدب صورة العقل[٥]

٦٨ لا حياء لحريص

٦٩ كثرة الوفاق نفاق وكثرة الخلاف شقاق

٧٠ رُبَّ أمل خائب

٧١ ربّ رجاء يؤدّي إلى الحرمان

---

١ ا: (بدو)، ربما تقرأ (بذؤ)، فقد سقطت بعض النقط والهمزة من هذه النسخة. ب: (بذا). ط، خ: (بذى)، ولا نجدها في القواميس.

٢ ا، و، ط: (الشرّ). ب: (البخل). رواية الدستور، ١:١٣٣ مثل رواية خ التي أثبتُّها.

٣ ب: (العداوة شغل القلب). خ: (العداوة تشغل القلب). ط، ث: سقطت الكلمة.

٤ خ: (القلب إذا أكره عمي). ط: (إذا أُكره القلب عمي). ب: (روّحوا القلوب فإنّ القلب إذا أُكره عمي). ث: سقطت الكلمة.

٥ ط: (الرجل). ث، خ: سقطت الكلمة.

53 Your success over one who sinned against you suffices as intercessor for forgiveness.

54 Many a person strives to attain a thing that will harm him.

55 Do not depend on hope, for it is a fool's commodity.

56 Acceptance is a free man, anticipation a slave.

57 If you have weak friends, you will be crushed by your enemies.[85]

58 With every sip, you choke; with every bite, you gag.

59 A man whose anus is entered will act immodestly and speak obscenely.

60 The happy man is one who learns from the example of others.

61 Wisdom is the believer's lost camel.

62 In gluttony are united all the worst faults.

63 An intelligent man's suppositions are clairvoyant.

64 One who observes learns.

65 Hatred consumes.

66 If the heart is forced, it is blinded.

67 Manners are the manifestation of intelligence.

68 The covetous have no shame.

69 Agreeing too much is a sign of two-facedness; disagreeing too much a sign of enmity.

70 Wishes can remain unrealized.

71 A hope sometimes leads to deprivation.

٧٢ ربّ أرباح يؤدّي إلى الخسران

٧٣ ربّ طمع كاذب

٧٤ البغي سائق إلى الحين

٧٥ من كثر فكره في العواقب لم يشجع

٧٦ اذا حلّت المقادير ضلّت التدابير

٧٧ اذا حلّ القدر بطل الحذر

٧٨ الإحسان يقطع اللسان

٧٩ الشرف بالفضل والأدب لا بالأصل والنسب[1]

٨٠ أكرم الأدب حسن الخُلُق

٨١ أكرم النسب حسن الأدب

٨٢ أفقر الفقر الحمق

٨٣ أوحش الوحشة العُجب

٨٤ أغنى الغنى العقل

٨٥ الطامع في وِثاق الذلّ

٨٦ احذروا نفار النعم فما كلّ شارد بمردود

٨٧ أكثر مصارع العقول تحت بروق الأطماع

٨٨ من أبدى صفحته للحقّ هلك[2]

٨٩ إذا أملقتم فتاجروا اللهَ بالصدقة

٩٠ من لان عوده كثف أغصانه

٩١ قلب الأحمق في فِيه

٩٢ لسان العاقل في قلبه

---

١ خ: (الشرف بالعقل والأدب لا بالأصل والحسب). ب: (الشرف بالعقل والأدب لا بالحسب والنسب).

٢ و: (من أبدى صفحته للحقّ ملك). ب: (من أبدى صفحته للحقّ ملك ومن أعرض عن الحقّ هلك).

72 There are profits that lead to loss.

73 An aspiration sometimes remains unattained.

74 Treachery will drive you to your death.

75 Whoever mulls too long over consequences will not gather the courage to act.

76 When the fates descend upon you, plans go awry.

77 When fate descends upon you, caution does not help.

78 Generosity cuts off your detractor's tongue.

79 Honor comes from merit and refinement, not from lineage and ancestry.

80 The best manners are from good character.

81 Good manners are the noblest ancestry.

82 Foolishness is the most indigent poverty.

83 The loneliest loneliness is brought on by conceit.

84 Intelligence is the best wealth.

85 The covetous will be tethered with the hobbling rope of shame.

86 Beware lest your blessings bolt. Not all camels that break loose can be recovered.

87 Most shattered minds have been felled by lightning bolts of covetous desires.

88 Whoever challenges the truth will perish.

89 If you lose your wealth, make a deal with God by giving alms to the poor.

90 If your trunk is pliant, your branches will be overly thick.[86]

91 A fool's heart is located in his mouth.

92 An intelligent person's tongue is located in his heart.

٩٣ من جرى في عنان أمله عـثر بأجله

٩٤ إذا وصلت إليكم أطراف النعم فلا تُنفّروا أقصاها بقلّة الشكر

٩٥ إذا قدرت على عدوّك فاجعل العفو عنه شكراً للقدرة عليه

٩٦ ما أضمر أحد شيئاً إلّا ظهر في فَلَتات لسانه وصفحات وجهه

٩٧ اللّهمّ اغفر رمزات الألحاظ وسقطات الألفاظ وسهوات الجَنان وهفوات اللسان

٩٨ البخيل مستعجل الفقر يعيش في الدنيا عيش الفقراء ويحاسب في الآخرة حساب الأغنياء

٩٩ لسان العاقل وراء قلبه

١٠٠ قلب الأحمق وراء لسانه

93 Whosoever gallops forward loosening the reins of his hopes will stumble into death.

94 If the fringes of God's blessings reach you, do not drive away the favors yet to come with a lack of gratitude.

95 If you catch your enemy, forgive him, in gratitude to God for giving you dominion over him.

96 A person cannot conceal something in his heart without it showing in the slips of his tongue and the planes of his face.

97 O God, forgive us the lapses of our eyes, the blunders in our words, the errors of our hearts, and the slips of our tongues.

98 A miser hastens his own poverty: He spends his life on earth with the destitute, yet is held to account in the hereafter with the wealthy.

99 An intelligent man's tongue is located behind his heart.

100 A fool's heart is located behind his tongue.

Notes

1 Q Baqarah 2:269.

2 Q Shūrā 42:11.

3 These marks are missing from our manuscripts.

4 This is a pun on the word *fāḥishah*, which has both the specific connotation of adultery and the general meaning of abomination.

5 Q Hūd 11:45 and Tīn 95:8.

6 Or: Whosoever associates with the learned gains dignity, and whosoever associates with the base becomes despicable.

7 It is reported that the prophet would tie a belt tightly around his waist to alleviate pangs of hunger; some add that he would put stones in it. See e.g. Muslim, *Ṣaḥīḥ*, report no. 2040; Ibn Ḥanbal, *Musnad* 3:44.

8 The Qur'an narrates that when Moses left Egypt, and crossed the desert to arrive at the Midian oasis, he found Jethro's daughters attempting to water their flocks, and he helped them. Then he went to rest in the shade, and said, «My lord, I am in need of whatever good you send down to me.» (Q Qaṣaṣ 28:24). The exegetes add that Moses was so emaciated from his long journey that the green color of the desert plants he had been eating could be seen through the skin of his stomach. (See al-Ṭabarī, *Jāmiʿ al-bayān*.)

9 Q Naml 27:44 and Qaṣaṣ 28:16.

10 Q Hūd 11:47.

11 Q Anbiyā' 21:87.

12 Q Āl ʿImrān 3:185.

13 Q Mu'minūn 23:86.

14 Q Kahf 18:45.

15 Q Najm 53:31.

16 Q Hūd 11:15–16.

17 Q Ḥadīd 57:20.

18 Grammatically modified version of Q Shuʿarā' 26:128–9.

19 Q Fuṣṣilat 41:15.

20 Q Qaṣaṣ 28:58.

21 Q Ṭā Hā 20:111.

22 Q Mu'minūn 23:100.

23 Grammatically modified version of Q Infiṭār 82:4.

24 Q ʿĀdiyāt 100:10.

25 Slightly modified version of Q Yūnus 10:30.

26 Q Najm 53:31.

27 It is considered virtuous to pray the dawn prayer early.

28 See Bayard Taylor, "The Wisdom of Ali," *Poems of the Orient.*

29 Q Nisā' 4:78.

30 Q Āl ʿImrān 3:154.

31 Q Luqmān 31:17.

32 Referring to the prophet Muḥammad.

33 Q Aḥzāb 33:21.

34 Modified version of Q Zumar 39:47, and grammatically modified version of Aʿrāf 7:95.

35 Vocalizing "Bikālī" following Ibn Abī l-Ḥadīd, *Sharḥ Nahj al-balāghah* 10:76–77.

36 This is the middle of the lunar month of Shaʿbān, thus a night with a full moon, and one considered particularly holy, to be dedicated to prayer.

37 Q Naḥl 16:128.

38 Q Ibrāhīm 14:34.

39 In the Arabic, the answers rhyme with the questions.

40 Mālik is the name of the gatekeeping angel of hell.

41 Q Ḥajj 22:11 and Zumar 39:15.

42 I.e. there are only some things he is permitted to know about the antichrist. The meaning "God knows where you will stand on the day of judgment" is also possible.

43 Q Nāziʿāt 79:34.

44 Q Anʿām 6:158.

45 Q Nūḥ 71:10–12.

46 These verses are: «Everything in the heavens and the earth extols God; he is the mighty, the wise. The kingdom of the heavens and the earth belongs to him, he gives life and he gives death, and he has power over all things. He is the first and the last, the manifest and the hidden, and he has knowledge of all things. He is the one who created the heavens and the earth in six days, then he sat upon the throne; he knows what enters into the earth and what comes out of it; what descends from the sky and what rises up to it; he is with you wherever you may go; and God sees all that you do. His is the kingdom of the heavens and the earth, and all things return to him. He makes the night give way to day, he makes the day give way to night, and he knows all that is in your hearts.» Q Ḥadīd 57:1–6.

47 These verses are: «He knows the unseen and the visible, he is the merciful and the compassionate. He is God other than whom there is no god, the king, the holy, peace, the preserver, the guardian, the almighty, the subjugator, the exalted—glorified be he above the partners they ascribe unto him. He is God, the creator, the originator, the one who gives shape. His are the most beautiful names, and he is the almighty, the wise.» Q Ḥashr 59:22–24.

48 Modified version of Q Taghābun 64:9.

49 Modified version of Q Taḥrīm 66:8.

50 Echoes Q ʿAnkabūt 29:41.

51 Modified version of Q Kahf 18:45.

52 The "Heavenly House" (*al-bayt al-maʿmūr*), lit. "the much-frequented house," is considered to be the heavenly prototype for the Kaʿbah.

53 Q Aʿrāf 7:171.

54 In *al-Ṣaḥīfah al-Sajjādiyyah*, this prayer is ascribed to ʿAlī's eponymous grandson, ʿAlī ibn al-Ḥusayn, better known as Zayn al-ʿĀbidīn. See William Chittick, *The Psalms of Islam*, no. 43, pp. 140–42.

55 Q Anbiyāʾ 21:101.

56 The Arabic text of the gong's "words" is rhythmic, to match what would be the beats of the gong. The rhythm is manifest in a set of equal beats (dong dong dong dong, dong dong dong dong / dong dong dong dong, dong dong dong dong); eight long syllables per hemistich, which is not a bona fide poetic meter in the Arabic Khalīlian system. The lines rhyme in a *muzdawijah* fashion, in the pattern xx, yy, zz. My translation follows approximately the same beat as the Arabic, and also applies an ad hoc loose rhyme.

57 I.e. death.

58 A reference to Q Aʿrāf 7:179 and Furqān 25:44.

59 Echoes Q ʿAnkabūt 29:41.

60 Modified version of Q Kahf 18:45.

61 Grammatically modified version of Q Mu'minūn 23:74.

62 Q Dhāriyāt 51:11.

63 Lit. "pharaohs."

64 Q Furqān 25:63.

65 Q Mu'minūn 23:11.

66 Christians, Jews, Sabians, and others. See "protected peoples" in the Glossary.

67 Q Baqarah 2:196, 211, Āl ʿImrān 3:11, Mā'idah 5:2, and many other places. The two epithets occur together in 5:98.

68 Q Yūnus 10:107 and many other places.

69 It is virtuous to preface any kind of prayer with blessings on the prophet (*ṣalawāt*); the belief is that since God will certainly respond to the prayer asking him to bless the prophet, he will surely answer any prayers that are offered with it.

70 According to Ibn Saʿd (s.v. *dhikr al-adhān*), this call to gather was the original call to prayer. See Qutbuddin, "Khuṭba," p. 208, for details.

71 Notice the pun: the word used for yellow here is *muzabraq*, a derivative of whose root, *zibriqān*, the full moon, is perhaps evoked retroactively with the next phrase comparing ʿAlī to the full moon using the more common word *badr*.

72 These poems were composed after the Battle of Uḥud in 3/625.

73 In addition to "jackal," *thaʿlab* also means "spear point." Here, the word puns on both meanings: the jackal (one of the disbelievers) killing the lion (Muṣʿab), and the spear-point piercing his body.

74 ʿAlī slew ʿAmr ibn ʿAbd Wadd in the Battle of the Trench (al-Khandaq), also called the Battle of the Confederates (al-Aḥzāb), in which the Meccans and their allies attacked Muḥammad in Medina 5/627.

75 Al-Majlisī, *Biḥār al-anwār* (20:279), explains that the three who lined up against Islam were the two pagan tribes of Quraysh and Ghaṭafān, and the Medinan Jewish tribe of Qurayẓah. The one "taken out" was Quraysh, when ʿAlī slew ʿAmr ibn ʿAbd Wadd and Nawfal ibn ʿAbdallāh. Al-Jubūrī, *Dīwān ʿAlī* (p. 189, note * [*sic*]), explains it differently, saying three individuals lined up against Islam, namely ʿAmr ibn ʿAbd Wadd, who was killed, and two others, who escaped.

76 A reference to the prophet's expulsion of the Jewish tribe of al-Naḍīr from Medina in 3/625.

77 Likely composed following the Battle of Badr in 2/624.

78 Among the Qur'an's many designations for itself is the Book of Demarcation (*al-Furqān*), something that explains the difference between right and wrong.

79 The reference is unclear.

80 According to al-Kaydarī, ʿAlī recited this verse after ordering the burning of a group who persisted in ascribing divinity to him (*Dīwān ʿAlī*, pp. 231–32).

81 Likely composed following the Battle of Ṣiffīn in 36/657.

82 Al-Khwārizmī has a different chain of transmission.

83 The *One Hundred Proverbs* may be part of the lost sections of Ibn Abī Ṭāhir's literary anthology *al-Manẓūm wa-l-manthūr*. I thank Shawkat Toorawa for suggesting this possibility.

84 The veil is the body; removing the veil is a reference to death.

85 Lit. "As for him whose lower parts are weak, his higher parts will be hard."

86 Al-Waṭwāṭ (*Maṭlūb kull ṭālib*, p. 57, my translation) explains this as follows: "One who is too soft is disrespected by his subordinates, and they do not obey or esteem him."

Glossary of Names and Terms

I provide here contextual explanations of key terms mentioned in this volume, and brief biographical information about the following people: individuals mentioned in the reports in the *Treasury*; principal transmitters of these reports, comprising ʿAlī's direct interlocutors and al-Quḍāʿī's principal recurring sources; the two scholars mentioned in the *One Hundred Proverbs*; and key persons mentioned in my Introduction and A Note on the Text.

ʿAbbād ibn Qays (fl. first/seventh c.) is one of ʿAlī's interlocutors in the *Treasury* (5.14). Perhaps ʿAbbāḍ ibn Qays is a transcription error for Qays ibn ʿAbbād (d. after 80/699) from the second generation of Muslims, a resident of Basra, who is said to have narrated hadith from ʿAlī. Alternatively, ʿAbbād may be a mistranscription for al-Aḥnaf, al-Ashʿath, or ʿAbd Allāh, all sons of Qays.

ʿAbd Allāh ibn Sinān al-Asadī (d. between 75/694 and 83/702) was a second generation Muslim of the clan of Banū Khuzaymah and a resident of Kufa. He was with ʿAlī at Ṣiffīn. He narrated ʿAlī's words as well as prophetic hadith transmitted by ʿAlī, ʿAbd Allāh ibn Masʿūd, and Mughīrah ibn Shuʿbah.

Abū ʿAṭāʾ (fl. first/seventh c.) is an interlocutor of ʿAlī in the *Treasury* (5.13) whom I have not been able to identify.

Abū Jahl (d. 2/624) was a fierce enemy of Muḥammad, polemically called Abū Jahl ("Father of Ignorance"). He belonged to Makhzūm, a clan of the Quraysh. He was killed by the Muslims at the Battle of Badr.

Abū Surādiq (fl. first/seventh c.) was a man from the clan of Dārim who, according to the *Treasury* (8.2), was part of the delegation that came to ʿAlī in Medina asking him to beseech God for rain.

Adhriʿāt is a town in southwestern Syria, known today as Darʿah (Deraa). In the early days of Islam, Adhriʿāt was the center of an important Jewish colony. Several members of the Medinan Jewish tribe of al-Naḍīr took refuge there upon their expulsion from Medina in 3/625.

al-Aḥnaf ibn Qays (d. 73/692) was a chieftain of the tribe of Tamīm from the clan of Banū Saʿd and a resident of Basra. He remained neutral in the Battle of the Camel but fought with ʿAlī at Ṣiffīn.

ʿĀʾishah (d. 58/678) was the wife of the prophet Muḥammad, from whom she narrated many hadith, and the daughter of Abū Bakr, the first Sunni caliph. She fought ʿAlī in 36/656 at the Battle of the Camel, so named because she rode a camel onto the battlefield.

ʿajwah is a special kind of date grown in Medina. A hadith ascribed to the Prophet says "*ʿAjwah* dates are from paradise."

ʿAlid refers to a descendant of ʿAlī ibn Abī Ṭālib, or a thing connected with him.

ʿAmr ibn ʿAbd Wadd (d. 5/626) was a famous pagan warrior whom ʿAlī slew in single combat at the Battle of the Trench. He belonged to the clan of Banū ʿĀmir ibn Luʾayy.

Aṣbagh ibn Nubātah (d. early second/seventh c.) was a close companion of ʿAlī and a prolific transmitter of his words, including the famous testament to Mālik al-Ashtar. An account of the killing of al-Ḥusayn at Karbala is also ascribed to him. He belonged to the tribe of Tamīm, was a resident of Kufa, and fought alongside ʿAlī at Ṣiffīn.

Badr is the name of a group of wells near Medina, site of the first major battle between the Muslims and the Meccan pagans in 2/624, in which the Muslims were victorious.

al-Barāʾ ibn ʿĀzib (d. 72/691) was a companion of the Prophet from among the Helpers (Anṣār), of the Medinan tribe of Aws. He was a prolific transmitter of hadith and a military commander during the early Muslim conquests. He moved to Kufa and died there. He is said to have fought alongside ʿAlī at the Battle of the Camel, Ṣiffīn, and Nahrawān.

Caesar (Ar. Qayṣar) is the title of the Byzantine emperor who ruled over the Eastern Roman Empire with his capital at Constantinople when Muḥammad began preaching Islam. In Islamic tradition, the term became a symbol of power and wealth.

Chosroes is the Greek form of the Persian name Khusraw (Ar. Kisrā), the given name of several Persian emperors who ruled in the late Sassanid period, shortly before the coming of Islam, including Khusraw Anūshirwān

(r. AD 531–79) and Khusraw Aparwīz (r. AD 591–628). In Islamic tradition, the term became a symbol of power and wealth.

dāʿī is a Qurʾanic term literally meaning "one who calls" to God. For the Ṭayyibīs, the *dāʿī* is their highest spiritual authority during the concealment of the Imām.

Dajjāl the antichrist, is according to Islamic tradition an evil, one-eyed man, who will appear at the end of time, signaling the approach of judgment day. He will gather an army to conquer the world, and will initially be successful. After forty days, or forty years, he will be vanquished, and killed by the Messiah: Jesus in the Sunni tradition, the divinely guided redeemer (Mahdī) in the Shia tradition.

Dārim was a clan from the tribe of Tamīm in the line of Zayd Manāt. Their area of residence was northeast of Medina, roughly in the center of the Arabian Peninsula.

David (fl. tenth c. BC, Ar. Dāʾūd) is the biblical King David and a prophet in the Islamic tradition. He is mentioned several times in the Qurʾan as someone granted kingship, wisdom, and justice. Several prophetic hadith stress David's fervor in prayer and fasting.

al-Dhayyāl ibn Ḥarmalah (fl. late first /seventh–eighth c.) of the Asad tribe, was a resident of Kufa who transmitted hadith from ʿAlī's close companion Jābir ibn ʿAbd Allāh.

Fāṭimah al-Zahrāʾ (d. 11/632) was ʿAlī's wife and Muḥammad's youngest daughter, about whom he is reported to have said, "Fāṭimah is the mistress of the women of paradise." She had four children with ʿAlī: al-Ḥasan, al-Ḥusayn, Zaynab, and Umm Kulthūm, all of whom played key roles in the political and religious life of early Islam.

Fatimids are an Ismāʿīlī Shia dynasty tracing descent from the prophet Muḥammad, and from ʿAlī ibn Abī Ṭālib and Fāṭimah, Muḥammad's daughter. The Fatimids, whose seat was first in North Africa, then Egypt, ruled over a large part of the Islamic empire in the tenth and eleventh centuries. They built the city of Cairo in 358/969.

Fīq is a town in the Levant between Damascus and Tiberias, also called Afīq.

Fihr is a clan of the Meccan Quraysh tribe.

Furqān is one of the names by which the Qurʾan refers to itself, meaning "The Demarcation" between good and evil.

Gabriel (Ar. Jibrīl or Jibra'īl) is the archangel who, in Islamic tradition, served as God's messenger in bringing revelation to prophets, including the Qur'anic revelation to Muḥammad.

hadith are words or deeds attributed to Muhammad, sometimes translated as "traditions" of the Prophet.

al-Ḥārith al-Hamdānī (d. 65/685) a resident of Kufa, was a staunch supporter of ʿAlī, and a learned man. He belonged to the Ḥūth clan of the Hamdān tribe. A famous set of verses addressing him by name is attributed to ʿAlī.

Ḥamzah ibn ʿAbd al-Muṭṭalib (d. 3/624) was the Prophet's uncle, lauded by Muslims as the Lion of God, who fought at the Battle of Badr, slaying several Meccan warriors in single combat. He was killed the following year at the Battle of Uḥud. Muḥammad is reported to have grieved deeply for him, and to have recited the funeral prayer for him 72 times.

al-Ḥasan ibn ʿAlī (d. 49/669) was the oldest son of ʿAlī and Fāṭimah, and for the Shia, the Imām after his father. The Prophet is reported to have said, "Al-Ḥasan and al-Ḥusayn are the leaders of the youth of paradise." Al-Ḥasan was active in ʿAlī's service. After his father's death in 40/661, he received the pledge of the caliphate in Kufa. He abdicated six months later, and, eschewing active politics, returned to Medina. According to some sources, he was poisoned by Muʿāwiyah.

Ḥawtharah ibn al-Hirmās is reported in the *Treasury* (8.2) to have witnessed the delegation from the Dārim tribe to ʿAlī in Medina.

Ḥimyar is the name of an Arab tribe based in Yemen which wielded political hegemony in southern Arabia between AD 100 and 590. The center of their kingdom was Saphar on the plateau south of modern Yarīm. From there, they gradually conquered the ancient Southern Arabian kingdoms of Qatabān, Saba', and Ḥaḍramawt. In the mid-fourth century, Judaism and Christianity began to spread in these regions. Repeated ruptures of the dam of Ma'rib attest to a general decline starting in the sixth century. In AD 597, South Arabia became a province of the Sassanid empire.

Ḥisl is a clan of Dārim, as it appears in the *Treasury* (8.2); there are a number of clans belonging to other tribes also called Ḥisl.

Hubayrah ibn Abī Wahb (d. after 8/630) was a Meccan pagan from the Makhzūm clan of Quraysh, who was married to ʿAlī's sister Umm Hāni' and had two children with her. He was one of six horsemen who stormed the trench outside Medina in the Battle of the Trench (Khandaq). It is reported that when Muḥammad conquered Mecca, Hubayrah fled to Najrān and died there.

Ḥuḍayn ibn al-Mundhir (d. after 96/715) was a resident of Basra, a chieftain of the Rabīʿah tribe, and standard-bearer for ʿAlī's side at Ṣiffīn.

Ḥunayn is the name of a valley between Mecca and al-Ṭāʾif, site of a major battle fought between Muḥammad and his followers against the tribe of Hawāzin and its subtribe of Thaqīf in 8/630, soon after the conquest of Mecca, which ended in a decisive victory for the Muslims.

al-Ḥusayn ibn ʿAlī (d. 61/680) was the second son of ʿAlī and Fāṭimah, and Imām after his older brother, al-Ḥasan. Al-Ḥusayn was martyred in 61/680, when Umayyad forces killed him, his male family members, and his companions, in the plain of Karbala. His shrine is an important pilgrimage site for the Shia who also commemorate the day of his martyrdom, called ʿĀshūrāʾ.

Ibn ʿAbbas, ʿAbd Allāh (d. 68/687) was the son of Muḥammad's uncle ʿAbbās, and one of the greatest scholars of the first generation of Muslims. Many hadith are attributed to his transmission. He supported ʿAlī's claim after the death of the Prophet, and was a close advisor to ʿAlī during his caliphate; he also served as governor of Basra.

Ibn Abī Ṭāhir Ṭayfūr, Abū l-Faḍl Aḥmad (d. 280/893) was a Baghdadian litterateur and historian whose works include a partially extant anthology of prose and poetry (*al-Manthūr wa-l-manẓūm*) and one volume of a significant work of history (*Kitāb Baghdād*).

Ibn Durayd (d. 312/933) was a lexicographer, linguist, and grammarian. He was born in Basra, and lived in Oman, Nishapur, and Baghdad. His major books include a lexicon titled *Jamharat al-lughah*, a grammar work titled *Kitāb al-Ishtiqāq*, and an anthology of wise sayings titled *al-Mujtanā*.

Ibn Muljam (or Ibn Muljim) (d. 40/661) of the Kindah tribe was the Khārijite who assassinated ʿAlī. He was executed by ʿAlī's son, al-Ḥasan.

Imām literally "leader," refers either to the supreme leader of the Muslim community, or to an exemplary scholar or prayer-leader. In Shia doctrine, the term denotes a man descended from the prophet Muḥammad and his legatee ʿAlī, who inherits their role of spiritual and temporal leadership, who is divinely guided, and who is the sole legitimate leader of the Muslim community.

Ismāʿīlīs are a denomination of Shia Muslims, who, after Jaʿfar al-Ṣadiq (d. 148/765), maintain the continuity of the imamate through his son Ismāʿīl. The Fatimid dynasty of North Africa and Egypt claimed descent from his line. After the death of the Fatimid Imām-Caliph al-Mustanṣir in 487/1094, the Ismāʿīlīs split into two further denominations, Niẓarī and Mustalawī (the latter known through their Ṭayyibī branch).

Jābir ibn ʿAbd Allāh (d. ca. 78/697) was a companion of the Prophet and one of the Helpers (Anṣār). A resident of Medina from the tribe of Khazraj, he pledged allegiance to Muḥammad at ʿAqabah before the Emigration. Jābir was a prolific narrator of hadith and of ʿAlī's words. He was a staunch supporter of ʿAlī, and fought with him at Ṣiffīn. He died in Medina in his nineties.

Jesus (Ar. ʿĪsā) is a prophet in Islam, referred to in 15 different surahs and 93 verses in the Qur'an, as the son of Mary, the Messiah (al-Masīḥ), the Word (*kalimah*), and the Spirit (*rūḥ*).

Kaʿb ibn al-Ashraf (d. 4/625) was an opponent of Muḥammad in Medina and leader of the Banū l-Naḍīr, a Jewish tribe. Kaʿb was killed by the Muslims on Muḥammad's orders, shortly before the expulsion of the Banū l-Naḍīr from Medina.

Khārijites literally "Seceders," are so named because they seceded from ʿAlī's following subsequent to the Arbitration at Ṣiffīn. Condemning the Arbitration, and ʿAlī too, with the dictum "Judgment belongs to God alone" (*lā ḥukma illā li-llāh*), they attacked and slew any who disagreed with this doctrine. ʿAlī fought and defeated them at the Battle of Nahrawān in 38/658. Most Khārijite factions eventually died out and they survive today as the milder Ibāḍī denomination in Oman and North Africa.

Kumayl ibn Ziyād (d. 82/701) was a close companion of ʿAlī who fought with him at Ṣiffīn, and served during his caliphate as governor of Hīt, a frontier town in the north of Iraq. He narrated ʿAlī's words, and the famous "Kumayl's Prayer" is one he is said to have learned from ʿAlī. The Umayyad governor of Kufa al-Ḥajjāj ibn Yūsuf executed him along with several other vocal supporters of ʿAlī.

Magians (Ar. Majūs) are followers of the ancient Iranian dualist religions associated with fire worship. The Magians are referred to in the Qur'an in a list of six forms of religion, including believers (= Muslims), Jews, Christians, Sabeans, and polytheists (Q Ḥajj 22:17). Some legal schools consider them "people of the book" (i.e. followers of a divinely revealed scripture), as followers of Zoroaster.

Moses (Ar. Mūsā) is a prophet in Islam, mentioned by name 136 times in the Qur'an, more than any other prophet.

Muʿāwiyah ibn Abī Sufyān (d. 60/680) a major enemy of ʿAlī, became the first Umayyad caliph. Second cousin of the third Sunni caliph ʿUthmān and governor of Syria under ʿUmar and ʿUthmān, he refused to accept ʿAlī as caliph and fought him with the people of Syria at the Battle of Ṣiffīn in 37/657. After ʿAlī's death in 40/661, Muʿāwiyah became the undisputed ruler of the Islamic lands. He ruled from his seat at Damascus until his death.

Muḥammad (d. 11/632) was the prophet of Islam, often referred to as God's messenger (*rasūl Allāh*). He is also referred to in the *Treasury* by two of his other names, Aḥmad and Muṣṭafā.

Muṣʿab ibn ʿUmayr or *Muṣʿab al-khayr* (d. 3/624) was one of the earliest Muslims. A Meccan from the Prophet's tribe of Quraysh, he was part of the migration to Abyssinia (modern-day Ethiopia). He returned to join Muḥammad, and was standard-bearer in the Battles of Badr and also Uḥud, where he was killed.

Muʿtazilah is the name of a rationalist school of Islamic theology which used the dialectical methods of Greek philosophy. Its subscribers called themselves "people of unity and justice," meaning they were strictly non-anthropomorphic proponents of God's oneness, and advocates for his justice and thus for human free will.

al-Naḍīr were a Jewish tribe who were expelled from Medina by the Prophet in 3/625 for breaking their covenant with the Muslims and plotting with the Meccans against him. They took refuge with their co-religionists in the northern oasis of Khaybar and the Syrian town of Adhriʿāt.

Nawf ibn Faḍālah al-Bikālī (fl. first/seventh c.) was a companion of ʿAlī. He was a member of the Banū Bikāl, a clan of the Yemenite Ḥimyar tribe.

al-Nazzāl ibn Sabrah (fl. first/seventh c.) of the Hilāl tribe and a resident of Kufa, was an associate of ʿAlī who transmitted his teachings as well as prophetic hadith. He is reckoned among the companions of the Prophet.

Niftawayh (d. 323/935) was a philologist, grammarian, historian, a scholar of hadith, and a Ẓāhirite jurisprudent.

protected peoples (Ar. *ahl al-dhimma*) are members of the revealed religions to whom the medieval Islamic state provided "protected" status.

Qadarites (Qadariyyah or Libertarians) are an early Islamic, proto-Muʿtazilite, theological school advocating human free will. The name is derived from the word *qadar*, meaning "power," used to denote the capacity of humans to choose between good and evil. The competing school is that of the Jabriyyah, or Predestinarians.

qāḍī means judge.

Qanbar ibn Ḥamdān (d. latter half of first/late seventh or early eighth c.) was ʿAlī's servant, also reported to have carried out his legal penalties. He was with him during the Battle of Ṣiffīn, and is said to have collected his orations after he died. The Umayyad governor of Kufa, al-Ḥajjāj ibn Yūsuf al-Thaqafī (d. 95/714), tortured and executed him along with several other supporters of ʿAlī.

al-Rabīʿāh were a large tribe, many members of which were residents of Basra in ʿAlī's time. They formed one of the largest blocs in ʿAlī's army: four thousand fought in the Battle of the Camel, and they comprised the entire left wing at Ṣiffīn.

Rifāʿah ibn Shaddād al-Bajalī (d. 66/685) was a second-generation Muslim, a chieftain of the Bajīlah tribe, and a resident of Kufa, who served as ʿAlī's judge in Ahwaz. He fought on ʿAlī's side in the Battles of the Camel and Ṣiffīn, where he was standard-bearer and orator of his tribe. After the Karbala tragedy, he became one of the Kufan Penitents who lamented their passivity in preventing the killing of al-Ḥusayn. He later participated in al-Mukhtār's revolt against the Umayyads, during which he was killed.

Rightly Guided Caliphs are, according to the Sunnis, the first four successors of the prophet Muḥammad, namely Abū Bakr, ʿUmar, ʿUthmān, and ʿAlī.

Sābūr is the Arabic form of Persian "Shāpūr," the name of several powerful Sassanid emperors. These include Shāpūr I, son of Ardashīr Pāpakān (r. AD 239 or 241 to 270 or 273), who is said to have founded the city of Jundīshāpūr, and Shāpūr II, son of Hormizd II (r. AD 309–79), who is known for his military might.

Salmān al-Fārisī (d. 35/655) was a prominent early companion of the Prophet, who came from Persia. A hadith ascribed to Muḥammad says "Salmān is one of us, the People of the House." He was also a close companion and staunch supporter of ʿAlī. Governor of Ctesiphon in ʿUmar's reign, he died and was buried there.

Ṣaʿṣaʿah ibn Ṣūḥān al-ʿAbdī (d. ca. 56/676) was a devoted supporter of ʿAlī who fought with him in all his battles and attempted to persuade the Khārijites to return to ʿAlī in the negotiations leading to the Battle of Nahrawān. He was a poet and orator, and chieftain of his tribe of ʿAbd al-Qays. After ʿAlī's death, he is reported to have discoursed eloquently and boldly on ʿAlī's merits in Muʿawiyah's court. In some reports, Muʿāwiyah exiled him to Bahrain, the traditional homeland of the ʿAbd al-Qays, where he died.

Ṣayfī ibn ʿĀʾidh is said in the *Treasury* (5.6) to be the antichrist (Dajjāl). It was also the name of a Meccan pagan who had indirect connections to the Prophet: brother of the former husband of Muḥammad's wife Khadījah, and grandfather of the Prophet's trading partner in his early Meccan years.

al-Shaʿbī, ʿĀmir ibn Sharāḥīl (d. between 103/721 and 110/728) was a resident of Kufa, and a famous early legal expert, exegete, and transmitter of hadith. He was from the Shaʿb clan of the tribe of Hamdān, and said to be descended from a chieftain of Yemen.

Shāfiʿī is the name of one of the four major Sunni schools of law, so called after its founder of the same name al-Shāfiʿī (d. 206/855). Shāfiʿīs are currently found mostly in Egypt and southeast Asia.

sharīf literally "a man of noble birth," commonly denotes descent from the prophet Muḥammad through his grandsons al-Ḥasan or al-Ḥusayn, typically the former; the term *sayyid* is generally used to denote the latter.

Shaybah ibn Rabīʿah (d. 2/623) was part of the Meccan opposition against Muḥammad. He was killed at the Battle of Badr.

Shurayḥ ibn al-Ḥārith (d. ca. 80/699) was a judge during the caliphates of ʿUmar, ʿUthmān, ʿAlī, and Muʿāwiyah. He was also a jurist, hadith scholar, and litterateur. ʿAlī chastised Shurayḥ more than once during his tenure, as in the report in the *Treasury* (7.7).

Shia literally means "followers" and is the shortened form of Shīʿat ʿAlī or "followers of ʿAlī." The Shia believe that the Prophet through divine revelation appointed ʿAlī to lead the Muslim community after him as Imām, and that, as such, ʿAlī was the rightful successor to Muḥammad in both his temporal and spiritual roles. Three major branches of the Shia evolved, subscribing to different lines of Imāms: Twelver (or Imāmī), Ismāʿīlī, and Zaydī.

Ṣiffīn is a place in north central Syria on the north bank of the Euphrates, and the site of a major battle in 37/657 fought by ʿAlī and his Iraqi force against Muʿāwiyah leading a Syrian army. The battle ended in arbitration.

Solomon (fl. tenth c. BC, Ar. Sulaymān) is the biblical king of Israel, son and successor of King David. He is revered as a prophet in the Islamic tradition. He is frequently mentioned in the Qur'an, particularly in connection with his knowledge of the language of the birds, and his command over the jinn and the winds.

sunnah literally meaning "well-trodden path to a watering hole," refers to the accepted practice of pious forbears, and when used without qualifiers, usually to Muḥammad's practice.

Sunni means "emulator of the Prophet's practice." The Sunnis believe that Muḥammad died without appointing an heir, and that the community accepted Abū Bakr as his successor. They venerate the first four leaders of the community as the "Rightly Guided Caliphs." The term Sunni emerged from the earlier, mainly political appellation, "people adhering to the sunnah and the majority group."

surah is a chapter of the Qur'an. There are 114 surahs in the Qur'an of varying lengths, between 3 to 286 verses.

Ṭalḥah ibn Abī Ṭalḥah (d. 3/624) of the Qurashite clan of ʿAbd al-Dār was part of the Meccan opposition to Muḥammad. He was the Meccans' standard-bearer during the Battle of Uḥud, where he was slain by the Prophet's uncle Ḥamzah, and where two of his brothers and four of his sons were also killed.

Ṭayyibī is the appellation of a denomination of Shia Muslims from the Fatimid-Ismāʿīlī branch, who believe the twenty-first Imām, al-Ṭayyib, went into concealment in 524/1130, and that the imamate continues, father to son, in his line. During his concealment, the Imām is represented among his followers by a continuous chain of dāʿīs, presently based in India.

tharīd is a savory porridge made of bread and broth.

Ṭūbā is the name of a tree in paradise, referred to in a Qur'anic verse promising «Ṭūbā and a good return» to «those who believe and perform good deeds.» (Q Raʿd 13:29). For some exegetes it is an Indian or Ethiopian term for paradise itself, for others an abstract notion of "bliss" or "bounty."

Tubbaʿ was, according to the lexicographers, the royal title of the kings of the second Ḥimyarite kingdom (ca. AD 300–525). The "people of Tubbaʿ"

(*qawm Tubbaʿ*) are an extinct community mentioned twice in the Qurʾan, which states that they—among several other pre-Islamic groups—were punished because they refused to believe in God and obey God's prophets (Q Dukhān 44:37 and Q Qāf 50:13).

al-Tustarī, Abū ʿAbd Allāḥ (d. ca. 400/1010) was a Cairene hadith scholar and one of al-Quḍāʿī's sources for prophetic hadith and for ʿAlī's words. (Not to be confused with Sahl al-Tustarī, the Shia scholar and mystic.)

Twelver Shia are a denomination of Shia Muslims, who, after Jaʿfar al-Ṣādiq (d. 148/765), maintain the continuity of the imamate through his son Mūsā al-Kādhim. Their twelfth Imām is the awaited redeemer, Muḥammad al-Mahdī. Currently, they are concentrated in Iran, Lebanon, Syria, and Bahrain.

Ubayy ibn Khalaf (d. 3/624) was a bitter enemy of Muḥammad. On the night Muḥammad migrated to Medina, Ubayy was one of the Meccans who tried to assassinate him. During the Battle of Uḥud, the Prophet is said to have killed Ubayy with his own hand.

Uḥud is the name of a mountain outside Medina, site of the second major battle between the Muslims and the Meccans in 3/625, in which the Muslims suffered heavy losses.

Umayyads are the first dynasty to rule the Islamic world, beginning with Muʿāwiyah ibn Abī Sufyān, who became caliph following ʿAlī's death in 40/661. From their seat in Damascus, they ruled till 132/750, when they were overthrown by the Abbasids.

ʿUtbah ibn Rabīʿah (d. 2/623) was one of the leaders of the Meccan opposition against Muḥammad. He was killed at the Battle of Badr by the Prophet's uncle Ḥamzah. His daughter Hind (wife of Abū Sufyān and mother of Muʿāwiyah) avenged her father's death by having a slave murder Ḥamzah at Uḥud.

ʿUthmān ibn Abī Ṭalḥah (d. 3/624) of the ʿAbd al-Dār clan, was part of the Meccan opposition to Muḥammad. He was slain by the Prophet's uncle Ḥamzah during the Battle of Uḥud, as were his two brothers and four nephews.

waṣī means "legatee." The Sunnis and the Shia both refer to ʿAlī as Muḥammad's *waṣī*, the one to whom Muḥammad entrusted the execution of his legacy. According to the Shia, this title endorses ʿAlī's rightful succession to the Prophet's role as spiritual and temporal guide for the Muslim community.

Zayd ibn Aslam (d. 136/754) was a second-generation Muslim and a resident of Medina, who is reported to have taught hadith and jurisprudence in the Prophet's mosque. His company was reportedly sought by the Shia Imām, Zayn al-ʿĀbidīn.

Zayd ibn Ṣūḥān al-ʿAbdī (d. 36/656) was referred to by the Prophet as "Zayd the Good" (Zayd al-khayr). When one of his hands was severed in an early battle, the Prophet is reported to have said that his hand preceded him to paradise. Like his brother Ṣaʿṣaʿah, Zayd was a staunch supporter of ʿAlī. He was killed fighting in the Battle of the Camel.

Zaydīs are a denomination of Shia Muslims, who, after Zayn al-ʿAbidīn ʿAlī ibn al-Ḥusayn (d. 95/712), uphold the imamate of his son Zayd (d. 142/740), and after him of any ʿAlid who combines religious learning with a will to wield the sword. They are concentrated today in Yemen.

Bibliography

Primary Sources

Abū l-Saʿādāt Asʿad ibn ʿAbd al-Qāhir al-Iṣbahānī (fl. seventh/thirteenth c.). *Maṭlaʿ al-ṣabāḥatayn wa majmaʿ al-faṣāḥatayn*, edited by Ṣādiq al-Ḥusaynī al-Ishkivarī. Tehran: Pazhūhishigāh-i ʿUlūm-i Insānī va-Muṭālaʿāt-i Farhangī, 1385/[1965].

Abū Nuʿaym al-Iṣfahānī (d. 430/1038). *Ḥilyat al-awliyāʾ*. Beirut: Dār al-Kitāb al-ʿArabī, [1985].

Āmidī, al- (d. 550/1155). *Ghurar al-ḥikam wa-durar al-kalim*. Sidon: Maṭbaʿat al-ʿIrfān, 1931.

Baḥrānī, Maytham al- (d. 679/1280). *Sharḥ al-ʿālim al-rabbānī Kamāl al-Dīn Maytham ibn ʿAlī ibn Maytham al-Baḥrānī (qaddasa sirrahū) ʿalā l-Miʾat kalimah li-amīr al-muʾminīn ʿAlī ibn Abī Ṭālib (ʿalayhi l-salām)*, edited by Mīr Jalāl al-Dīn al-Ḥusaynī al-Armawī al-Muḥaddith. Qom: Manshūrāt al-Mudarrisīn fī l-Ḥawzah al-ʿIlmiyyah, 1970. Available online at http://gadir.free.fr/Ar/imamali/Nhj/Serh100/7/book_60/01.htm/.

Dhahabī, al- (d. 748/1347). *Tārīkh al-Islām wa-wafayāt mashāhīr al-aʿlām*, edited by ʿUmar ʿAbd al-Sallām Tadmurī. Beirut: Dār al-Kutub al-ʿIlmiyyah, 1987.

Ḥabbāl, Abū Isḥāq Ibrāhīm ibn Saʿīd ibn ʿAbdallāh al- (d. 482/1089). *Wafayāt qawm min al-Miṣriyyīn wa-nafar siwāhum*, edited by Maḥmūd Ḥaddād. Riyadh: Dār al-ʿĀṣimah, 1987.

Ḥājjī Khalīfah (d. 1067/1657). *Kashf al-ẓunūn*. Beirut: Dār al-Kutub al-ʿIlmiyyah, 1993.

Hodazādeh, Abdülaziz Efendi (d. 1025/1616). *Hazrat-i Ali'nin Yüz Sözü*, edited by Ādem Ceyhan. Istanbul: Buhara, 2011.

Ibn Abī l-Ḥadīd (d. 655/1257). *Sharḥ Nahj al-balāghah*, edited by Muḥammad Abū l-Faḍl Ibrāhīm. Cairo: Dār Iḥyāʾ al-Kutub al-ʿArabiyyah, 1965.

Ibn ʿAsākir, Abū l-Qāsim ʿAlī ibn al-Ḥasan ibn Hibat Allāh al-Shāfiʿī (d. 571/1176). *Tārīkh madīnat Dimashq*, edited by Muḥibb al-Dīn ʿUmar ibn Gharāmah al-ʿUmarī. Beirut: Dār al-Fikr, 1995.

Ibn ʿAṭiyyah al-Andalusī (d. 541/1147). *Fihris Ibn ʿAṭiyyah*, edited by Muḥammad Abū l-Ajfān and Muḥammad al-Zāhī. Beirut: Dār al-Gharb al-Islāmī, 1983.

Ibn Ḥamdūn (d. 562/1166). *Al-Tadhkirah al-Ḥamdūniyyah*, edited by Ihsān ʿAbbās. Beirut: Dār Ṣādir, 1996.

Ibn Hishām (d. 218/833). *Al-Sīrah al-nabawiyyah*, edited by Aḥmad Ḥijāzī al-Saqqā. 4 parts in 2 vols. Cairo: Dār al-Turāth al-ʿArabī, n.d.

Ibn al-ʿImād (d. 1089/1678). *Shadharāt al-dhahab fī akhbār man dhahab*, edited by ʿAbd al-Qādir al-Arnaʾūt and Maḥmūd al-Arnaʾūt. Damascus: Dār Ibn Kathīr, 1401/[1981].

Ibn Khallikān (d. 681/1282). *Wafayāt al-aʿyān*. Beirut: Dār al-Thaqāfah, n.d.

Ibn Mākūlā, al-Amīr Abū Naṣr (d. 475/1082). *Kitāb al-Ikmāl fī rafʿ al-irtiyāb ʿan al-muʾtalif wa-l-mukhtalif min al-asmāʾ wa-l-kunā wa-l-ansāb*. Beirut: Dār al-Kutub al-ʿIlmiyyah, 1990.

Ibn Manẓūr (d. 711/1311). *Lisān al-ʿArab*. http://www.baheth.info/. Accessed on January 18, 2012.

Ibn al-Ṣabbāgh (d. 855/1451). *Al-Fuṣūl al-muhimmah fī maʿrifat al-aʾimmah*, edited by Sāmī al-Ghurayrī. Qom: Ḍār al-Ḥadīth, [2001].

Ibn Taghrībirdī (d. 874/1470). *Al-Nujūm al-ẓāhirah fī mulūk Miṣr wa-l-Qāhirah*, edited by Muḥammad Ḥusayn Shams al-Dīn. Beirut: Dār al-Kutub al-ʿIlmiyyah, 1992.

Jāḥiẓ, al- (d. 255/869). *Al-Bayan wa-l-tabyīn*, edited by ʿAbd al-Sallām Muḥammad Hārūn. Cairo: Maktabat al-Khānjī, 1985.

———. *Rasāʾil al-Jāḥiẓ*, edited by Muḥammad Bāsil ʿUyūn al-Sūd. 4 vols. Beirut: Dār al-Kutub al-ʿIlmiyyah, 2000.

Jahshiyārī, al- (d. 331/942). *Kitāb al-Wuzarāʾ wa-l-kuttāb*, edited by Muṣṭafā al-Saqqā, Ibrāhīm al-Ibyārī and ʿAbd al-Ḥāfiẓ Shalabī. Cairo: Muṣṭafā al-Bābī al-Ḥalabī, 1980.

Kaydarī (or Kaydharī), Quṭb al-Dīn Muḥammad ibn al-Ḥusayn al-Bayhaqī al- (d. after 576/1180). *Dīwān al-Imām ʿAlī*, also titled *Anwār al-ʿuqūl min ashʿār waṣī al-rasūl*, edited by Kāmil Salmān al-Jubūrī. Beirut: Dār al-Maḥajjat al-Bayḍāʾ, 1999.

Khwārizmī, Abū l-Muʾayyad Muwaffaq ibn Aḥmad al-Bakrī al- (d. 568/1172), *Manāqib al-Khwārizmī*. Najaf: al-Maktabah al-Ḥaydariyyah, 1965.

Majlisī, Muḥammad Bāqir al- (d. 1699). *Biḥār al-anwār al-jāmiʿah li-durar akhbār al-aʾimmah al-aṭhār*. Tehran: Dār al-Kutub al-Islāmiyyah, [1956].

Maqrīzī, al- (d. 845/1441). *Al-Khiṭaṭ al-Maqrīziyyah*. Full title: *Kitāb al-Mawāʿiẓ wa-l-iʿtibār bi-dhikr al-khiṭaṭ wa-l-āthār*. Beirut: Dār Ṣādir, n.d.

———. *Kitāb al-Muqaffā al-kabīr*, edited by Muḥammad al-Yaʿlāwī. Beirut: Dār al-Gharb al-Islāmī, 1991.

Mas'ūdī, al- (d. 344/956). *Murūj al-dhahab wa-ma'ādin al-jawhar*, edited by Sa'īd Muḥammad al-Laḥḥām. Beirut: Dār al-Fikr, 2000.

Qālī, al- (d. 356/967). *Kitāb al-Amālī*. Cairo: Dār al-Kutub al-Miṣriyyah, 1926.

Quḍā'ī, al- (d. 454/1062). *Daqā'iq al-akhbār wa-ḥadā'iq al-i'tibār*. Istanbul: al-Maktabah al-'Āmirah, 1883.

———. *Dustūr ma'ālim al-ḥikam wa-ma'thūr makārim al-shiyam min kalām amīr al-mu'minīn 'Alī ibn Abī Ṭālib (karrama Allāhu wajhahū)*. (1) Edited by Jamīl al-'Aẓm, commentary by Ibrāhīm al-Daljamūnī. Cairo: al-Maktabah al-Azhariyyah, 1914. (2) Edited by 'Abd al-Zahrā' al-Ḥusaynī al-Khaṭīb. Beirut: Dār al-Kitāb al-'Arabī, 1981. (3) Edited by Barakāt Yūsuf Habbūd, with a commentary by him titled *Bawāriq al-ishārāt wa-l-tawjīhāt limā fī l-Dustūr min al-maṭālib wa-l-ma'āthir wa-l-'iẓāt*. Beirut: Dar al-Arqam, 1997. (4) Edited by Ḥasan al-Samāḥī Suwaydān, commentary by Ibrāhīm al-Daljamūnī. Damascus: Dār al-Qalam 2003. (5) Online: http://gadir.free.fr/Ar/imamali/kutub2/Destur_Mealimul_Hikem.htm.

———. *Kitāb al-Inbā' 'an al-anbiyā'*, edited by 'Umar Tadmurī. Beirut: al-Maktabah al-'Aṣriyyah, 1999.

———. *Musnad al-Shihāb*, edited by Ḥamdī al-Salafī. 2 vols. Beirut: Mu'assasat al-Risālah, 1986.

———. *'Uyūn al-ma'ārif wa-funūn akhbār al-khalā'if*, edited by 'Abd al-Raḥmān 'Alī. [Amman]: Dār al-Yanābī', 1997.

Raḍī, al-Sharīf al- (d. 405/1014). *Nahj al-balāghah*, edited by Husayn al-A'lamī, commentary by Muḥammad 'Abduh. Beirut: Mu'assasat al-A'lamī, 1993.

Sayf al-Dīn, Ṭāhir (d. 1385/1965). *Risālah Ramaḍāniyyah: Tadhkirat al-labīb*. Bombay: Ṭayyibī Da'wat Publications, 1369/[1950].

Shāfi'ī, al- (d. 204/820). *Dīwān*, edited by Na'īm Zurzūr. Beirut: Dār al-Kutub al-'Ilmiyyah, 1984.

Silafī, Abū Ṭāhir al- (d. 576/1179). *Mashyakhat al-shaykh al-ajall Abī 'Abd Allāh Muḥammad al-Rāzī*. N.d., n.p.

Subkī, al- (d. 771/1370). *Ṭabaqāt al-Shāfi'iyyah al-kubrā*. Cairo: al-Maṭba'ah al-Ḥusayniyyah, [1906].

Ṭabarsī, al- (d. 548/1153). *Nathr al-la'ālī*, in *Proverbia quaedam Alis, imperatoris Muslimici: Et carmen Tograi, poetae doctiss. nec non dissertatio quaedam Aben Sinae*, edited by Jacob Golius. Leiden: Elzevir, 1629.

Tha'ālibī, al- (d. 427/1035). *Al-I'jāz wa-l-ījāz*, edited by Ibrāhīm Ṣāliḥ. Damascus: Dār al-Bashā'ir, 2001.

Wāṭwāṭ, al-Rashīd al- (d. 578/1182). *Maṭlūb kull ṭālib min kalām ʿAlī ibn Abī Ṭālib.* (1) Edited by M. Heinrich Leberecht Fleischer. Leipzig: W. Vogel Sohn, 1837. (2) Edited by Ioannes Gustavus Stickel, with grammatical parsing. Jena: Sentibus Croeckerianis, 1984. (3) Edited by Adem Ceyhan, with a further Ottoman Turkish commentary by Hocazade Abdulaziz Efendi. Istanbul: Buhara Yayınları, 2011. (4) Online: http://lib.ahlolbait.ir/.

Yāfiʿī, al- (d. 768/1367). *Mirʾāt al-jinān wa-ʿibrat al-yaqẓān.* Cairo: Dār al-Kitāb al-Islāmī. 1993.

Yāqūt al-Ḥamawī (d. 625/1229). *Muʿjam al-buldān.* 5 vols. Beirut: Dār Ṣādir, n.d.

Zayn al-ʿĀbidīn, ʿAlī ibn al-Ḥusayn (d. 94/713). *Al-Ṣaḥīfah al-Sajjādiyyah,* translated by William Chittick, as *The Psalms of Islam: Al-Ṣaḥifat al-kāmilat al-Sajjādiyya.* London and New York: The Muhammadi Trust of England and Northern Ireland, 1988.

ʿAlī's Gnomologia in Translation

Cleary, Thomas. *Living and Dying with Grace: The Counsels of Hadrat ʿAli.* Boston and London: Shambhala, 1996. [Translation of the wisdom section in al-Raḍī's *Nahj al-balāghah.*]

Fleischer, M. Heinrich Leberecht. *Ali's hundert Sprüche.* Leipzig: Friedr. Christ. Wilh. Vogel, 1837. [Text and German translation of a manuscript containing al-Waṭwāṭ's commentary of al-Jāḥiẓ's *Miʾat kalimah,* al-Ṭabarsī's *Nathr al-laʾālī,* and a further brief selection of proverbs.]

Kuypers, Gerard. *Ali ben Abi Taleb Carmina.* Leiden: John Hasebroek and Bernhard Jongelyn, 1745. [Edition and Latin translation of ʿAlī's gnomic verse.]

Ockley, Simon. *Sentences of Ali, Son-in-Law of Mahomet and his Fourth Successor (translated from an Authentick Arabick Manuscript in the Bodleian Library at Oxford).* London: Bernard Lintot, 1717. [Translation of an anonymous medieval compilation of ʿAlī's sayings.]

Taylor, Bayard. "The Wisdom of Ali." In *Poems of the Orient.* 1855. http://en.wikisource.org/wiki/The_Wisdom_of_Ali. Accessed August 15, 2011.

Waenen, Cornelius van, *Sententiae Ali ebn Abi Talib.* Oxford: Clarendon, 1806. [Edition and Latin translation of four compilations: (1) al-Ṭabarsī's *Nathr al-laʾālī,* (2) an excerpt from al-Āmidī's *Ghurar al-ḥikam,* (3) al-Naysābūrī's *Amthāl,* and (4) al-Maydānī's *Amthāl.*]

Weston, Stephen. *Moral aphorisms in Arabic, and a Persian commentary in verse: tr. from the originals; with specimens of Persian poetry; likewise additions to the author's Conformity of the Arabic and Persian with the English language.* London: S. Rousseau, 1805. [Translation of al-Ṭabarsī's *Nathr al-laʾālī.*]

Yule, William. *Apothegms of Alee, the son of Abo Talib Son in Law of the Moslem Lawgiver Mahummid and Fourth of the Khlifs . . . with an Early Persic Paraphrase and an English Translation.* Edinburgh: Marshall Leslie, 1832.

Secondary Sources

ʿAbd al-Zahrāʾ, al-Sayyid al-Ḥusaynī al-Khaṭīb. *Maṣādir Nahj al-balāghah wa-asānīduhū.* 4 vols. Beirut: Muʾassasat al-Aʿlamī, 1966.

Baghdādī, Ismāʿīl Pāshā al-. *Hadiyyat al-ʿārifīn: asmāʾ al-muʿallifīn wa-āthār al-muṣannifīn.* Beirut: Dār al-Kutub al-ʿIlmiyyah, 1992.

Carruthers, Mary. *The Book of Memory: A Study of Memory in Medieval Culture.* Cambridge: Cambridge University Press, 1990.

Gutas, Dimitri. "Classical Arabic Wisdom Literature: Nature and Scope." *Journal of the American Oriental Society*, 101, no. 1 (1981): 49–86.

Kassis, Riad Aziz. *The Book of Proverbs and Arabic Proverbial Works.* Leiden: Brill, 1999.

Lanham, Richard. *Analyzing Prose.* New York: Charles Scribner, 1983.

Marāghī, Abū l-Wafāʾ al-. *Al-Lubāb fī sharḥ al-Shihāb.* Cairo: Al-Majlis al-Aʿlā li-l-Shuʾūn al-Islāmiyyah, 1970.

Ong, Walter. *Orality and Literacy: The Technologizing of the Word.* London: Methuen, 1982.

Pellat, Charles. "Nouvel essai d'inventaire de l'oeuvre Ǧāḥiẓienne." *Arabica*, 31, no. 2 (1984): 118–164.

Qutbuddin, Tahera. "The Sermons of ʿAlī ibn Abī Ṭālib: At the Confluence of the Core Islamic Teachings of the Qur'an and the Oral, Nature-Based Cultural Ethos of Seventh Century Arabia." *Anuario de Estudios Medievales*, 42, no. 1 (2012): 201–228.

Rebhan, Helga. *The Wonders of Creation: Manuscripts of the Bavarian State Library from the Islamic World.* Wiesbaden: Harrassowitz Verlag, 2010.

Schoeler, Gregor. *The Genesis of Literature in Islam: From the Aural to the Read.* In collaboration with, and translated by, Shawkat M. Toorawa. Rev. ed. Edinburgh: Edinburgh University Press, 2009.

———. *The Oral and the Written in Early Islam.* Translated by Uwe Vagelpohl and edited by James E. Montgomery. London and New York: Routledge, 2006.

Ṣafwat, Aḥmad Zakī. *Jamharat khuṭab al-ʿArab fī l-ʿuṣūr al-ʿarabiyyah al-zāhirah.* 4 vols. Cairo: al-Maktabah al-ʿIlmiyyah, 1933–4.

Ṭabāṭabāʾī, ʿAbd al-ʿAzīz. "Ahl al-bayt fī l-maktabah al-ʿarabiyyah." *Turāthunā*, 4 (1406/[1986]). http://www.rafed.net/books/turathona/4/t4-6.html. Accessed April 27, 2011.

Further Reading

Cleary, Thomas. *The Wisdom of the Prophet: Sayings of Muhammad. Selections from the Hadith.* Boston and London: Shambhala, 2001.

Dakake, Maria Massi. *The Charismatic Community: Shiʿite Identity in Early Islam.* Albany, NY: State University of New York Press, 2007.

Jafri, S. H. M. *The Origins and Early Development of Shiʿa Islam.* Oxford: Oxford University Press, 2000. First published by Longman Group and Librairie du Liban, 1979.

Kohlberg, Etan. "ʿAli b. Abi Taleb." In *Encyclopedia Iranica*, ed. by Ehsan Yar-Shater. London: Routledge and Kegan Paul, 1982, 1:838–48.

Lakhani, M. Ali, ed. *The Sacred Foundations of Justice in Islam: The Teachings of ʿAli ibn Abi Talib.* Bloomington, Indiana: World Wisdom, 2006.

Madelung, Wilferd. *The Succession to Muhammad: A Study of the Early Caliphate.* Cambridge: Cambridge University Press, 1997.

Qutbuddin, Tahera. "ʿAli ibn Abi Talib." In *Arabic Literary Culture*, 500–925, ed. by Michael Cooperson and Shawkat M. Toorawa. Detroit, Michigan: Thomson Gale, 2005, pp. 205–224. *Dictionary of Literary Biography*, 311.

———. "Khuṭba: The Evolution of Early Arabic Oration." In *Classical Arabic Humanities in their Own Terms: Festschrift for Wolfhart Heinrichs on his 65th Birthday*, ed. by Beatrice Gruendler with the assistance of Michael Cooperson. Leiden: Brill, 2008, pp. 176–273.

Shah-Kazemi, Reza. *Justice and Remembrance: Introducing the Spirituality of Imam ʿAlī.* London and New York: I. B. Tauris, 2006.

Ṭabarī, al- (d. 310/923). *Tārīkh al-rusul wa-l-mulūk*, edited by Muḥammad Abū l-Faḍl Ibrāhīm. Cairo: Dār al-Maʿārif, 1977. Translated as *The History of al-Ṭabarī*, general editor Ehsan Yar-Shater. Albany, NY: State University of New York Press, 1985–2007. Adrian Brockett, translator, *The Community Divided.* Vol. 16, 1997. G. R. Hawting, translator, *The First Civil War.* Vol. 17, 1996.

Index

About the NYU Abu Dhabi Institute

The Library of Arabic Literature is supported by a grant from the NYU Abu Dhabi Institute, a major hub of intellectual and creative activity and advanced research. The Institute hosts academic conferences, workshops, lectures, film series, performances, and other public programs directed both to audiences within the UAE and to the worldwide academic and research community. It is a center of the scholarly community for Abu Dhabi, bringing together faculty and researchers from institutions of higher learning throughout the region.

NYU Abu Dhabi, through the NYU Abu Dhabi Institute, is a world-class center of cutting-edge research, scholarship, and cultural activity. The Institute creates singular opportunities for leading researchers from across the arts, humanities, social sciences, sciences, engineering, and the professions to carry out creative scholarship and conduct research on issues of major disciplinary, multidisciplinary, and global significance.

About the Typefaces

The Arabic body text is set in DecoType Naskh, designed by Thomas Milo and Mirjam Somers, based on an analysis of five centuries of Ottoman manuscript practice. The exceptionally legible result is the first and only typeface in a style that fully implements the principles of script grammar (*qawāʿid al-khaṭṭ*).

The Arabic footnote text is set in DecoType Emiri, drawn by Mirjam Somers, based on the metal typeface in the naskh style that was cut for the 1924 Cairo edition of the Qur'an.

Both Arabic typefaces in this series are controlled by a dedicated font layout engine. ACE, the Arabic Calligraphic Engine, invented by Peter Somers, Thomas Milo, and Mirjam Somers of DecoType, first operational in 1985, pioneered the principle followed by later smart font layout technologies such as OpenType, which is used for all other typefaces in this series.

The Arabic text was set with WinSoft Tasmeem, a sophisticated user interface for DecoType ACE inside Adobe InDesign. Tasmeem was conceived and created by Thomas Milo (DecoType) and Pascal Rubini (WinSoft) in 2005.

The English text is set in Adobe Text, a new and versatile text typeface family designed by Robert Slimbach for Western (Latin, Greek, Cyrillic) typesetting. Its workhorse qualities make it perfect for a wide variety of applications, especially for longer passages of text where legibility and economy are important. Adobe Text bridges the gap between calligraphic Renaissance types of the 15th and 16th centuries and high-contrast Modern styles of the 18th century, taking many of its design cues from early post-Renaissance Baroque transitional types cut by designers such as Christoffel van Dijck, Nicolaus Kis, and William Caslon. While grounded in classical form, Adobe Text is also a statement of contemporary utilitarian design, well suited to a wide variety of print and on-screen applications.

About the Editor-Translator

Tahera Qutbuddin (Harvard University, Ph.D. 1999) is Associate Professor of Arabic Literature at the University of Chicago. She has also taught at Yale University and the University of Utah. After school in India, she studied Arabic language and literature in Cairo (Ain Shams University, B.A. 1988, Tamhīdī Magister 1990). Her scholarship focuses on intersections of the literary, the religious, and the political in classical Arabic poetry and prose. She is the author of *Al-Mu'ayyad al-Shīrāzī and Fatimid Da'wa Poetry: A Case of Commitment in Classical Arabic Literature* (Leiden: Brill, 2005). Her current book project is *Classical Arabic Oratory: The Rhetoric and Politics of Public Address in the Islamic World*, for which she was awarded a fellowship by the Carnegie Corporation of New York. She has also published articles on the Qur'an, Muḥammad, the sermons of 'Alī ibn Abī Ṭālib, Fatimid and Ṭayyibī literature, Arabic in India, and Islamic preaching.